OTHER BOOKS BY JOHN FULFORD

The Cat Cook Book and Dictionary, 2011

The Complete Guide to English Spelling Rules, 2012

Hitchhiking to Serendip, 2013

Last Plane to Cochabamba, 2014

To Reach the Sea, 2014.

MY 60-JOB RESUME

Or, How Quitting 60 Jobs in 30 Years
Added Up to an Extraordinary Life

By

John J. Fulford

My Sixty Job Resume by John J. Fulford

Copyright © 2016 by John J. Fulford

Published by Astoria Press, Long Beach, CA

Author services provided by Pedernales Publishing, LLC
www.pedernalespublishing.com

Cover by Jana Rade
jrade@impactstudiosonline.com

Editing services by Barbara Ardinger, Ph.D.

Library of Congress Control Number: 2015959129

ISBN Number: 978-0-9963799-0-8 Paperback Edition
              978-0-9963799-1-5 Digital Edition

Contents

Prolog .... *vii*

Chapter 1: Haberdashery *1*

Chapter 2: Repairing Antiques *6*

Chapter 3: White-Collar Office Work *17*

Chapter 4: Making Terrazzo Tiles *26*

Chapter 5: Rustic Furniture *28*

Chapter 6: The Illegal Wood Shop *30*

Chapter 7: The Metal Fabricators *32*

Chapter 8: The Assembly Line *34*

Chapter 9: The Royal Air Force *37*

Chapter 10: Making Movies *48*

Chapter 11: Fleet Street Man *59*

Chapter 12: Chocolate Taster *69*

Chapter 13: Computer Expert *74*

Chapter 14: Summer Jobs in Canada *78*

Chapter 15: Deconstruction in Kitimat *81*

Chapter 16: Dish Washing *94*

Chapter 17: The Cement Factory *100*

Chapter 18: The Fish Cannery *105*

Chapter 19: Picking Fruit *114*

Chapter 20: The Airline *116*

Chapter 21: Danger in the Forest 125

Chapter 22: Forest Firefighter *129*

Chapter 23: Surveyor *146*

Chapter 24: The Grain Elevator *166*

Chapter 25: On the Pipeline...................................... *179*

Chapter 26: On the Green Chain 186

Chapter 27: Geologist *197*

Chapter 28: The One-Room School.......................... *208*

Chapter 29: Mountain School................................... *232*

Chapter 30: Teaching Law *244*

Chapter 31: Teaching in Spain.................................. *251*

Chapter 32: Winter in Winnipeg............................... *256*

Chapter 33: Getting to California.............................. *265*

Chapter 34: The School in Orange County 268

Chapter 35: Motel Manager *278*

Chapter 36: Bilingual Teacher................................... *292*

Epilog *294*

Prolog

I left school in 1947 when I was fifteen. I left because I was bored and restless and learning nothing. During the Second World War, almost all the male teachers in England had been put into uniform and most of the female teachers had found that they could make more money working in factories than in classrooms, so the schools had to grab any live body they could find and haul out of retirement some who were barely alive. As schools were bombed or children were evacuated, the schools became more and more overcrowded and quickly ran out of even the most basic equipment. After the war, the returning teachers just would not accept the miserable pay and the terrible working conditions, so there was little, if any, improvement for many years.

Because my siblings and I were evacuated and the family moved many times, we children went to over a dozen different schools. I like to think that we survived those years simply because we were all excellent readers, we were all extremely independent, and we all had an intelligent curiosity about life and the world around us that did not depend on the wretched schools we had to put up with.

There was no fuss when I left. I simply walked away. I doubt if the school even noticed. There were no school counselors in those days and I had never received one word of advice from my teachers and absolutely no guidance from my parents.

Actually, since no adult had ever discussed my future with me, I had not the faintest idea what to do with myself. I knew that I was a dreamer and a loner and not very good at passing exams. I just wanted to leave school and get out into the world. At that time I never thought that one day I would become the first member of the family to earn a university degree and become a teacher, and love it.

I took evening classes after I left school. There was a wide variety of classes offered by various government departments, and I chose subjects that interested me, whether academic or fun, and somehow, no matter what job I had, I usually managed to attend a night school class. There was a time, for example, when I was interested in painting and found myself in a class of watercolor enthusiasts. Then I found that I liked oils better, and the instructor encouraged me. However, the other students objected to the smell of the oils, so I had to sit at the back of the class. I got my revenge when one of my oil paintings was chosen for a small exhibit, and none of the watercolors were.

I knew that my mathematics was very weak so I enrolled in a math class and struggled mightily. The class helped a lot, but to this day I still have trouble with higher math. Similarly, I always wanted to learn Spanish and signed up for night classes. Twice a week for many months, I managed to get to my classes through the dark and the rain, eating supper in some steamy fish and chips shop while mumbling Spanish irregular verbs to myself. I didn't learn much, but it gave me a good foundation when I eventually did study Spanish seriously.

Today, as a retired teacher with nearly forty years of experience at all grade levels from kindergarten to adult education, I really should not say this, but looking back, I think I owe more to what I picked up from the various jobs I had and to voracious reading than to what I learned at most of the schools I attended.

Chapter 1
Haberdashery

My first paid employment was a Saturday job in a large department store. I was still at school and had set my heart on a new bicycle, a lovely red sports model with dropped handlebars and the latest gears. Father would not lend me a penny, of course, but my brother-in-law, Harry, offered to co-sign on condition that I got a part-time job and kept up the payments. The only job I could find that paid enough was in a large department store.

I was put in the notions department, which was always busy on Saturdays, and very quickly found myself, along with five women, selling buttons, zippers, colored thread, skeins of yarn, pinking shears, knitting needles, and a host of other similar items. The time passed quickly, and I rather enjoyed myself and took pride in finding just the right item for each customer, then writing the bill with a flourish and popping it into the vacuum tube that hissed off through the ceiling to unknown regions. I liked working with people, even the impatient housewives who were not always in the best of humor. One Saturday, I was moved to the menswear department, where I spent much of my time helping middle-aged ladies choose birthday presents for their husbands. They would take a long time looking at various things, then would invariably choose a couple of pairs of dark blue socks or a dark blue tie. Menswear was nowhere near as much fun as the notions counter.

Now and then a bunch of school friends would march through in their soccer jerseys and boots and make rude comments about my wasting a perfectly good Saturday. This never worried me because I didn't much like playing soccer. I preferred riding long distances and exploring England on my sports bicycle. When the bike was fully paid for, I gave up my Saturday job.

My first full-time job was almost the same thing. I was hired by the manager of a small, exclusive menswear shop who had seen me working on Saturdays and liked the way I handled bad-tempered customers. The problem was that his shop was so exclusive that only a trickle of customers came in. There were just the two of us. My employer handled suits and jackets while I took care of ties and monogrammed handkerchiefs. He was pleasant enough, but not the talkative type, and so I spent hours polishing the dark oak fittings and poking through the dozens of little wooden drawers that lined the walls.

Some of the stock had been there for years. There were extra long shoe laces from the days when everybody, even gentlemen, wore boots that required long laces. There were cuff links, tie tacks and boxes of collar studs, too. One day, when I came across a drawer full of stiff collars, the manager showed me how to attach a collar to a shirt with a couple of studs. But first he had to search around in the upstairs store room for a collar-less shirt. "Not much call for this type of shirt these days," he said. After fumbling with a stiff collar, two studs, and a tie for five minutes, I was not surprised that there was not much call for those old-fashioned shirts.

In another drawer there were things like cut-off sleeves designed to protect a clerk's shirt cuffs from ink while he was writing and quite a wide selection of braces (suspenders). There were drawers of men's garters that were used to hold men's socks up, clumsy, elastic and metal clip things that looked most uncomfortable but came in a wide variety of colors. When I asked if we carried any spats, the manager laughed and said, "Haven't seen spats in many a long year. Pity, really." He himself wore braces and garters and large cuffs with gold cufflinks. He always had a stickpin in his wide tie and invariably wore a waistcoat with a gold chain draped across the front. He also wore a black homburg and carried a tightly rolled black umbrella, no matter what the weather.

Yes, the manager was always a perfect English gentleman with beautiful diction. But there was one thing that cracked the façade: he loved cod roe. There were three fishmongers close to the shop, and every afternoon, when things were quiet, he would leave me in charge and check them out. About once a week he was lucky and hurried back with a large, well-wrapped package of cod roe, which he would tenderly tuck away in the coldest part of the back office until it was time to go home. Then he would wander around the shop as happy as a child on Christmas Eve; his accent would slip into broad Lancashire as he rubbed his hands with anticipated pleasure of eating fish eggs. I never did find out how he cooked the stuff, but I took some home once, and my mother battered and fried it. It was rather good.

It wasn't long, however, before I was utterly bored with men's wear. I really did not see myself behind a counter for the rest of my life, even in a very exclusive shop. I tried changing the somber ties in the window for the brightest and gaudiest ones we had in stock in the faint hope that this would bring in younger and livelier customers, but all that did was get me banned from window dressing.

Then, one bright day, my uncle Jack dropped into the shop. Uncle Jack, a very practical man who always took a friendly interest in my family, was in the construction trade and doing quite well.

At closing time that day, he took me out for a cup of tea and asked about my work. After listening to me for several minutes, he said, "You're wasting your time there. Give him your notice. I'll find you something better."

Some years later, and a few thousand miles to the west, I once again found myself behind the counter in the men's department. I was now a university student in Vancouver and, as usual, almost broke. A large department store in the city needed extra help over the Christmas holidays and I was hired immediately. My job was to wander among the customers and help them come to decisions. My instructions were simple: "Don't let anybody leave without buying something, even if it's only a pair of socks." Thanks to my earlier experience, this was not difficult and I enjoyed myself.

My most interesting customer appeared late one Saturday evening. He was a weather-beaten fellow whose clothes were very grubby, though he was clearly not a bum. He shoved a credit card into my hand and proceeded to gather up a complete set of clothing, from underwear to tie. I followed him to the changing room with my arms piled high and a pair of scissors to cut off the labels. Over the door, he explained that he had been "living in a tent up the coast" and doing some research and had spent the last couple of months in the same clothing. When he emerged he was a new man, all neat and tidy, except for his well worn but obviously expensive boots. With a huge smile, he waved at his old garments and said, "You can burn those."

The next summer, I was in exactly the same position. I had spent the summer "living in a tent up the coast" and had been in the same clothing for weeks. When I got back to Vancouver I, too, indulged myself and bought an entirely new outfit except for the boots. But instead of dumping my old clothes with orders to burn them, I wrapped them carefully and took them to a laundry.

Chapter 2
Repairing Antiques

When Uncle Jack rescued me from haberdashery, I thought that he had found me a job in construction as a carpenter's assistant or something like that. But he had something better in mind.

Early on a Monday morning, I presented myself at a large four-story building in London, not far from the British Museum. It looked like any other Victorian house with nothing but the house number on the door. I was greeted by a fussy little man in a pinstripe suit and bowler hat who introduced himself and showed me to his tiny office on the ground floor. The rest of the floor space in the house was taken up by a wonderful collection of antique furniture all crowded together but in perfect showroom condition. Mr. Lummis, the manager, proudly informed me that I was standing in the repair facility of the most prestigious antique dealers in London, if not the world. He also informed me that I was to wear a clean white carpenter's apron at all times and to make myself scarce if there were any visitors around.

Then he took me upstairs. On the first floor, he opened the door and said, "This is the electrical department. Mr. Taylor doesn't like to be disturbed when he's working." I tip-toed in and found myself in a forest of shimmering crystals. From the ceiling hung dozens of magnificent chandeliers of every size and shape and all the space on the floor was covered in small table lamps. Some of the fixtures were lit, and their light added to the light coming in the windows, creating a sparkling, rainbow fairyland that was eerily silent except for occasional faint tinkles when a draft blew through the door. Against the wall were rolls of fine electric wire. When I glimpsed a vague human shape almost lost in the glistening forest, I didn't need to be told that it was Mr. Taylor and that he was converting the chandeliers to electricity.

The second floor was different. "Upholstery," Mr. Lummis informed me. "Most of that material costs a fortune, so always wash your hands before touching it." The large room was packed with antique chairs and sofas of every shape and size, in every state of disrepair. Along the walls were racks of colored material and the floor was littered with bright pieces of cloth and stuffing. Where the electrician's floor had been a cool and silent forest, this was a vibrant country garden. Three or four women and a man were hard at work in a sea of canvas and stuffing and lengths of beautiful cloth, chatting while they worked.

On the top floor, I was handed over to a short, elderly man who nodded silently and showed me where to hang my jacket. This room contained half a dozen workbenches and enough space to hold pieces of furniture that were being repaired. Each workbench was packed with hand tools of every kind, and the walls were covered in racks with even more tools. The men at the workbenches looked me up and down but carried on working as the foreman handed me a broom and told me to sweep the floor. It didn't seem like much, but it took all morning because the floor was a sea of sawdust and wood chips and there was dust everywhere. It coated all the racks of tools, and each workbench was covered in light brown dust. Some looked like they hadn't been cleaned in decades. I soon found out why.

At the far end of the room was a large alcove where the French polishers worked. There were three of them and they were friendly and helpful, but they hated to have any dust in the air. I had hardly started sweeping, in fact, when one of the polishers came up and showed me how to hold the broom and slide it slowly along so that I moved the wood chips but didn't raise any dust.

"Always ask one of us before you sweep," he said. "And never open any window." I looked around and saw that there were windows but they had not been opened in decades and were gray with grime. I also noticed that nobody was smoking. There might be dust on everything, but the air was clean.

The polishers did their work the hard way. From stripping down the old surface to applying the final high gloss varnish, they used only what they mixed themselves from ancient glass containers stored under a stained workbench. They rubbed everything slowly and patiently by hand, using wads of soft cotton and often applying eight or nine coats of varnish. If it was a large table, they worked as a team, walking slowly around and rubbing in a circular pattern for hours, reversing direction every half hour to give their arms a rest. It sometimes took days, but the results were worth it. The table would glow with a deep, deep shine that no commercial varnish in a can could ever equal.

Most of the antiques were much too heavy and awkward to carry up the narrow stairs, so in the far corner was a very large and very old hand-operated freight lift. It had an iron gate to prevent anybody falling down the shaft, but the lift itself was merely a platform with a pair of ropes flapping against the walls. I soon learned that it was my job to operate it. To go down, I pulled the correct rope, which was strung around a giant wheel in the attic, and winched the platform down. If the lift was empty, only a slight tug was enough, but if there was a heavy load, the rope would slide through my hands fast enough to raise blisters. Coming up was the same, except that a heavy load called for some serious rope pulling on my part. Since there was no button or even a bell on the lift, the only way to summon it was to yell down the shaft or for me to run down to the ground floor and bring it up myself.

Near the end of my first day on the job, I realized that, for a workshop containing nearly a dozen people, the house was extraordinarily quiet. The cabinetmakers, like most skilled craftsmen, were completely absorbed in their work, though they did make a remark or two or even crack a joke when they relaxed. At mid-morning, they all stopped for a large mug of tea and chatted quietly about sports or gardening or the weather. I kept the tea pot filled. At noon, most of them ate their sandwiches at their benches and read the newspaper. There was no radio, and no traffic noise reached us.

I was there several days before I noticed the most important feature (and the reason for the silence). There were no electric tools anywhere. In fact, there were no electric outlets in any of the walls and, except for the powerful electric lights overhead, it could have been the nineteenth or even the eighteenth century. When I asked one of the men why there were no electric tools, he smiled, shook his head, and said, "We're repairing antiques, not building garages." Then he picked up an ancient wooden plane and ran his hands lovingly over it and said, "My dad used this. We do it properly. Only hand tools here."

Another of my tasks was to tend the glue pots. On the ancient gas stove in the corner, one burner was used for the kettle for brewing tea. The other three burners held hot water containers in which sat small pots of glue which had to be heated up first thing every morning. The glue arrived in hard brown chunks and gave off a slight smell when it was melted. I never did find out what it was made of, but whatever it was, it was powerful. Throughout the day, when one of the men called for glue, I had to hurry some over and then watch as he skillfully painted a joint or a repaired break. Then he would clamp it or I would hold the joint together for five minutes.

Nobody used nails. Almost everything was fastened with glue and a variety of connections, such as dovetails and tongue-and-groove joints. Many of the pieces called for wooden pegs or butterfly connections. Each was done by hand in exactly the way it had been originally made and almost always using the exact same type of wood. Sometimes the men spent hours searching in the stacks of wood that were parked on the landing outside, looking for a perfect match, Once a messenger delivered a small length of very rare wood from an importer in the East End. There were a few boxes of screws gathering dust, and, on very rare occasions, I would be called to hold an object while the cabinet maker gently tapped in a tiny nail he called a "pin" to hold everything together while the glue dried.

While the men could all handle anything that arrived, they did specialize. There was a tall, silent man with a remarkable collection of chisels who could carve anything. It didn't matter whether it was a giant four-poster bed or a tiny jewelry box. He would carefully cut away the damaged part, replace it with a block of wood, draw some simple guidelines in blue chalk, and then, when the glue had dried, carve his way along and create a perfect match with no visible join. One of the other men told me that the carver had been a ship's carpenter in the Royal Navy at the battle of Gallipoli. (All of them had served in the Second World War, but they never talked about it.)

Another man specialized in anything inlaid or veneered. There were shelves near his bench that held a tangle of finely cut veneers, some almost paper thin, and small chunks of exotic woods in a wild variety of colors. He could reach into his collection of wood and within minutes find a match for almost anything. He loved the strange woods and knew the names and countries of origin of most of them. I liked to watch him cut tiny pieces with a razor sharp chisel, which he then used to move the pieces because his fingers were too big. Each tiny fragment fit to perfection. He spent much of his time repairing the doors of grandfather clocks.

Another man had a remarkable collection of planes. There were shelves of them and nearly all were edge planes. Today, when a cabinetmaker needs a special edge trim, he reaches for his router and puts in the appropriate bit. But they didn't have electric routers when those antiques were created. The planes were narrow and their bottoms were carved to the required shapes. The steel blades were also ground to the very same shape, which meant sharpening them was quite tricky. All the men had a wide range of planes and chisels and much time was taken sharpening them by hand with whetstones or putting an extra keenness to them so that they would not damage the wood.

One day the foreman gave me an armful of well-worn whetstones and took me down to the basement. It was packed with marble statues of every kind and size. There was just one light in the center, and under the light there was a table with a large flat stone and a can of greasy water. My job was to rub the whetstones on the wet block and get them back to a perfect flatness. It was hard, slow work. Rubbing one stone against another was boring, and I soon began to lose my initial enthusiasm. But when I stopped, I realized that all the statues were facing toward me. It was deathly quiet in the gloomy basement and I was being watched by an army of marble nymphs and maidens, Roman emperors and British colonels, and unknown ancestors, all long dead. At first, it was just creepy, but as the time went by, my feeling of being watched increased. I began to rub faster and faster. All I wanted was to finish the job and get away from that multitude of cold, white eyes. I splashed more water on the stone and put some real muscle into my grinding while I tried to think of anything amusing to keep myself from just grabbing everything and running upstairs. It was the thought of having to explain myself to everybody that kept me there, madly scrubbing until all the whetstones were relatively smooth. Eventually the job was done, and I left the gloomy basement, never to return.

Running messages around London was a part of the job I liked. Sometimes the work would pile up, so smaller pieces were sent out to trusted craftsmen, but usually it was something that our shop did not handle, such as a lock. Many of the antiques had locks, which the foreman would carefully remove and label and give me detailed instructions for an address somewhere in London. I would pick up the bus fare from Mr. Lummis, who would repeat the instructions in even more detail, and head off into the great city.

I usually took the oldest locks to a tiny workshop in the Paddington area, where the locksmith was a friendly, middle aged man. He never touched the modern Yale locks, but he knew all about the older locks and eagerly explained how they worked and showed me how to pick them with a bent piece of stiff wire. He would open up the lock and study its innards for a few minutes, then search through boxes of blank keys of every size and shape until he had one that fit. He would then file all the grooves and cut the notches so that the key would navigate the maze of wards inside the lock.

"You realize," he once said, "that the ancient Egyptians had locks very much like these modern Yale things." He tapped the old lock that he was working on. "And this thing hasn't changed much in the last 500 years, either." One of the reasons this locksmith was so popular with the antique dealers was because he knew his history. The fashion in keys changes over the years, but he could look at a lock and tell immediately just what kind of key it needed. He had boxes of keys of every description and could pick up any key, study its design and the decorative style, then make an accurate guess as to what period and to what piece of furniture it belonged.

Keyholes went to another specialist in another part of London. Most keyholes were simple brass or bronze inserts that protected the wood, but they too have changed over the years. I took ours to a tiny, one-man foundry where the owner either tried to match it from his collection or made a mold and poured a new one. Other keyholes were decorated with fancy metal plates, and the foundry man searched through his rack of wooden drawers until he came up with a match. If he could not find a match, he had to make the part and I had to return with detailed sketches and measurements. Since making the keyhole was a complex operation, I never actually saw it done, but went back a week later and picked up a perfectly aged, antique keyhole, complete with a few dents and scratches.

One craftsman who would not let me watch was the jigsaw man, who worked alone in a large, empty basement seated on a cleverly designed, foot-operated jigsaw that he had obviously made himself. There was one powerful light, he had no radio to distract him, and his work bench was bare except for a few boxes of the finest, most delicate blades, some of them almost hair thin. I took to him intricate fretwork and complicated veneer work that needed a great deal of time and serious concentration. These were carried in a lined box, and if I had to wait, he made me sit on the steps outside while he performed his magic.

Going to the antique showroom in the West End was Mr. Lummis' job. As he bustled off in his bowler hat, clutching his rolled umbrella, he let me come along only once, and that was a quick trip to deliver a parcel. But I did sneak a quick look into the showrooms, where a surprisingly friendly clerk showed me around. It was a magnificent collection of carefully selected and tastefully arranged items, all in perfect condition. I was strangely proud to be part of the team that created such beauty.

One day Mr. Lummis had to leave when we were expecting a delivery, so I was detailed to guard the office while he was gone. When an immense, red and yellow Bugatti pulled up, a short and rather portly man marched in. "Where's old Lummis?" he demanded in a cheerful tone. I explained that the manager would be back very soon. The man said, "Don't worry, I'll find it myself," and disappeared into the tangle of antiques. A few minutes later he came out and found me standing at the door drooling at the sight of the priceless classic car.

"She's a beauty, isn't she?" he said proudly. Then he laughed. "Only four ever built. Probably because the fuel gauge goes down as fast as the speedometer goes up! Tell Lummis I'll phone." And he disappeared into the monster and roared off down the road.

I had not the faintest idea who the man was, but when I told Mr. Lummis about the Bugatti, he informed me that I had had the privilege of talking to one Mr. Harris, the owner of the business. He went on to explain just how rich and well connected Mr. Harris was, but the only thing that impressed me was his splendid old car.

Another time I was minding the office when a dark car appeared at the door and an exquisitely tailored gentleman slipped into the office and in a soft voice asked for Mr. Lummis. I explained that he was out and offered to show the visitor around. He was looking for a particular antique that was being prepared for his mother, he said, but Lummis had not explained the system to me and I had not the faintest idea where it was. So the man apologized for wasting my time, and the car drove off.

When Mr. Lummis returned and I described our visitor, he almost had a heart attack. "Good heavens, boy! That was the Duke of Windsor."

At lunchtime, some of us usually went across the road to a café, but one day a cabinetmaker who was particularly friendly and had seen me admiring his collection of chisels persuaded me to go with him to a nearby secondhand market. "Let's see what they have in tools," he said.

It was a typical side street market of wheeled stalls called "barrows," all of them overloaded with a wild collection of odds and ends. Two of the dealers had nice selections of well used tools. The cabinetmaker picked over them carefully, commenting on them and explaining their uses and looking at the quality of the metal. "You can make your own handles," he said, "but they don't make good steel the way they used to." On the way back he told me of other little back-street markets where old tools could sometimes be bought for a song and hinted that it was never too early to start building up a decent set of tools.

I had worked there for about a year when I began to get restless. Although I was part of a team of craftsmen who did marvelous things, I was not actually allowed to do anything. There must be something more, I thought. More than sweeping the floor and running errands. I thought I could sweep floors and maybe make better money without having to ride the tube for an hour each way every day. What I did not realize, and nobody ever explained to me, was that I was receiving an education just by watching and helping. I had already learned more about the art of fine woodworking by watching it done by experts day after day than I ever could have learned from books or classroom lectures. I was not an apprentice, but I was in the same position. After years of observing and assisting, I would have mastery of a trade.

I also lacked tools. A craftsman has to have tools, and I had nothing. The pay was barely enough to pay my tube fare, buy lunch, and give my mother something for board, and yet I was supposed to be building up a collection of tools large enough to handle any repair job. Craftsmen do not lend or borrow their valuable tools, and it would take me years to buy my own. When Uncle Jack dropped by one day and asked how things were going, I didn't have the heart, or the verbal skill, to explain that I was deeply frustrated. One day I just gave my notice and quit.

I have often wondered how different my life would have been if I had continued there. Undoubtedly, I would have been a superior craftsman in a highly respected trade with skills learned from masters. And I would have married a local girl and settled down somewhere in London to a pleasant, middle-class life.

But I would never have traveled the world and wandered over six continents. I would never have gone to university, earned two degrees, and become a teacher. I doubt if I would have emigrated to North America, and I certainly would never have ended up happily married and living in a nice house in southern California. Thinking about my life's path now, I feel that, although I didn't know it at the time, I took the right turn in the road.

Chapter 3
White-Collar Office Work

Mother said nothing, but I think she was rather pleased that I had given up the job in London because she had always wanted me to have a white-collar job closer to home. My next job was as a pay clerk at a factory just a five-minute bike ride from our house. The office manager was a youngish man who had absolutely no control over the three women clerks, who talked incessantly. My job was to collect the time cards, run messages, and check other people's figures. Since our office was separate from the main building, it was very relaxed and, as long as we got the pay packets out on time every Friday, we were left alone. The main office was a converted country house with a permanent gardener and a huge lawn that ran down to the river. The gardener spent much of his time mowing and rolling the lawn in geometrically exact diagonal lines. It was a perfect lawn. Only senior staff were allowed to walk on it.

The men in the factory checked in and out by sliding their cards into the time clock, which stamped the time on the card. Because being more than one minute late meant the loss of a quarter of an hour's pay, the men had developed a number of ways to fool the machine. The most popular was to have somebody else clock them in on time, and it was common to see one man standing in front of the machine clutching half a dozen cards. Another was to bang the card up and down a number of times so that the resulting inky mess was illegible and the worker had to have the benefit of the doubt. Otherwise, there could be union trouble, perhaps even a strike. A third trick was to smear a greasy thumb print across the inked time or even drop the whole card on the wet ground. Part of my job, accordingly, was to chat with the foremen about these disputed time clock marks and come to a decision. The foremen usually sided with the workers. Since the office work was boringly simple, I didn't mind wandering around the factory holding time cards in my hand and pretending to look for a foreman. It was a very interesting place.

The factory made and repaired huge tanker trucks. After the truck chassis arrived stripped of everything except the cab, it was soon swarming with welders who attached a score or more brackets. Sparks flew in all directions, dazzling lights flashed, and there were loud buzzings and cracklings, along with the smell and smoke of burning metal. Nearby, other welders were joining huge sheets of steel which had been precisely curved in a giant roller to form the tanks. An overhead crane set the tank on the prepared chassis and still more welders attached it. The end pieces were next welded on, plus various pipes and fittings until the tanker truck stood gleaming, large, and unpainted, waiting for a pressure test.

Almost everybody employed there seemed to be a welder, and they hurried around the cavernous building in their protective helmets in a sea of smoke and sparks like creatures in a science fiction movie. I had come from a quiet world of wood and glue and delicate construction slowly and carefully done by hand, so this was a completely different world. I was fascinated by it.

There was one part of the factory, however, that I avoided whenever I could. This was where the tanks that were in for repair were descaled (rust and grime were removed). This was done in a separate building called the boiler shop by a gang of men who would crawl through an opening cut into the end of the tank and attack the walls with pneumatic chisels, grinders, and high-speed wire brushes. They left the inside of the tank gleaming like the outside, but at a heavy price. The noise of half a dozen high-powered chisels on the inside of a huge steel tank was beyond deafening, and so the boilermen, as they proudly called themselves, were almost all partially deaf. Everybody in the shop was issued ear plugs that ranged from little rubber stoppers that were almost useless to huge cup-shaped things that were heavy and uncomfortable. As they worked in that extraordinary noise all day long, even with the best of ear plugs, it was inevitable that their hearing would be damaged. And they didn't always wear the regulation ear protection. Some of the older men had long ago given up trying to save their hearing because the pay was extraordinarily good and the work, though hard and dirty, took little skill and no training. They were obviously trading good pay for good hearing. We could always tell a boilerman when he came into the office because he would shout when he spoke and we had to shout when we replied.

Despite their handicap, though, they were a cheerful bunch. During one lunch break, a particularly old and gnarled boilerman told me, "I got into this business the hard way. Thirteen, I was. Worked on the steam trains cleaning the boilers. Crawled into them things with just a hammer and chisel. No fancy electric tools in my day."

The boiler shop was always dusty. Some days, the air was heavy with a reddish fog of powdered rust, and there was a lot of coughing and spitting. The company issued nose and mouth masks for the men, but almost all of them said they were for sissies and refused to use them. Not surprisingly, many of the men had permanent coughs. Nobody wore helmets or hard hats of any kind, either.

Apart from what I picked up in the factory, I learned very little in that job. During a visit to the main office, I once saw a blueprint machine and a draftsman showed me how they made blueprints and explained why they come out blue. I also learned a bit from the old gardener who was even prouder of his forget-me-nots than of his immaculate lawn.

The office work was simple. The men were paid in cash every Friday. We had to check and double-check each little brown envelope and have the time cards ready for the inevitable complaints. The only excitement was when the office manager took his heavy leather bag to the bank to get the money. It wasn't far enough to drive, so he walked, but the head office insisted that he have a bodyguard. It was my job to go down to the factory and choose the biggest, ugliest man available at the time. Since the bodyguard would get paid for taking a nice stroll in the middle of the working day, the chore was very popular. Nobody worried about the danger. I must have chosen well because they were never robbed.

As the months went by, I became increasingly bored with this job. The travel bug had already bitten me very hard and I had been cycling greater and greater distances, taking weekend trips and stopping in youth hostels or sleeping in barns. But a bicycle is limiting as far as distance goes, and I wanted to see much more of the world, so one day I gave my notice, bought a stout pair of shoes, took the train to Dover, and went hitch-hiking on the Continent. It was a wonderful experience. ˋ

In the early 1950s, there were very few high-speed roads in Europe except for the German autobahns. Traffic was slower, people were friendly, and there was no danger in hitch-hiking. Some days I covered many miles, and some days I walked more than I rode. Everywhere I went was wonderfully new and exciting as I wandered from country to country, thoroughly enjoying myself. Paris. Amsterdam. Copenhagen. Hamburg. Vienna. Venice. Rome. Monte Carlo. The Alps. The Pyrenees. The Danube. I saw them all. Inevitably, as the long summer began to turn to cold autumn, I discovered I had used up my small savings. It was time to go home

Having seen some of the major cities of Europe, I now had an urge to take a job in the heart of London, which to me was—and still is—the greatest city of them all. A large travel agency just off Piccadilly had an opening for a cost clerk, and so, with the vague idea that there might be travel opportunities, I jumped at the offer.

I was disappointed from the first day. In a huge room crowded with busy clerks at small desks, four of us junior clerks sat at a large table with narrow file boxes of used tickets from all over Europe and the world. We had to count them and compare the results with the official records, then get another box and do the same thing. That's all we did all day—count tickets.

One bright spring day, I skipped lunch and took a stroll in Green Park, one of the royal parks off Piccadilly where the daffodils had appeared in their golden clouds. I spotted a vacant deck chair there in the mild sun, but I had hardly sat down in it before the attendant appeared. I paid the small fee and then decided to enjoy it and lie back to stare at the clear blue sky. It was the middle of the afternoon when I awoke. In a panic, I hurried back to the office, where I expected to be confronted by an angry manager. As I ran, I concocted a nicely complicated excuse…but I didn't need it. Nobody had missed me! I stood there and looked around at the sea of clerks, all of them wasting a beautiful day at fiddling little meaningless jobs. I took my raincoat out of the locker, and walked away.

A few blocks from the travel agency was a small shipping line that needed a cost clerk. Their ships, which went to the Far East, carried both freight and passengers, and I thought (again) that a future with this company could involve some cheap travel.

This was a very old company in a very old building with mahogany paneled corridors lined with beautifully detailed scale models of all the company's ships, going back for years, most of them now at the bottom of the sea or rusting away in a scrap yard. It was also a very old fashioned firm buried in tradition. The small costing office was on the very top floor of the ancient building. While there was a lift, junior staff could use it only to go up. Only senior staff could descend in it. Suits and ties were to be worn every day, except for Saturday morning, when we could wear a sports jacket, but still with a tie. Junior staff could not talk in the corridors, and whistling and smoking were completely banned for all staff…with the exception of directors and very senior managers, who smoked cigars. There was even a correct way to address any director or senior executive who deigned to talk to us lowly clerks. Naturally, we could not talk to visitors or even be seen by them.

The work was interesting enough, and the other clerks were friendly, but it didn't take me long to realize that I was frozen in a job with no chance of promotion and no chance to move to a more interesting department. The office manager had been there over twenty years and had never even seen one of the company ships.

When I heard of a job doing almost the same work for nearly twice the pay, I quickly moved to a new company on Oxford Street. The company was indeed new but their clerical department was not.

I found myself in yet another large room filled with clerks huddled over desks adding up columns of figures and writing in ledgers. They were giant ledgers, hardly changed since the days of Charles Dickens, though we wrote in them with fountain pens instead of feather quills. I didn't stay there very long.

The thrill of working in the heart of London had worn off by now, and I no longer wanted to be a little cog in a big machine. So I looked around home for another job. Mother was pleased when I found a costing job close by in a factory that made built-in cabinets and other wooden items. Working there was interesting and I learned quite a lot. When the order department sent us a detailed description of an item, we worked out exactly, to the fraction of a penny, how much it would cost to manufacture. This information then went off to the sales department for final pricing.

It was amazing how many items went into making something as simple as a cupboard. We measured every scrap of wood and calculated its cost, every knob and hinge was valued, and every nail, screw, or drop of glue was taken into account. Then we worked out how many minutes it would take to cut, assemble, and paint the item, plus the time it took to move it to the warehouse. Even the time required for the paint to dry was carefully noted.

However, summer came, and I was itching to travel again. I could not afford to go back to the Continent, so I planned a bike trip around England. One fine day I gave my notice, packed a sleeping bag on my bike, and set off. It was a glorious summer as I coasted through the countryside with no specific plan, no timetable, and no worries, wandering down side lanes and stopping where and when I wanted. I didn't go home until the nights had become cooler and I had run out of money.

When I returned from my trip I found a job near home in the office of a cable manufacturing company. This job proved to be quite useful. I learned to count.

Most of my time seemed to be spent in adding up huge columns of figures and comparing my sums with those from other huge columns of figures. The electronic calculator had not been invented yet, and the office had just one mechanical adding machine, which was heavy and clumsy. Since the UK was still using the complicated pre-decimal currency with ha'pennies and farthings and twelve pennies to a shilling with twenty shillings to a pound but twenty-one shillings to a guinea…well, adding up prices and receipts was much more complicated than it sounds.

There were eight people in the office, eight people who needed the adding machine. As I was the newest person there, I was at the bottom of the priority list. Since my chance at the machine was very slight and the work had to be done, I was forced to add up the figures in my head. For days, I struggled with a note pad and a pencil and gradually learned that if I concentrated very hard and cut out all distractions, I could add more quickly. I worked out a few short cuts and tricks to speed up my work, and within a month I could slide my pencil down a long column of figures and get a result almost as fast as the mechanical adding machine did.

Inevitably, it wasn't long before I became bored with the job. Whenever somebody had to go into the factory to get some figures, I found myself volunteering. The other clerks, who were mostly middle-aged women, hated to go into the noisy, dusty factory where the cable was made, so it became my job.

Most of the factory was taken up by an enormous wheel that towered up almost to the ceiling and was decorated with a score of smaller wheels. The first time I saw this monster, it was slowly spinning, and so were the smaller wheels. At the back of the shed, a thin wire ran from a giant spool, through the giant spinning wheel, and out through the back door. But what was most amazing was the fine cobweb of wires that led from each of the smaller wheels in a great cone of shimmering colored light as they slowly wrapped themselves around the core.

Stacked against the walls were spools of wire of every kind. There were copper wire and steel wire, wire of every thickness, wire of every conceivable color. There were also spools of various types of paper and material that I couldn't identify. It was both mysterious and fascinating.

As the office job got more and more boring, I found myself making up excuses to visit the great wheel. The foreman was friendly and answered all my questions and showed me how the tangle of reels all fed into the core to produce the required cable in all its complexity. One day he pointed to some dark paper that was being wrapped into the cable and smiled. "Don't touch that stuff with your bare hands," he said. "It's soaked in rat poison. Those buggers just love to chew on cables."

My problem was that the factory fascinated me more than the office. Unfortunately, the office manager, a thin-faced, elderly woman with a bad temper, sensed my feelings and soon took me aside to "have a little talk." Ten minutes later I was happily riding my bike down the road, quite convinced that working in an office was not for me.

Chapter 4
Making Terrazzo Tiles

I had greatly admired the terrazzo tiles in the lovely old churches and palaces in Italy, so when I learned that a local company specialized in making terrazzo tiles and an extra hand was needed, I applied. It was close enough to home that I could ride my bike, and it sounded interesting, although the pay was barely enough for me to give my mother some housekeeping money and take a girl to the cinema once a week.

There were four other workers, the oldest of whom showed me the ropes. "So," he said, "you want to learn how to make these fancy tiles, eh?" I was soon filling the cement mixer, greasing the forms, and helping pour the special terrazzo mixture into the forms. Since the twelve-inch-wide tiles were made top-down, the marble chips and the color had to be sprinkled carefully on the bottom of the form before the cement was poured. The sprinkling was done by one of the two managers, who used color charts and small measuring cups to keep the finished product consistent.

"Now we have to shake them down," said my guide, as we set the filled molds on a small metal table. "Better take off that wrist watch," he said. "This little toy will shake the innards out of it." And then he switched the table on. The table's vibration was powerful, and it took some strength to keep the molds from sliding off. After a minute, my guide seemed satisfied. "You get to lug them out into the yard where they'll dry in the open air," he told me. "That's if it don't rain."

The terrazzo tiles dried for a few days, then they were gently removed from their molds. "We polish them while they're still green," the clerk said. "Get a much nicer shine that way." We lifted the tiles onto benches, where one of the men polished them by machine until the marble chips gleamed.

Although I helped everywhere, my main job was to stack the uncured tiles in long rows in the yard. It was back-breaking work, as every tile had to be placed on edge one inch from the next tile and tilted gently to lean against its neighbor and harden in the open air. The finished tiles were very beautiful.

But I lasted less than a month. One day I was in a hurry and accidentally knocked one of the tiles with the tip of my shoe. Like dominoes lined up on the kitchen table, the whole long line of uncured tiles fell and every single one broke in half. It was a day's output, and I was genuinely sorry. But the senior manager had seen it happen. He looked at me and through tightly gritted teeth said, "I don't think we will be needing you anymore."

Chapter 5
Rustic Furniture

A few days later, I passed a shop where they made rustic garden furniture out of peeled logs and branches. The furniture was cleverly done so I stopped to look at the display and saw the *Man Wanted* sign. Making furniture looked like interesting work, so I went inside and applied.

When I turned up next day, I was shown how to fit a branch into a low clamp and how to use a draw blade, which was a two-handled knife that I had to pull toward me to peel the bark off the branch.

"That tool hasn't changed in a couple of thousand years," said the older of the two men who ran the place. "Probably used it in Bible days."

I soon got the hang of it and peeled branches out in the back yard in the fresh air. The bark was piled up by the gate to be carted off, and the cleaned limbs, all white and shiny, were stacked against the wall according to height. For about a week, I was content, but then I asked if I could lend a hand in the actual construction of the furniture or even apply the finishing varnish.

The other men reacted as if I were trying to deprive them of their jobs and told me to stick to my peeling. "Look," said one, "you've got a nice job here, and it will keep you out of the army." I must have looked surprised, so he explained. "This is classified as agricultural, see? We're working with natural wood, and anybody classified as an agricultural worker can request an exemption from national service, same as them coal miners and fishermen." He winked as broadly as a clown in the circus and half whispered, "You stick with us and you won't be called up to be a soldier."

But the thought of two years of peeling branches was worse than the thought of being conscripted. At least the army might teach me a useful trade, so I smiled politely and quit.

Chapter 6
The Illegal Wood Shop

Near the lumber yard was a place that manufactured wooden garages and garden sheds. They always seemed to need men, so I applied and was hired immediately...which should have made me suspicious.

The great woodlands that once covered most of England are long gone, and even the famous Sherwood Forest is now all farmland. England thus has to import almost all of its lumber from Canada or Scandinavia. At that time, lumber was heavily controlled and regulated.

I was teamed up with an older man to make sections of prefabricated garages, a very simple operation. There were three or four other teams, too, all making more or less the same buildings. The first thing I noticed was the quality of the work. We just threw those buildings together. The owner was constantly wandering around, urging everybody to work faster and suggesting short-cuts to speed up the work. The delivery crew always seemed to be waiting impatiently for loads, so those atrociously built sheds just flowed out of the door.

On the very first day, when I was carefully screwing something together, my partner snapped, "Don't waste time. Just use your hammer and bash the bastards in." So I drove in the screws with a hammer. Nobody ever used a carpenter's square, and when the owner caught me using one he snorted, "Hit it hard enough and it'll fit. Anyway, that's the assembly crew's problem."

I have always had a great respect for craftsmanship and have been called a perfectionist more than once when doing something around the house. The slap-dash work we had to do to keep up with the owner's nagging soon became very irritating. He paid well, but I certainly would never buy one of his buildings.

Another thing I noticed in the very first hour I worked there was the quality of the wood. Even the lowest grade lumber should be given a few days to dry before going off to the planer mill. Nobody in his right mind would build something with green lumber, which shrinks and warps very quickly. But the junk we used was wet with sap and had obviously been a live tree just a few days before it reached us. When I pointed this out to my partner, he said, "Oh, it's fresh all right. Fresh off the black market!" He stopped and looked around for the owner, then lowered his voice. "This stuff is delivered at night. The trees are cut illegally, but you can't watch every tree in England, can you?" Then he laughed. "Some of it is poached. Fancy that. Poaching trees! I can see borrowing a few rabbits or a nice pheasant now and then, but poaching a tree?"

I had been there about a month when a car full of men in belted rain coats and shiny black shoes drove up. They were obviously police or government inspectors. At noon the next day, we were told to pick up our tools and collect our pay.

Chapter 7
The Metal Fabricators

I found another job almost immediately in a clean, airy, efficiently-run place just a bike ride from home. This was a company that fabricated sheet metal. They made everything from simple steel storage bins to strangely shaped stainless steel or aluminum things that only the draftsmen understood. It was precision work, and I was only a helper, but after my experience at the previous places, it was an interesting change, even though it was probably one of the noisiest places I've ever worked in.

Within a couple of weeks, I was cutting sheet metal as if it were paper, driving rivets, bending angles, punching holes, and creating showers of hot sparks with the grinder. Although I operated the simpler machines, I was never allowed to learn how to weld, though nobody hesitated to show me how to use a tool or a machine. I learned the hard way when to wear heavy gloves. Some of the older men who disdained gloves had hands that were thick and ugly with calluses and scars.

Nevertheless, it was a good job and a very interesting one, and I might have been there until I was called up for my national service. But one day I came very close to disaster. I was helping an older man feed sheet steel between a pair of rollers on a bending machine. It was a large, powerful machine with absolutely no safety features. The noise level, as usual, was deafening. I was feeding the metal with my bare hands while the older man operated the switches. Suddenly I felt a tug on one of the fingers of my right hand. I'd been grabbed by the rollers! It was a very slow machine, and I tried to pull my hands back. But it was too late.

Suddenly the machine stopped. As the rollers reversed a few inches and released my hand, I staggered back into the arms of the older man who sat me down on the floor and inspected my hand. Blood was flowing from one finger, but I was not yet feeling any pain. "Christ! It's a good job I was looking at your face," he said, "Soon as I saw that expression on your face, I guessed what had happened. Your eyes was as wide as balloons." He shook his head. "Another few seconds and it would have torn your arm right off." That's when I fainted.

A few years later, I had a summer job in Toronto that involved using a huge paper cutter called, appropriately enough, a guillotine. It could slice neatly through ten or twelve inches of paper with no effort at all and had all possible safety devices. When I had the paper positioned and clamped down, I had to keep one hand on the starter button as a metal grid slid out and firmly pushed my other hand away. If the grid was blocked or even felt a bit of pressure, it would stop the machine instantly. Every time I used the guillotine, I remembered the steel rollers in that metal working shop.

Chapter 8
The Assembly Line

When my mother saw my bandaged hand she almost fainted, too. She refused to let me go back to that job. Thanks entirely to my partner's quick action, the bone in my finger was not crushed so I spent a few weeks as a pampered invalid before heading out again to look for work.

Not far from home was a large factory that made adding machines, calculators, cash registers, and similar machines. Before the electronic revolution, these machines were marvels of precision engineering with their cogs and levers and cams and shafts. They were all assembled by hand by rows of women sitting at tiny workbenches and fitting the precisely engineered bits and pieces together, their bandana-covered heads bent over their work and their hands moving quickly and almost magically.

When I applied for work, some genius in the employment office assigned me to a section where they were assembling adding machines on piece work terms. A fast worker could make excellent money.

It was not a good idea.

Being an assembler was not just a matter of putting bits together. The assemblers had a selection of files and other tools so that they could make minute adjustments as they worked and smoothed away the slightest irregularity. The finished machines were carefully tested and they had to work as well as an expensive watch. I found it extremely difficult work. My fingers were too big to handle the tiny parts, and I did not have the delicate touch needed to file away just a hairsbreadth of metal. Various supervisors hovered around and gave me advice, but I produced just a tiny fraction of my quota. Before the week was up, I was moved to the department where the bits and pieces were made and I learned to adjust the machines.

The female workers all made good money, but it was based on how much they produced, so they wanted their machines to work at maximum efficiency. A jammed machine or one that was slow meant money out of their pockets. I was shown how to crawl under an ailing machine and find what needed to be adjusted. Usually, it was very easy. What was difficult was keeping the women happy.

Stamping out the same widget for eight hours a day is an extremely boring activity. The monotony would drive a man crazy, but some of those women operators had been doing it for years. The secret was piece work. For the women, it was not a career or a profession, nor did they expect (or want) advancement. Their lives revolved around their families, and the job was simply a way to bring home as much money as possible. The company, on the other hand, wanted to get as much as possible for its money, so I was kept busy by the women and the department manager was constantly checking my work.

The fun part was the compliments I got from the women when I improved the performance of their machines. These ranged from a smiling "Ta, love!" from the younger ones to "Ooo, you're a darlin' boy!" often accompanied by a hug and a fat kiss on the cheek, from the older ladies.

The man who never got a nice word from the ladies was the time and motion expert. He appeared without warning at uneven intervals through the year with his clipboard and multiple stop-watches. An invisible cloud of gloom seemed to hover over his head as he stood and silently watched each operator for a precisely measured time, taking notes and clicking stopwatches. Then, without a comment, he vanished. Soon he would be back with his notes to make small but vital changes in the way the woman operated. Sometimes he had me adjust the height of her chair or the angle of a lever, sometimes he produced a newly designed parts tray, but often his improvement was something as simple as moving a parts box from one side to the other or changing the order in which the woman moved her hands.

I found it extremely interesting and admired the way he almost always increased production without increasing the actual work. He often made the operator more comfortable, too, but the ladies hated him. He increased productivity, yes, but then he recalculated the number of widgets that ought to be produced in a work day. The generous piece work pay did not start until production went over the base figure that he calculated. He was highly disliked, whereas I and my tool box became ever more popular.

A few days after my eighteenth birthday, I received a registered letter. I had a new job with the British government.

Chapter 9
The Royal Air Force

My birthday greetings from His Majesty's Government contained a one-way ticket to a depressing little town in the north of England, where I would begin my military service, and a money order for two shillings. Inflation had taken its toll and the King's Shilling of Nelson's day was now two. This was my first week's pay. Just enough to buy a tot of rum.

After basic training, where I became quite good at polishing buttons and boots but not very good at hitting the target on the shooting range, I was posted to a base in the south of England, where the RAF, in all its wisdom, tried to make a radio mechanic out of me. I never could work out the difference between ohms, watts, and volts and failed so many courses that one day, when I was feeling particularly low, an officer looked at me and said, "Fulford. I have a job for you."

Along with about twenty other men who were six feet tall, good looking, and smartly dressed—and were also failing the course—I was moved to another barracks, where we were made into a special ceremonial squad. Our job was to keep our dress uniforms in perfect condition at all times, polish our Lee Enfield 303 rifles until they gleamed, and be ready to turn out for any ceremonial duty that came along, not only at our camp, but at any RAF base in the south of England. It was a lot better than struggling with ohms and volts, and I enjoyed every minute.

Three or four times a week, we would scramble into our truck and head off through the dawn to a new destination, where we would line up near the gates and an orderly would fuss with our uniforms and waggle a feather duster over our gleaming boots. Then, after the usual long wait, we would present arms to some important visitor. The honored guest would solemnly inspect us and we stood motionless until the VIP and all the brass had gone their ways. We saw a lot of politicians and royalty and quite a few foreign visitors, and we were sometimes inspected by the same person who had inspected us at another base. We often wondered what would happen if he, or she, actually recognized us, but it never happened. They all just walked by with politely serious looks on their faces and boredom in their eyes.

We served a useful function. No base commander wants the bother and disruption of turning out a ceremonial guard at short notice, especially if one phone call can get one sent along. For that reason, we were always treated to a decent meal in the mess while our officer visited their officers club. Since our officer rode in a comfortable staff car and we rode on wooden benches in the truck, it was easy for our driver to get lost on the way home, which of course forced us to stop at the first likely looking pub to get directions…and try the local brew. Some of us became quite expert at identifying the different ales of southern England.

Funerals were our specialty. We spent hours practicing the slow march and firing three blank rounds. Unfortunately, not all cemeteries have neatly mowed lawns, and so we often had to contend with weeds, shrubs, and piles of wet dirt. Nevertheless, we always gave the departed a good send-off.

Once, in a gloomy coal mining village in south Wales, we were plagued with a swarm of little brats who ran in and out of our neat ranks, stomping on our boots and pulling at our rifles. As it happened, the front door of the tiny row house where the deceased had been laid for viewing was too narrow to allow both the coffin and the bearers to get through at the same time. We watched, horrified, as the bearers struggled in the rain, trying desperately to tilt the coffin without dropping it while the brats shrieked with laughter as they ran between their feet and under the coffin. It was not one of our better days. On our way home, we were forced to stop a couple of times to wash away the memory.

When business was slack, some of us were sent off to guard RAF exhibits at various locations. During Battle of Britain week, for example, three of us were assigned as night guards for the Second World War airplanes on show outside the Palace of Whitehall in London. There were a Spitfire, a Hurricane, a Messerschmitt, and a couple of others, authentic planes that still wore the scars of long service, though they would never fly again. They stood under the street lamps in that most historic of locations, silent reminders for one week of the summer of 1940, barely a decade earlier, when a handful of young men held off almost the entire German air force. Their average age was twenty, and over a thousand young men died.

One night, when the great city lay sleeping, I climbed into the Spitfire and sat in the pilot's seat, which was uncomfortably low because I had no parachute under me. I sat there for an hour, thinking about those young men and wondering what it must have been like to be in such a great battle. That was the closest I ever came to being an RAF pilot.

One sunny day, a very young officer walked into our barracks, looked at us for a while, then said, "Get into your truck. You can wear shoes and don't bring the rifles. Maybe you'll learn something." He rode next to the driver as we went to Biggin Hill in Kent, which had been the most important of the airfields used by the RAF during the Battle of Britain. The officer explained to us where we were and the significance of the place, then he left us alone.

I wandered off through the deserted buildings. All the wartime fixtures and fittings had been removed, but there was old trash on the floor and the walls were still decorated with torn and weathered posters, charts, and notices. It was strangely quiet as I studied the walls and scuffled at the trash looking for mementos of the brave young men, mostly my age, who had once been there. Outside, the runway was still grassy. I stood in the doorway and pictured the Spitfires bouncing across it, their pilots racing to get into the air, eager for the fight from which many never returned.

Next day, still without explanation, we went to an abandoned American airfield in Norfolk, which the officer explained had been used by the American Eighth Air Force. The buildings were all gone, and there was nothing left except for an enormous concrete runway stretching off into the tall grass. We stood in the wind in the middle of the empty runway, and the officer told us how this had been one of the many airfields from which so many American airmen took off in their massive bombers, hundreds of them, to fly over Germany and, all too often, never to return. Twenty-six thousand men of the Eighth Air Force died.

On the way home, we stopped at Cardington, where we took a look at the old airship (dirigible) hangar. From a distance, it had looked like a very large barn, but up close it was simply enormous. The great roof was completely self-supporting, and standing in the middle of it, I felt as awe inspired as I did in any medieval cathedral. The doors were especially fascinating. They looked like the largest and heaviest doors in the world.

"This is where the R101 was built." said the officer. "She was the largest airship in the world before the Germans built the

Hindenburg." He paused, then continued. "Left here in 1930 on her maiden voyage. Crashed in France. Killed a lot of important people." Somebody mentioned that they had read something about the *Hindenburg.* "Yes, she burned and crashed a few years later," the officer said. "Quite a few of those monsters were built, but they all eventually crashed." He soon had a small group of men around him discussing helium and airships, to which I listened. I learned that in civilian life he was a history student at Cambridge and that our trips were not just historic sight-seeing; he was gathering data for his thesis.

Another time, six of us were put on night guard duty at an exhibit in Battersea Park, London, which at that time was a very rough neighborhood. We were to guard a Second World War Wellington Bomber that had been trucked there in pieces and reassembled under the trees. The day crew had been dressed as the flight crew and had sat inside pretending to use the various navigation instruments and fly the plane. They also had to answer all the visitors' questions...even if they didn't know the answers.

We arrived to find a very angry day crew. The visiting public had stolen everything that was movable and even some things that were not. Knobs had been unscrewed, fittings had been torn off, all the navigation instruments had vanished, and even the hard leather seat cushions had been spirited out, all under the noses of the phony flight crew. Exasperated, the officer in charge had closed the exhibit. But people then began to steal parts from the outside of the plane. As one angry airman told us, "The bastards even tried to steel one of the bloody propellers! They got the cap loose. Take a look." The cap was high off the ground, but it was indeed quite loose.

If we thought we would have easy nights at that duty station, we were wrong. Even during the earliest hours of the morning, there were people wandering around. We had to be on our toes for vandals and looters, but we had our revenge when they asked questions. Since none of us knew the slightest thing about the plane, it was delightfully easy to let our imaginations run loose. The most common question was "How did you get the plane here?" A Somerset farm boy in our group came up with the best answer. "Well, you see that there river?" He pointed over the embankment at the Thames. "We put pontoons on this 'ere plane and landed it on the water. Then we just hoisted 'er up and stuck 'er wheels back on." He looked entirely serious as he added, "Quite a bit o' work, it were." What surprised me was that almost everybody swallowed the story and walked off impressed by the ingenuity of the RAF.

I was eventually kicked out of the radio mechanic training unit and posted to another camp. This was a bomb dump or, more correctly, an unexploded ordinance storage facility. If they could not make a radio mechanic out of me, I suppose they thought they would turn me into an armourer with expertise in unexploded bombs. Or, with a bit of luck, I would blow myself up. The camp, which was in a forest, was little more than a dismal cluster of unheated metal huts with no facilities, no hot water, and terrible food served by permanently drunken cooks. The officers lived some miles away in a commandeered country house with an inside heated swimming pool. They rarely visited us.

The explosives, most of them left over from the Second World War, were scattered for miles in huge stacks in the forest and included giant blockbusters as big as two oil barrels, incendiary bombs, 20 mm shells, hand grenades, and boxes of fuses and detonators. Our work was mainly moving these stacks from one place to another and looking for any trouble we could get into. Out of sheer boredom and natural curiosity, a few of us studied the various explosives very carefully. We pulled things apart, unscrewed whatever could be unscrewed, broke open what we could, and tested the various explosive powders on the ground.

Today, I shudder when I think of the nonchalant way in which we opened up old hand grenades or twisted the shell out of a cartridge to get at the powder, or the way we unscrewed the detonators from 500-pound bombs that had been lying for years, rusting in the weeds, or the casual way we treated the phosphorus that oozed out of decaying incendiary bombs. The timers, fuses, and detonators had been neatly packed in greased paper in boxes and were still in perfect condition. We spent hours trying to guess how they worked and trying them out on various bombs to see if they fit. It was all very interesting, but, in the long run, a waste of time. About the only thing of practical use that we learned was that when making a big firework out of a cardboard tube and powder extracted from 20 mm ammunition, it is vital to mix in plenty of dry sawdust. Without the sawdust the result will be quite spectacular but rather dangerous.

Although we were supposed to be training as armourers and learning how to handle unexploded bombs, there was very little attempt to teach us anything useful. We rarely saw any of the officers, though once or twice an obviously bored officer would turn up in a staff car, give a quick lecture on fuses or detonators to a group of us seated on the ground, then dash off in his car before anybody could ask a question. The real unexploded bomb problem throughout England was handled by the Royal Engineers. As these extremely well trained soldiers took care of old mines that washed up on the beaches or rusty old bombs uncovered in plowed fields, there was no need to train airmen to do the job. So nobody did.

In the middle of the forest was a meadow with a large crater in it. Now and then a truck load of old explosives was dumped into the hole and an officer would arrive to supervise the demolition.

But almost all the old munitions were loaded onto trucks or rail cars and taken down to the coast where they were loaded onto landing craft and dumped into the sea.

One day as I was fooling around, I broke my glasses. As our little camp had no medical facilities whatsoever, I was sent to a much larger RAF base that was swarming with military police. While I waited for new glasses, I wandered around the hangars and the airfield, staring at the surprisingly wide variety of new and obviously experimental aircraft. In one hangar there were two or three shiny new jet fighters surrounded by a group of NATO pilots in a variety of uniforms. There was also a ring of military police surrounding the foreign pilots, so I gave them all a wide berth. Since I was just a humble airman, nobody paid any attention to me.

Twenty years later, my brother George, who had been at that time a pilot in the Royal Canadian Air Force and stationed in France, happened to mention visiting a very hush-hush base in England and seeing all the latest aircraft. When we compared notes, we learned that we had been in the same place at the same time. Perhaps he had been one of the pilots in the group that I had so carefully walked around.

One of the men in my bunkhouse was a genuine poacher who came from a family that lived off the game from other men's land. He showed us how to make rabbit snares and where to set them. I tried it once and was delighted to catch a rabbit, but when our surly cooks refused to cook it, we roasted it over an open fire in the woods. It turned out as tough and tasteless as leather. Another day, a small group of us, including the poacher, walked down to the nearby village. It was a picture post card English village with charming thatched cottages, a cute little church, and willows leaning over the stream. However, the villagers hated all servicemen and would not serve us in the charming old pub or in the quaint village store with leaded windows, so we rarely went there.

That day, as we were walking over the low bridge, the poacher suddenly stopped and made us freeze. Near the bank was a large trout. Slowly and silently, we tiptoed off the bridge and stood near the bank where our shadows would not reach the water. The poacher took off his jacket, rolled up his sleeves, and wriggled to the edge of the stream. Then he dipped his arm into the water and very, very slowly slid his fingers behind the trout, which was floating almost motionless and facing upstream. Gradually he worked his fingers forward, occasionally letting them touch the trout like a piece of waterweed, and then, with astonishing speed he slipped two fingers into the trout's gills and tossed it far up onto the grass, where we quickly covered it with his jacket. I had read about "tickling trout" but had only half believed it. Now I had seen it done with my own eyes.

While we were admiring the prize and congratulating the poacher, another, slightly smaller trout appeared in almost exactly the same place. I was closest, so I took off my jacket, rolled up my sleeves, crawled to the edge of the stream, and slipped my arm into the surprisingly cold water. I did exactly as the poacher had done, curving my fingers as he had done, moving them along the trout as slowly and as gently as he had done. But when I was almost at the gills, the trout leaped away and vanished. I have never had the opportunity to try my hand at tickling trout since that one time, but I still know how to do it. And the cook on duty that day surprised us by actually offering to cook the trout for us if we washed the dishes. It made a delicious afternoon snack.

That trout changed my luck. It had been a miserable, cold winter with heavy snow and rain, and I had requested an overseas posting. A few weeks later, my orders came through and by sheer good luck I ended up at an RAF base in Southern Rhodesia that had a beautiful swimming pool and where, by tradition, all work stopped at noon and we spent the afternoons lying around the pool, basking in the hot, dry, African sun.

I was given a clerical job that included making out leave passes. It was wonderful just to be in Africa. But I wanted more. I wanted to travel around Africa and see as much as I could. Unfortunately, I had no form of transport, no car, no motorbike, not even a bicycle. So I hitchhiked. Almost everybody assured me that it was not only highly dangerous to hitch-hike, but probably impossible, but I had hitchhiked all over Europe and never had any serious trouble. I was in Africa about eighteen months, and in that short time I hitchhiked all over southern and northern Rhodesia and into Nyasaland and Mozambique and even managed to get into the Congo for a couple of days. I also went south to Johannesburg, Durban, Kimberly, and Cape Town. I had a wonderful time and learned a great deal about colonial Africa. Recently, when I looked at my old diaries and thought about how much I had enjoyed myself and what I had learned about Africa in the 1950s, I wrote a book and published it under the title *Hitchhiking to Serendip.*

I left the RAF after three years without regret. It had been an interesting job, and the British taxpayer had given me a free trip to Africa, which I greatly appreciated, but I had not learned a useful trade. I had, however, learned something more useful: I was setting my sights too low.

The conscription process had included an education test and a rather primitive intelligence test. Those who fell below the line were shunted into the army, whereas those above the line were placed in the RAF (the Royal Navy took only volunteers). That's how I found myself mixed in with young men of my own age with roughly the same education and the same middle class background and way of speaking. My new friends came from an extraordinary variety of trades and professions. There was a man keen on photography, another in real estate, two or three studying aircraft engineering, a church organist, and one particularly cheerful young man who saw a lucrative future in embalming and undertaking. None of them had wandered from job to job looking only for a good pay check, as I had. I was slightly embarrassed and kept my mouth closed and never talked about the jobs I had had. Whenever I was asked, "What are you going to do when you get out?" I just said that I wanted to travel a lot. I also thought seriously about my parent's constant battle to make sure that all their children spoke correctly. Now I was beginning to understand what my mother had been trying to say when she insisted that I find a job where I wore a jacket and tie.

I wasn't home from Africa and out of uniform very long before I was off again, hitchhiking around Europe. This time I wandered through the Alps and the Pyrenees and only stayed away for a month because I was eager to find a profession, to find something that I could do well, and start making something of myself.

Chapter 10
Making Movies

Every aspect of movie making is interesting, even glamorous, so when a girl friend who worked at a large film processing plant on the western edge of London told me they were hiring, I applied and was delighted when they accepted me on the spot at a pay rate that was extremely attractive. That alone should have made me suspicious.

When I reported for work, I was given a white lab coat and taken upstairs to a large room dominated by two glass-walled cabinets that stretched the full length of the room. The floor gleamed, the walls were white and bare, there were no windows, and everything was as sterile and dust-free as a hospital operating room. The room was also temperature controlled and silent except for the hum of the machines.

My floor supervisor explained in great detail that the glass walled cabinets contained various chemicals and the master prints of a number of movies that the processor automatically developed and made copies of for distribution. He pointed out the film making its way up and down over hundreds of sprockets as it moved through the various sections of the giant processor. He explained that it was a twenty-four hour operation and emphasized, "The processor must never stop! If the machine stops for even ten seconds," he explained, "everything in it is ruined." He then led me to a work bench near the end of the processor. "You'll work here," he said, and vanished.

The man sitting on a stool at the work bench beckoned me over, and I watched as he slipped a film can down a slot in the tabletop. He then reached up, pulled down the end of a reel of film with one hand, slipped a plastic roller onto a sprocket in front of him, and expertly inserted the end of the film. He then touched a button, and the film began to wind quickly onto the sprocket. We watched as the roll grew wider and wider. I could see that the film came overhead from the processor about ten feet away. Suddenly he grunted and pointed at a small white marker attached to the film. We watched it carefully. When the marker reached the bench, he stopped his motor, snapped the film with his fingers exactly at the white marker, slipped the reel of film off the sprocket, laid it in a film can, slapped a lid on it, and slid it down the chute. Within a few seconds, he had another plastic roller on the sprocket and the whole process began over.

It looked so easy when he did it, but I soon discovered two major problems. First, tearing the film was impossible. He handed me a length, and I spent ten minutes trying to tear it. It would not tear like paper. Instead, it bunched up and stretched between my fingers and became even harder to break. Eventually, he showed me how to hold the film and how to place my fingers in just the right position so that it would snap exactly where I wanted it. When I asked why we didn't use scissors, he said, "That would take too long." He made me practice snapping the film until I had the hang of it. Sure enough, it was much faster than using scissors.

The second problem was speed. The main film processor could not be stopped, so the film kept pouring out while I loaded and dumped the can and fitted a new spool and struggled to work the film end into the tiny slot. At the end of the processor was a complicated system of weighted pulleys and sprockets that was designed to take up the slack whenever there was a holdup. The finished film wound itself around a dozen spools on a bar that slowly descended to the floor as it collected the excess film. In an emergency, it could hold up to 100 feet of film.

My instructor, bored but politely patient, stayed with me for a couple of hours until he felt that I had the knack. Then he left, and for the rest of the morning, I sat on the tall stool, my eyes glued to the approaching black ribbon of film, waiting anxiously for the little flash of white. With beating heart and sweaty fingers, I hurried to break the film and start a new reel, not breathing until the full can slid down the slot, while all the time the bar of the take up system, with its load of shimmering black film, inexorably descended like some slow motion guillotine.

Every two hours, somebody relieved me for ten minutes. Across the room and behind me, there was another man on the take-up machine for the second processor, but he was too far away for me to talk to him. Every few hours, a man came through with a vacuum cleaner, which he poked carefully into every corner, but he, too, had no time to stop and talk.

The lunch break was a full hour, but there was nobody in the spotlessly bare lunchroom to talk to as I ate my sandwich. During one lunch break I walked down to the other end of the room and met the men who loaded the film into the processor, but they were always busy and had no time for conversation. Once I went downstairs to see where the film cans ended up. I found two men operating film projectors that were set on very high speed. Although they spent their days watching movies, they were not actually *watching* the movie. Their job was to check that the color was correct and that there were no obvious flaws in the prints before the reels were shipped out. They, too, were much too busy to talk.

After a few days the floor supervisor came and watched me for a while. He seemed to be pleased with my work and offered me the night shift. Since the pay would be appreciably higher, I accepted. This was the first time I had worked a real night shift, and going home as all the clerical staff were arriving was a strange experience. Going to bed in the daytime also took some getting used to, as did having a hearty breakfast at ten in the evening. But the worst part was my ruined social life. Everybody else was at work when I was free, and they were off having fun when I was busy working. All I saw of my girl friend, who worked in the office, was a figure hurrying up the stairs in the morning at the exact time that I was hurrying down. I was very lonely.

It didn't take me long to build up speed, and then of course the boredom set in. All night long, I sat or stood at the bench in front of a blank wall watching a small black spot expand rapidly into a large black plate. A few seconds of work, and there was another black spot in front of my eyes already expanding rapidly. The building was silent. Nobody dropped by except the man who relieved me during my breaks and the vacuum cleaner man. I didn't even see who brought up my supply of empty film cans and fresh spools. The company did not allow portable radios, and reading was impossible because the reels of film were not all the same length, so I had to keep my eyes on the film at all times, watching for that little white marker.

I worked the night shift for barely six weeks. At first, I was only slightly bored, and I cheered myself up by thinking of the money I was making. But the boredom deepened to the point where I began to hate going to work. I asked to be put back on the day shift, but although there were more people about and my social life got back to normal, working days in that sterile room did nothing to dull the monotony. I soon realized that, money or no money, I hated that job.

One day disaster struck. I missed the white tag. The reel grew much larger than the largest can and kept on growing. While I was wondering what to do, it wobbled awkwardly and the film began to topple off the reel. I pushed it back with my hands and shouted for help, but suddenly the whole mess came off the reel and unwound itself all across the bench and onto the floor while more and more film added itself to the tangle.

I knew what to do. I shut off my machine, snapped the film, placed a fresh roller on the sprocket, connected the film, and started a new reel. Pleased with my quick thinking, I began to kick the now scratched and damaged film across the floor and into the corner where, I hoped, the vacuum cleaner man would know how to dispose of it. But, in my haste I had not put the reel on the sprocket firmly enough. Although the motor was running, nothing was turning. I heard a shout and turned to see that the emergency rollers had rapidly filled up with excess film and the dreaded guillotine had almost reached the ground. While I stood there, horrified, the bar touched bottom and film started to spill out all over the floor. I felt like Mickey Mouse trying to tame the brooms in *The Sorcerer's Apprentice*. The film looked like a glistening, twelve-inch-deep pile of black spaghetti. It was alive, growing by the second, and creeping eerily across the floor.

Fortunately, that first warning cry had brought the floor supervisor. He was quickly joined by others, and soon there were half a dozen senior management types in dark suits and ties scrabbling around in the black swamp trying to find what had gone wrong. Eventually, somebody forced the reel onto the sprocket, cut away all the ruined film, and got the take-off machine running properly. But the film had to be fed painstakingly back and forth over the reels on the safety mechanism and that took time and effort. Meanwhile, the processor was steadily doing its job, pouring out more film.

The supervisor found me standing near my bench trying hard to look invisible. He said not a word, but just shook his head and jerked his thumb toward the door. I understood him perfectly.

A few days after I left the film processing plant, I got a phone call from my girl friend. "Everybody is talking about what you did," she told me. "The other girls think it's hilarious. Daddy laughed and told me to ask you over for tea." Then she whispered, "I think he has a job for you."

Daddy worked for an American film company. In the middle of tea, he asked me, "Have you ever done any costing?" When I told him that I had and that I was quite good at it, he asked, "How would you like to work in Rome?"

Travel to Rome? "I'd love to," I managed to stutter, trying not to spill my tea.

"Good. The company is making a film there and it's gone way over budget. I think they need another man in their costing department." He further explained, "Because of currency freezes and red tape, you'll have your salary paid into your bank here in sterling and a smaller salary in Italian lira, which you can only spend in Italy. The people over there mostly stay in hotels. The company will pay for that, of course."

I sat with my mouth half open. I had a job in the movie industry. In Rome. Expenses paid. Fat salary! I was so dazed that I didn't even ask what movie was being made.

A couple of days later, I was sitting on a plane bound for Rome. I'd received minimum instructions and had even fewer ideas about what I would actually be doing, but I wasn't worried. I knew that I would enjoy it. I was met at the airport by a big, black limousine and an English-speaking chauffeur who drove me to a first-class hotel on a quiet, tree-lined street close to the heart of the city. The staff had a room ready for me, and the driver told me that he would pick me up next morning at eight. I spent the rest of the day wandering around in a daze, marveling at my extraordinary luck and lingering over an excellent dinner in the hotel dining room.

Next morning, exactly at eight, after the doorman ushered me into the big black limousine, I relaxed in solitary splendor as he drove me out to the studios. I felt like a Hollywood movie star. But not for long. The car stopped at three or four other places and picked up more people so that we were soon packed in like sardines. Two of the other passengers were English.

"The film company allows just so much for housing," one of the Englishmen said. "So we rent apartments, which are a damn sight cheaper than a luxury hotel. With the money saved, we can have our wives here with us." He smiled. "And get some good English cooking. Lord, how I hate olive oil on everything!"

The studio was a large, modern complex called Cinecitta, which had been built by Mussolini. It was very spread out, and everything seemed to be a long walk from everything else, and there were lots of people bustling about. I was fascinated. When somebody showed me to the costing department, I found myself the youngest of just three Englishmen in a small office. After introductions, my first question was, "What movie are we making here?"

The older man, who turned out to be a hardened cynic, answered, "Some god-awful tripe called *Helen of Troy*. It's 100 percent over budget already and is nowhere even close to finishing on schedule."

The other man was younger and had a better sense of humor.

"These Italians just love to waste time and money," he said. "It drives the Americans crazy. Sometimes I think they do it on purpose."

It didn't take me long to see what was driving the Americans crazy. Using the phone was a waste of time because nobody ever phoned back, no matter how sincerely they swore they would "phone you right back." My job was to do the running around, finding costs and figures, and bringing back the information that the other two needed. This gave me a close-up view of the complete lack of record keeping and the expensive or wasteful decisions that were constantly being made by the producer, the director, and everyone else.

Almost every day a young, very fashionably dressed Italian would wander into our office. He spoke beautiful English and would perch on the edge of a desk and waste hours of our time telling us all the latest gossip about the leading lady and her amorous adventures and other activities on the set. I would be deep into calculating just how many rubber-headed arrows had been bought and where they all were, and he would be giving an eyewitness account of the tantrums of some second-level actress trying to impress the Hollywood crew. He had all the gossip and scandals about everybody and enjoyed passing it all on, and although he was a nuisance, he was impossible to ignore. I never did learn what his job was, or even if he was working in the studio at all.

Part of my job was to check the medical records of all the stuntmen who were used in the film. There were dozens of them, and almost all of them ended up in the hospital at one time or another. Falling off walls, fighting even with blunted swords and spears, and jumping off cliffs invariably resulted in accidents. One scene called for the hero and heroine to jump off a high cliff. The stuntmen who did the scene had to repeat it a number of times because the one who played the female just did not look female enough, especially when his wig fell off in mid-air. Eventually he dislocated his shoulder and they found a slimmer stunt man.

The daily rushes showed that, in one scene, the great gates of Troy had been left slightly open during a great battle scene. Other shots showed Greek warriors wearing wristwatches, or the massive stone walls quivering when touched. Every day, costly shots had to be redone. The money just poured down the drain. The script also called for a great armada of Greek ships to be hauled up on the beach, but our office had estimated the cost of building replica ships. It was too expensive, so they decided to build just one and use camera magic to make it look like a huge fleet. But it was taking so long to build the Greek ship, and was proving so expensive, that they eventually used an old barge with a lot of plywood and a clever paint job. When the movie was finished, this remnant of the great fleet of a thousand Greek ships was abandoned somewhere along the coast not of Troy but of Italy.

I was too busy tracking down such mundane items as hundreds of specially made sandals or thousands of meters of white cloth to ever get to see the actual filming, but our Italian friend reported that the intimate love scenes were so crowded with visitors, technicians, and every workman who could think of an excuse to wander in that it looked rather like a popular night club on Saturday night.

The oldest man in our office was most incensed by the number of holidays that interrupted the shooting. "Good heavens!" he grumbled. "They celebrate every saint in the book. Practically every other day they come up with another unknown saint and have to have the day off." The union was very powerful, however, and so the entire crew and even some of the extras were paid for these holidays.

"I think the Italians work to live while the Americans live to work," I suggested, and the younger man added, "And the

English are somewhere in the middle. They're not sure why they work."

I enjoyed the holidays because they let me wander around the Eternal City all day. I had been to Rome a year or two before, but I had been a poor hitchhiker then, walking everywhere and eating in the cheapest trattorias. Now I could eat in good restaurants and take a taxi when I wished. But I still preferred to walk down strange streets and discover curious statues or fountains or wander into beautiful little churches or just mix with the Roman crowds on the popular avenues. London and Rome are two great cities where a man could never see everything, even when he lived there.

But all good things must come to an end. When the overrun was three times the original estimate, Hollywood lost patience and one of the Warner brothers flew to Cinecitta. His cost cutting method was simple. Our door opened and a man asked, "How many people work here?" "Three, sir." As the door closed, I heard him say, "Get rid of one." As the youngest and the newest man there, I was the one to go.

That job at Cinecitta was my only attempt to break into the movie industry…except for the time, a few months later, when I voiced some foolish criticism of movie dialog in general and a visiting uncle, who just happened to be a scriptwriter, turned to me and said, "If you can write, if you think you can write, if you would like to write, if you would like to learn how to write, just be in my office Monday morning. You will be very welcome." I was too embarrassed to take him up on his offer.

Back home, our family lived very near the famous Pinewood Studios in Buckinghamshire (a bit west of London). My sister Josie, a very smart and ambitious girl, got a job in the typing pool there.

She worked hard, was eager to please, and eventually moved up to script girl, then quickly worked up to the continuity department. She was so good at her job that she soon became one of the top continuity girls in the business and her name has appeared in the credits of dozens of famous movies. One day she told my younger brother, Dominic, that they needed a clapper boy. He applied and was hired immediately and, through hard work and an extremely friendly manner, he worked his way up to assistant director. He, too, had his name in the credits of dozens of English movies and television series during the 60s and 70s. Perhaps if I had taken my uncle seriously, I might also have walked down that road.

Chapter 11
Fleet Street Man

When I got back from Rome and described to my parents what I had been up to, my father, who had never taken the slightest interest in my career, suddenly decided that perhaps I was not a useless wastrel who couldn't hold down a job. Perhaps, out of all of his five sons, I was the one that would follow in his footsteps to Fleet Street.

In those days Fleet Street was England's journalistic Mecca. Every newspaper of any importance had its head office on that stretch of road between the Law Courts and Ludgate. My father, who had been a Fleet Street journalist for years, could no longer compete with the younger, more aggressive breed of modern journalists, and so he had moved to the advertising side. At the time, he was handling the advertising for a provincial paper with a small office on Fleet Street. "Come to my office on Monday," he said. "I think I have a job that you just might be good at."

I turned up bright and early wearing my only suit and a sober tie and was introduced to a youngish man in a conservative but very expensive suit who explained that he had just started a small monthly magazine devoted to relatively unknown country homes and village churches that had great historic value and beauty but somehow never seemed to appear in tour guides or travel books.

I looked at a sample copy. It was very well laid out on high-quality paper with excellent color photographs. It was obviously expensive to produce. It was also obvious that it was sadly lacking in advertising. Even I could see that if that magazine were going to survive, it would need three times the amount of advertising it had.

The publisher asked me a few questions, and it soon became clear that he had serious doubts about me. He was looking for an experienced advertising manager, but all he saw was a young man with no experience and a lot of enthusiasm. I was genuinely eager to break into advertising, and as my father touted my wide business experience, my travel experience, my fine education, and my energy, coupled with an uncanny ability to learn fast and my unrivaled knowledge of London, I sat there trying hard to look like all of those things…. and trying not to feel like a stolen horse being sold by an Irish gypsy.

Eventually we settled on a one-week trial period. The publisher handed me samples of the magazine and a wad of rate cards, and I scuttled out of the office, keen and eager, but without the slightest knowledge of what I was supposed to do. My first step was to visit a friend in a nearby building who worked in advertising. He was slightly older than me and had been in the business since he left school.

He held up one of the rate cards and said, "Do you know what this is?" I didn't, and he sighed dramatically. "This, my friend, is your life, your rent, your bread and butter, your beer money. It contains everything you need to know about any ads of any size that a customer may want. Prices, deadlines, color, all that vital stuff."

And then he proceeded to make a space salesman out of me. I learned about column inches and color bleed off and circulation figures and target markets. I memorized the prices on the card and the deadlines. Our tutorial took so long that I treated him to stand-up lunch in a nearby pub, where we continued my lesson over brown ale. By late afternoon, he was satisfied that I was reasonably ready to go out into the hard, harsh world of advertising sales.

Next morning, I was back in the big city, standing on a corner staring at the great gray buildings and wondering which to try first. As luck would have it, the most inviting door was that of an insurance company. I went in and asked for the advertising manager. Within minutes, I was rattling off the speech my friend had made me memorize to a middle-aged lady who sat and watched me with a slight smile on her lips. She looked carefully at the sample copy, then glanced at the rate card and said, "Yes, I think we'll try a quarter page."

I nearly fell off my chair!

I had made a sale on my very first attempt. It was almost unbelievable. Fortunately, I had enough sense to produce the proper order sheets and necessary papers from the rather dilapidated briefcase that I had found somewhere. I tried to look casually businesslike while the lady filled them in. Then she shook my hand and wished me luck, and I floated out of the building six inches off the ground.

Five minutes later I was back in the magazine office, where I casually strolled into the publisher's office and slid the order form across his desk. He read it, then read it again. There was a long silence. Then he stood up and said, "Well, John, it looks like you have the job." I was the magazine's official advertising manager.

It was a nice title, but the magazine was seriously underfunded. It didn't have a Fleet Street office, and I didn't even have business cards. My boss was using an office on temporary loan from a journalist friend, and I was to use a desk and phone in the office of a provincial newspaper that had more space than they needed. By sheer good luck, it was the place where my friend worked; in fact, his desk was right next to mine. As we celebrated with a couple of ales in one of the many pubs that cater to Fleet Street people, I looked around at the crowd of journalists, editorial writers, and advertising executives and felt at home.

I worked my heart out for the next few months, knocking on doors, following the slightest tip, phoning endless lists of possible leads, and wearing out a lot of shoe leather. Everybody I met was very helpful and would offer possible leads whenever they could. But it took me a long time to learn all the tricks of the trade.

My first step was to move into London. I was wasting over two hours a day sitting in a train, which was not only expensive but also boring. One day I was scouting the Bloomsbury area where, at that time, many university students had rooms, and came across an ad for a room in Soho. The idea of a room in the very heart of the West End intrigued me. I took a look. It was a tiny attic room at the top of three flights of narrow, rickety stairs. It had a cold water sink, an electric hot plate, a bed, a table, and a chair. The little window had no view, and the only heating was a tiny gas heater, which had to be fed coins. It wasn't very much, but the rent was reasonable and I loved the location.

My little garret was on Carnaby Street, but that was years before the Beatles made it famous. The ground floor of the building was a tiny bakery. Next door were a hat-blocking shop and a scissors-repair shop. Down the street was a West Indian club where there was a fight every night and blood on the street at least once a week. Opposite was a very noisy pub where the prostitutes took their clients. Yes, it was a dark and grubby street, but it was also just minutes away from Piccadilly Circus and the real heart of London.

New home accomplished, my next step was to buy a motor scooter. I couldn't even dream of a car and was wasting a great deal of time and money on buses and trains, so a little scooter seemed a good idea. I found a second-hand one in south London and learned how to drive it the hard way—by getting on the thing and navigating it through the heart of London in Saturday traffic. For a small fee, a local parking garage allowed me to tuck it into a corner at night. I loved my little scooter and drove it everywhere in all kinds of weather, sometimes with a passenger on the back. It was cheap to run, easy to park, and I could wriggle my way through the worst traffic jam with ease.

Just about that time, my brother Paul in Montreal landed a job as a steward on a Canadian airline. At irregular intervals, usually past midnight, he would announce his arrival by hammering on my door with a bottle and demanding that I get myself out of bed and accompany him to some second rate night club or illegal speakeasy. Paul knew every sleazy joint in the west end of London, and I think we visited all of them, especially those with little peep holes in the doors. They invariably had the most watered-down booze.

My sisters likewise soon found my little place and began dropping in whenever they were in London. They would politely introduce themselves to my landlady, who ran the little bakery, and then dash up the narrow stairs. The problem was that the neighborhood was crawling with prostitutes, and my landlady was forever shooing them off her doorstep. When Marie claimed she was my sister, the landlady accepted her word. But then one day Josie turned up, and a few days later Monica appeared and claimed that she, too, was my sister, and then Anita and finally Susan showed up. Five extremely attractive young women were too many for the good landlady, so one evening she waylaid me and demanded some proof. It was sheer good luck that I had a photo album with enough old black and white snaps to convince her that I did indeed have ten brothers and sisters.

On the floor below mine lived a medical student about my own age. His hobby was uncovering strange and little-known facts about London, especially historically curious places in the West End. He got me interested in the subject and whenever we had the time we began to cruise through odd corners of London on my scooter.

Late one evening, we were down a grubby back alley studying a lamp post. According to our research, the gas for the light was actually methane from the sewers below, and it was the last relic of an ambitious experiment. We could see nothing from the ground, so my friend climbed on my shoulders and scrambled up the ancient rusty pole. He had just reached the top and was enthusiastically describing what he could see in the dim light when a London bobby appeared out of the gloom.

"Well now. And what might you two be up to?" he asked. It took a while to explain, but he accepted our explanation. He even added something we had not noticed. "I've always wondered why it doesn't have that little bar up there, where the lamplighters used to lean their ladders," he said. "Must be continuously burning." Then he frowned. "But this ain't the time of night to do archeological research. Run along now, the pair of you."

That week I saw a real lamplighter. Just about sunset a man on a bicycle carrying a long pole zigzagged his way down Carnaby Street going from street light to street light. As he passed each one, he raised his pole and deftly flipped the lever to allow the gas to flow. He didn't stop, in fact he hardly even looked up, but each light came on as he passed. Next morning, I got up extra early and waited in the pre-dawn cold and, sure enough, he appeared again with his long pole, flicking off the switches with the casual skill that comes from long practice. I felt like a man who has just seen the last of the dinosaurs.

My brother Paul would often dump a stewardess on me with instructions to "Show her the town." I would have to take time off from my work, which was a nuisance, but the Canadian girls always had a list of fancy restaurants that they wanted to sample after we had done the sights. As they always insisted on paying, I didn't complain too loudly.

As a typical Londoner, I had never actually been inside most of the historic places that I passed every day. I had never watched the changing of the guards at Buckingham Palace. Nor had I ever gone into the public gallery and watched Parliament in session. I had never watched a trial at the Law Courts. The Tower of London proved to be amazing, and so did the score of museums and markets of every type that I visited with the stewardesses. Many of the girls were so well prepared that they knew more about London than I did. It was a Canadian who took me to the great market in Petticoat Lane one Sunday morning.

Each girl also had to have a ride on the double-decker buses, though they all preferred to whiz around London on the back of my scooter. The stewardess uniforms at that time had very short, very tight skirts. This posed a problem which we eventually solved by the girl putting on my rain coat, then hitching her skirt up to her waist. It involved interesting wriggling every time she got on or off the scooter.

Meanwhile, back at the magazine office, I was making very little progress in advertising sales. Eventually, an old-timer took me aside and said, "It's a matter of contacts. Getting to know the people in the agencies. You have to take them out to lunch. Buy them a beer. Play golf with them. It takes time, but you have to make those contacts."

My heart sank. I had no expense account, and I rarely had enough money to buy myself lunch, certainly not enough to buy a couple of rounds for a bunch of hard drinking advertising agency types. As for golf, I didn't even play golf.

All I could do was step up my efforts and visit all the account managers in all the agencies and meet as many advertising managers as I could. The big agencies were a waste of my time, however, and the magazine struggled by on what I could squeeze out of individual companies. To make matters worse, I could have got plenty of full color pages for all kinds of alcoholic beverages and tobacco products, but the boss had made it quite clear that he wanted none of that advertising.

One day the publisher phoned from his estate near Cambridge and invited me to spend a weekend helping him proofread the next edition. I sped out on my scooter and spent an interesting couple of days learning how to scan the long strips of paper called galley proofs for typos, spelling or grammatical errors, and any inconsistencies in the articles. There was a checklist of special marks I had to use in the event that I found an error. Fortunately, there were very few.

On Sunday evening, the publisher told me that he had decided to take over the advertising. I could handle the circulation department, if I wanted to. This new job offered no increase in pay, but he would pay travel expenses up to a point. I accepted the offer.

My job was to visit the newsstands and book shops that carried the magazine and persuade the managers to keep it in the front at eye level, order more copies, and mention it to regular customers whenever they could. The magazine always had an attractive cover, but the newsstand managers knew that it did not sell well to the casual public. They were hard to persuade. Sex, crime, and political scandals always sell better than ancient castles. Our magazine was clearly the type of publication that sells best by subscriptions taken out by serious readers, not commuters looking for something to read on the bus.

Despite the uphill battle, I enjoyed the job. It was just perfect for somebody who loved to travel. Through rain and fog and sun, I scooted around London. I expanded my trips out to the suburbs, and eventually I was traveling rather far and stopping overnight in bed-and-breakfasts. My little scooter was not big enough or fast enough for the major roads, so I used the secondary roads and country lanes and of course took every opportunity to see the countryside and detour to all the little to places I had never visited. Fortunately, it was one of those rare English summers when the sun actually shone and there was very little rain.

I thoroughly enjoyed myself as a Fleet Street man, but my efforts did not show an increase in sales. It soon became very clear that I was wasting my time. The magazine was seriously underfunded and clearly needed a major campaign to drum up subscribers and boost advertising. If it relied on casual newsstand sales and weak advertising revenue, it would not last long. Sitting in the beautiful ruins of Fountains Abbey one day, eating a sandwich and wondering if I had enough money for a tank of petrol, I decided to quit.

I had learned a great deal about the advertising business, enough to know that it was not for me. I had also learned a bit about circulation and proof reading, but it was equally clear that I would never have a career in the publishing business. Also, I had traveled widely in Europe and much of Africa, but I knew there was a lot more of the world to see. With three brothers in Canada, there was a whole new world just across Atlantic.

I decided to emigrate. On my way home that afternoon, I dropped in on the magazine publisher and told him of my decision. Considering how very little I had done for the magazine, it was nice to hear him say that he regretted losing me. But he agreed that I would never be a real Fleet Street man.

A few days later, I gave up my Carnaby Street garret, moved back in with my parents, sold everything I possessed, including my beloved scooter, and applied for a visa. Then I looked around for a job that would pay enough for me to save up the air fare.

Chapter 12
Chocolate Taster

I had made up my mind to follow my brothers to Canada, but even after selling everything I possessed that had any value, I still didn't have enough for the air fare and basic expenses. I needed a well paid job and was prepared to exaggerate my training and my experience (just a little) to get it. I was determined to aim high, so when I came across an advertisement for an industrial chemist, I applied. The position was in the quality control lab of a famous chocolate maker, and the elderly gentleman in a lab coat and wire-rim glasses who interviewed me asked very few questions and did not seem interested in my training or experience. All he wanted to know was whether or not I would work the night shift. "It is a nuisance, I know," he said, "but it does pay much more than the day shift." That was music to my ears. I accepted the position immediately.

I worked the day shift for a few days until the department manager was satisfied that I knew what I was doing and would follow the routine. The work proved to be so simple, in fact, that the manager was soon satisfied and retired down the hall to his office, never to be seen again. There were two middle aged women in the lab who cheerfully showed me exactly what to do and how to do it and even showed me a few short cuts to speed up my work.

The department's job was to keep constant and carefully documented control over the quality of the chocolate. Every step in the long process was checked half a dozen times a day and every little detail was carefully logged. It was a very important job, but it did not need a highly trained chemist to do it. Within a week, therefore, I was on the night shift on the factory floor, where the men and women called me Sir as I wandered around in my gleaming white lab coat, my clipboard pressed to my chest and a solemn look on my face. It was fun.

Almost everybody loves chocolate, and every corner of the factory—and the streets around it, too—was heavy with the smell of chocolate, which even clung to my clothing.

"For the first day or two," one of the women in the lab told me, "you're going to be stuffing yourself on chocolates. But you'll get used to it." She laughed. "I've been here five years now and I don't even notice the smell." Then she added, "But I still like a nice chocolate now and then."

Part of my job was to actually taste the mixture at various stages of the mixing process. First, I would allow it to melt on my tongue, grinding it gently between my teeth to feel for sugar crystals that had not been ground down fine enough. Then I would take a sample back to the lab and measure the sugar crystals with a high powered microscope. The sugar grinding was the key to the quality and I was often down at the huge machines with their stainless steel rollers, getting the operators to tighten them up just another notch until the sugar was reduced to a fine powder.

Some of the mixing was done in vats that looked like bathtubs where stainless steel paddles slowly worked up and down or in larger tanks where the paddles revolved. Everything was heated to an exact temperature and it was nice to visit them on a cold and rainy night. The temperature inside the factory and that of the chocolate were thus a constant worry, so there were thermometers everywhere. I visited them hourly and compared them with the thermometer I carried and noted both figures in the log book.

Moving the raw chocolate from one place to another was done in stainless steel wheelbarrows. The workmen, who wore rubber boots, would climb into the tanks and shovel the mix out. To me, they looked rather like farmers cleaning the pig pens. Not an attractive sight.

The most interesting part of the factory, and the place where visiting dignitaries were rarely taken, was the "dropping and wrapping" area, where the chocolate mixture was turned into the finished product. Various automated machines dropped chocolate into trays of all sizes and shapes, where other machines decorated them or added things like nuts and raisins. I had no reason to go there, but I had to pass through part of it, and it was always painful.

The chocolate factory had been built well before the Second World War, and the machinery was rather antiquated, though still quite serviceable. The chocolates, which are made upside-down, lay in molds in metal trays that traveled along a conveyor belt to an area where there were dozens of irregular metal rollers. There the trays were bounced around until the soft chocolate was forced into every corner of the molds and the added ingredients were well embedded. The noise was horrendous. Dozens of metal trays rattling over metal wheels created harsh, ear-piercing noise that kept visitors far away. I always reached for the ear muffs I kept near the sound-proof rubber doors.

What I found most interesting was that on either side of the conveyor belt sat half a dozen women inspecting the trays and picking out irregular chocolates. They concentrated on their work, but they chatted among themselves at the same time. The noise was so loud that I couldn't hear a thing, yet these the women chatted away in normal voices, ignoring the noise. As one of the women in the lab told me, "They've been there for years. Just got used to the noise and now they ignore it." The other woman said, "Actually, the part of the ear that receives that particular sound has gone dead in these women. They just don't hear it anymore. If they took piano lessons, they wouldn't be able to hear some of the notes. Or so the company nurse says." She laughed and added, "None of them are going to learn the piano, so I suppose it's all right. They get good pay for it."

I was all alone on the night shift and had plenty of time to experiment with the scientific instruments. There was an enclosed scale that could weigh a speck of dust. All the samples had to be fed into it by remote control through a special panel. I had fun weighing various lengths of my hair. But the microscope was the best. I learned to look through it with both eyes open and kept trying to see how small an object it would magnify. Even when we ground the sugar down to the finest powder, I could still measure the width of the particles when I added various dyes.

Now and then, the night watchman would stop by for a chat as he made his rounds. He was an elderly gentleman, and I should not have played any tricks on him because he may have had a weak heart. But one night I caught a wasp on the window and put its head under the microscope, facing up. Then I turned it up to maximum magnification, and, when the watchman stopped by, I suggested that he take a peek, and he did. He could not have jumped so quickly or so high if he had touched a live electric wire. He let out a shriek followed by a string of words that elderly gentlemen should not use in public. But then, after he got his breath back, he laughed at the joke. "God!" he said, "That was the most horrible monster I've ever seen! Fair put the wind up on me, it did." He never peeked into the microscope again.

One morning, I was late leaving and got talking to a scientist from another department who had arrived early. He was Hindu and dark skinned. "I was working in your department," he said "I applied for the job you have. I have been here for five years and I have my university degree in chemistry. There is not the shadow of a doubt that I can manage the job." He spoke perfect English with only a trace of an accent. "Nobody said why I did not get the position," he continued. "I was simply moved to another department." Then he gave a resigned shrug. "The scuttlebutt is that management did not want to give the job to an East Indian." He smiled and hurried off, leaving me feeling slightly uncomfortable.

A few weeks later, I decided I had enough money for an airline ticket to Canada with a few dollars left over, so I gave notice and left the chocolate factory with its wonderful smell. It had been a memorable experience. And I still love chocolates.

Chapter 13
Computer Expert

When I arrived in Montreal, I was met at the airport by my older brother Paul. It was an icy cold day, but the sky was blue and everything appeared so refreshingly clean and fresh after the winter gloom of London that I decided immediately that I liked Canada. I had never met Paul's wife and children, so we celebrated, and I spent a few happy days adjusting to this bright new world I had entered. But Paul had no wish to be saddled with an unemployed younger brother, and so he was soon carefully scanning the men-wanted pages of the newspaper and making phone calls on my behalf.

I eventually found myself working in the head office of a large insurance company. It was a massive building in the middle of Montreal that seemed to employ an astonishing number of extremely pretty young French-Canadian girls...a feature that Paul was quick to point out. He also mentioned a more practical job benefit: the company had an excellent lunch room that served free lunches to the employees. Even if the pay was not high, I wouldn't starve. I learned later that three of my brothers (Paul, George, and Anthony) had worked at the same company, as another brother, Dominic, did when he arrived in Canada a few years later. Paul also found me a cheap basement apartment on a convenient bus route.

I was to start on the company's punch-card machines. All the complicated data of the insurance business was reduced to little rectangular holes in six inch cards, and it was my job to run the cards, thousands of them, through a high-speed sorter. There were six of these machines, all operated by young men of my age. We were surrounded by about thirty girls who worked at the machines that punched the holes in the cards.

The first thing I learned was that most of the girls were not particularly keen on humble sorters. They would switch from English to French whenever we tried to get friendly, even in the lunch room, and so I never got as much as one short date.

It didn't take me long to learn the job and the various idiosyncrasies of my machine. The only problem was that I had to be highly vigilant and check the cards carefully so they would flow smoothly through the machine. At the speed at which they moved, just one crumpled edge would cause a spectacular pile up and the machine would be jammed with shredded and torn cards. What's more, after the mess was cleared up, the guilty party would have to take each mangled paper corpse to one of the girls to be redone and suffer a minute or two of sarcastic criticism, fortunately *en français*.

One of the other sorters was a university student who was taking a year out to make some money. Through him, I got a room in a fraternity house near McGill University, right in the center of the city, and also found some very lively friends. As many of us were newcomers, we set about exploring the city and the area around it. At that time, Montreal was a wide open city, a wonderful place with an endless variety of bars and topless night clubs. Of course we tried to visit them all. We also tried skiing, but one trip to the slopes left me cold, wet, and convinced that skiing was definitely not the sport for me. When spring arrived, we explored the countryside south of the St. Lawrence River and discovered that some apple farmers brewed a potent, and thoroughly illegal, cider, which they proudly called *Champomme*. It left an equally potent headache. It was a wonderful time.

Meanwhile, back at the insurance company, a couple of us were given white lab coats and moved to the brand new computer that had been recently installed. A large glass-walled room with special air filters and its own carefully controlled air conditioning had been constructed for the monster, which consisted of two long rows of tall, gray-green cabinets with glass doors on some of them. On the front of many of these cabinets were giant spools of tape that would spin and stop at irregular intervals. The glass doors also revealed shelves of vacuum tubes of a multitude of sizes and a jungle of colored wires.

The monster was served by half a dozen silent, white coated servants. At a keyboard near the end of the cabinets sat the "expert" who received the punched cards and did magical things with them as he tapped out instructions to the monster in a secret code and scowled at the hieroglyphics printed on the endless sheet of paper that rolled out of the printer. I gathered that somebody had decided that I could be trained as a computer expert. Remembering the wasted efforts of the RAF to train me as a radio mechanic, however, I soon had my doubts.

As part of our training, we young trainees spent most of our time hunched over a table wiring the "breadboards." Nobody ever did explain this strange name. They were plastic boards, about eighteen inches square, with codes and numbers around the edges. Each side was covered with neat rows of holes into which we were supposed to insert various colored wires and string them to other holes, following a printed script. It was rather like finding some-where on a map by looking for D7 or M13, though smaller and a lot more difficult.

The breadboards were slipped in and out of their slots in the cabinets by the same man who changed burned out vacuum tubes. But we trainees were not allowed to touch anything else, nor were we given the slightest instruction on the actual workings of the monster. I did not like the endless fiddling around with bits of wire and was soon bored. Then I began to make mistakes.

The real expert growled like a watchdog whenever we attempted to see what he was doing at the keyboard. When I plucked up my courage one day and asked him if I would get any further training, he looked down his nose and asked, "Do you know any languages?" I thought quickly and lied. "I speak Spanish and a little French." At that, he laughed sarcastically and waved me away. "Computer language, you idiot!"

I slunk away, red with embarrassment. A week later, I was called into the manager's office where, after a very short discussion, we agreed that if I left at the end of the month, the company would not try to stop me.

Years later, after the invention of transistors and the wonders of micro-processing and miniaturization had reduced the monster to a gadget that could fit on my lap, I tried to describe that first computer to my class of high school students. Their faces went blank and their eyes glazed over. "What's a punch card?" one asked. "What's a transistor?" somebody else asked. I gave up and changed the subject.

Chapter 14
Summer Jobs in Canada

It was early summer when I left the insurance company and its massive computer, the perfect time to take a look at this vast and wonderful land called Canada. I had no car, so I decided to hitchhike to Vancouver, on the Pacific coast, three thousand miles across the continent. Traveling through the vast forests north of the Great Lakes was a wonderful experience, as was crossing the seemingly endless prairies to the magnificent Rockies and going down to Vancouver. The people I met were friendly, the weather was mostly good, and, although it was sometimes slow going, it was a fascinating and highly enjoyable journey. I fell in love with Canada and looked around Vancouver for work. My intention was to make that lovely city my home.

But first I had to visit my brother George, the pilot, who was newly married and had just been hired by United Airlines. He had moved to Seattle and was waiting for me when I stepped off the Greyhound bus.

We had a great reunion. He told me of his experiences at sea and in the Canadian Air Force and I told him of my adventures and travels in Africa and Europe. Of my five brothers, George was the sensible one. As my eldest sister Marie once said, "He's the only one of you boys who has his head properly screwed on."

One day he said, "You can't be a bum all your life. Go back to Vancouver and go to university. Get a degree."

I sat down, thoroughly surprised, and pointed out that I had dropped out of high school.

"Details," he said, "You know more now than some kid right out of high school, and what you don't know you can find in books." I must have still looked doubtful because he became more serious and said, "Here in America, you won't get anywhere without a university degree. You don't want to end up back behind a counter selling socks."

When I mentioned money, he brushed it aside. "Take out loans," he said. "Everybody has to take out student loans sooner or later. I'll sign for them and you can get summer jobs."

It was very generous of him and very far sighted, so I agreed to give it a good try. Despite my lack of a high school diploma, I was allowed to register as an ex-serviceman at the University of British Columbia, which is, after McGill, the best in Canada. I signed all the papers and then faced the prospect of finding a summer job that paid well.

Because I took a year out to teach school and changed my major halfway through, it took me six years to get my degree, which meant seven or eight summers spent looking for work. Some students found jobs in Vancouver so that they could live at home, and others found good jobs somewhere that they returned to summer after summer. Often these were boring jobs that just happened to pay well.

Reasoning that I would never again have such a golden opportunity to travel anywhere I wished and that I was free to work for one short summer in anything that caught my interest, I took any job I could find. During those summers, I knew I would also have experiences that I could never hope to have once I graduated and settled down to a serious job with a wife and a mortgage. There were summers when I made enough to last the whole winter, and there were also summers when I made less and had to take part-time jobs to eke out my dollars. But I rarely came back empty-handed and I never had a boring summer. I sometimes think I learned more from those summer jobs than I did from some of the university lecturers.

I took whatever job came along, from mailing packages to laying cement. Once, I tried my hand at selling pots and pans door-to door. I was a miserable failure. Another time I tried my hand as a hearing aid salesman for a sleazy firm that promised me an enormous commission. They dressed me up in a white coat with a name tag and a thermometer to look suspiciously like a doctor and gave me plenty of leads, but there too I failed. The weirdest selling job was when I was persuaded to sell cosmetics. I took a one-day training course and the company proclaimed me a "cosmetician," but I had hardly started to put my new-found skills to work when the company went out of business.

One Christmas I spent the holiday season as a temporary postman, and got bitten by a dog. Another winter I earned room and board as a sandwich maker and housekeeper in a boarding house and, for a couple of winters, I made good pocket money as a baby-sitter for faculty members. One way or another I managed to make ends meet.

Chapter 15
Deconstruction in Kitimat

By sheer good luck, on my first week in Vancouver I bumped into a school friend I had known years ago in England. He was doing well as an architect and generously allowed me to sleep on a cot in his basement while I looked for work. Next, a sympathetic lady at the university employment office told me about a man named McKenzie who was looking for half a dozen strong and healthy students to work on a construction job tearing down some buildings near Kitimat, which was over 500 miles up the coast. Since food, board, and transportation would be provided, I jumped at the offer. We all met in a hotel room, where McKenzie, a short, weather-beaten, older man, explained that he was dismantling a village of prefabricated houses that had been put up years ago when they were building a giant aluminum refinery at Kitimat.

There was only one problem. The site was almost inaccessible. That part of the Pacific coast is extremely rugged, and, since there were no roads to the site, the only access was by water. We would, therefore, have to drive inland and get to Kitimat by a roundabout route that could take two or three days, depending on the conditions of the roads. Then we would park the cars and take a small boat to our destination.

"Now if, for some reason, you don't like the job and want to quit," McKenzie informed us, "that's too bad. The only way out is in my boat. I'll pay you when the job is done. And don't worry—I'll see you get back in time for school." He looked around. "And don't think I'm going to gyp you. That lady up at the placement center checked me out real good."

Since I had no car, it was agreed that I would ride with him and the other deconstructionists would all ride in another car and share expenses. McKenzie drove like a maniac, but it still took us two and a half days to get to Kitimat, where we waited for the others.

Kitimat was a carefully planned company town built for the people who worked at the aluminum smelter and all the service industries around it. The town and the smelter lay at the head of a long fiord that cuts through the coast range. With a population of about 10,000, it had everything that a modern town should have, such as schools, hospital, theaters, and ballparks. The company kept it clean and attractive, so it would be a wonderful place to live… except for the fact that it was one of the most isolated communities in western Canada. The nearest town was Prince Rupert, which is hardly worth the drive. As we sat in the coffee shop, McKenzie said, "If you like hunting and fishing, this little town is paradise. But anybody who prefers the bright lights of the big city won't last more than one winter here. I guarantee that."

When the other members of the deconstruction crew arrived, we drove down to the docks, where there were a couple of bauxite ore carriers unloading, and parked the two cars. McKenzie's boat, a large aluminum open dinghy with a powerful outboard, was tied up and ready to go. It was a wild ride and I was soon wet from the cold ocean spray and wincing every time the boat slammed into a rock-hard wave. We went the full length of the fiord, then rounded the point and headed up the next fiord until, after a long, uncomfortable ride, we came to the very end, where there was an area of level ground among the towering mountains. We tied up at a tiny dock, from which we could see a small town of small, square, flat roofed cabins, all identical and all slowly disappearing in the brush and weeds that were reclaiming the land.

We stood there and looked at this ghost of a town. "This was put up to house the construction workers," McKenzie informed us. "They're all prefabricated and should come down pretty easy. I bought the whole town and I'm going to ship it back to Vancouver by boat." There was a hint of pride in his voice. "You can choose anywhere to sleep, but I'll cook the meals at my place," he said. "Can't have any food anywhere else because of the damn bears! They'll all come sniffing around if they think there's even a hint of something to eat." He gave us another minute to look at our summer home, then added, "I'll have supper in half an hour, then you can find some place that suits you."

He turned out to be a good cook, and when we had eaten we walked among the abandoned houses until we found one that was clean and in good condition and decided, considering his comments about bears, that it would be sensible to room together. That first night, we all slept on the floor, but as the days wore on, we found enough abandoned beds and other bits of furniture to make our place fairly comfortable.

After breakfast the next morning, the boss took us to the nearest house and showed us how it had been pieced together with standardized four by eight insulated plywood panels, some of which had windows or doors. Even the floors and the roof were panels. It was all quite ingenious, and when they had been first erected, complete with trim and a coat of paint, they must have looked very attractive. He showed us how he wanted the panels stacked and gave each of us an armful of assorted tools.

And so we set to work, starting with the nearest house and beginning with the roof. We worked as a gang and, since the weather
was beautiful and there were no mosquitoes or black flies, it was a
pleasure to work out in the crisp clean air. The time passed quickly.

At first, knowing that the houses were going to be resold, we
carefully removed all the trim and stacked it, then pulled the nails
and gently tapped the panels apart so that they were in good condition, considering they had been abandoned for nearly a decade. But
that was time consuming. The boss watched our progress carefully,
then compared it to the number of houses and decided that we had
to move twice as fast. "Can't reuse the trim," he said, "so don't waste
time on it. Don't piss around pulling every damn nail, either. Use
the crowbars."

At first, he told us to pile up the electric wiring and stack all
the water pipes, as they had salvage value, but as the days passed,
he became more impatient. "Leave the damn wires and pipes!" he
said. "Just get those panels out and stacked." We had first taken
the asphalt sheeting off the roofs by pulling the nails out with claw
hammers, but then he climbed up and showed us how to run a
wide shovel along the roof under the sheeting and either pop all the
nails or shear them off. He had a whole roof cleaned in a fraction of
the time it had taken us. "Well," one of my fellow deconstructionists
remarked, "he might be a bad-tempered old bastard, but he knows
a few things."

Gradually, we worked out a routine and began to work as a
crew. We were all students, eager to make some money and have an
interesting summer. Nobody was in charge, but we all knew what
had to be done, so there were no personality clashes. Surprisingly,
in this region of high rainfall, the weather remained beautiful. As
the days passed, the piles of panels grew and the houses began to
disappear faster and faster.

Many of the houses had a story to tell. The workers, or their wives, had usually done something to the rectangular boxes they lived in. Individualizing your residence seems, in fact, to be a human instinct. Most of the houses were almost bare, except for clues about the former occupants, such as books, hobbies and crafts, tools, records, and an occasional child's toy. Lots of the houses had once had little gardens in front, and it was surprising how many of the carefully tended plants had survived and even flourished during the years of neglect. Some houses had elaborate rose arbors over their doors, others had window boxes, and there were even tiny patches of front lawn. Although the houses in this high-rain-fall region had flat roofs, surprisingly few had collapsed, and the insides of most of them had hardly changed since the occupants left. There were even two or three houses that had been converted into little chapels.

Most of the refrigerators, stoves, and bathroom fixtures had of course been salvaged years ago, but the house we chose to live in still had a toilet and a kitchen sink. To our surprise, the water to that house was still turned on, too. It was a very weak flow, obviously coming from some gravity feed up the valley, but it was water and the toilet flushed. The local Indian tribe had taken all the pots and pans and useable kitchen utensils, but we didn't need them, anyway. The abandoned furniture ranged from old iron bedsteads and broken chairs to a dining room set complete with an empty china cabinet. In one house, we found a gorgeous dressing table that looked antique. It was heartbreaking to drag it out into the open air, where it would be ruined in the next rain.

The most intriguing house had a small lean-to that was heavily barred and locked. When we broke in, we found a large wooden barrel as big as a bath tub, some smaller wooden barrels, boxes of green glass bottles, and various tools. "Hey!" someone shouted, "a moonshiner!" "Can't be," another guy said. "There's no still." Then somebody pointed out. "Well, he was making something to go into those bottles, and he sure kept this place locked up tight." We looked around carefully, then one of us said, "Wine. This guy was making wine."

Sure enough, one of the shelves held a gadget for inserting corks and we also found a few corks lying on the workbench. "Where the hell did he get grapes this far north?" we wondered. We discussed it for a while and decided that one of the workers, probably an Italian immigrant, had wine grapes shipped in bulk from San Francisco. It must have been expensive, but, since the site was a no-alcohol zone, there must have been a very profitable market for the homemade wine. "I now declare this the furthest north winery on the Pacific coast. Napa Valley North," said the comedian in our group as he broke a ceremonial bottle across one of the barrels.

For the first few days, we kept our eyes open for bears, but it soon dawned on us that there was no game in the valley, or at least we city boys didn't see anything. There were plenty of birds and insects, but in our work we never disturbed a skunk or a raccoon, no squirrels chattered at us, and no cougar peered at us from the brush. Clearly, the deer had migrated up the mountains that towered over us, and the bears, smelling nothing worth eating, were off doing whatever bears do.

Because we were so far north and the days were wonderfully long, we worked as late as nine in the evening before we stopped for supper. We also worked six or seven days a week. Actually, nobody except McKenzie kept records. We had a job to do before leaving, and there was absolutely nothing to do in the evenings, so the long hours and the extended weeks didn't worry us. The quicker we finished the job, we figured, the sooner we would be out of there. So we worked quickly at a comfortable pace, and most evenings we simply washed up and went to sleep.

One morning, I looked at the bottle of milk on the table and said, "Mr. McKenzie, where do you get fresh milk?"

He shrugged and said, "At the store."

There was a dead silence, then everybody said at once. "There's a store here?" He nodded his head.

"You never told us."

He shrugged his shoulders again, "You never asked." Then he smiled and said, "I have to go up there this morning. Hop into the truck."

We bounced up the valley away from the ghost town and came to a cluster of abandoned buildings, and there in the middle was a small shop overshadowed by an enormous radio tower. A sign in the window proclaimed that it was also a post office and a telegraph office.

As a store, it was a little disappointing. It had once been quite an establishment, but now the shelves were bare except for the most basic necessities. Everything was packed or wrapped stoutly. After we introduced ourselves, my first question was, "Where do your customers come from?"

The storekeeper laughed. "Oh, we're not as isolated as it seems," he said. "You'd be surprised at just how many people have cabins in these woods. Mostly old-timers who like to be left alone. Sometimes a 'back-to-nature' family, too, but they never stay long. Had some religious nuts once." He made a face. "And Indians come in once in a while, and there's always hunters and fishermen and surveyors and engineers and such-like." He laughed again, "Why, I'm so busy I sometimes have two or even three customers in one week."

McKenzie interrupted him. "Can't make a living that way. Have you got a little gold mine hidden away in these hills?"

The storekeeper shook his head. "Nope. It's the taxpayer who keeps me in such luxury. I'm the post office and the telegraph office and the radio station and the police station and the ranger station and the game warden and the official voting place. If there were any children around here, I would probably be the teacher, too."

One of the other guys asked where he got his supplies.

"Heavy stuff comes in by boat from Kitimat," he said, "but other stuff comes in on the helicopter, along with engineers and big wheels from the company and such-like. Most everything is done by helicopter nowadays." He pointed to the rough piece of road outside. "That's my helipad."

The storekeeper obviously liked company and was only too willing to show us the mixer that turned milk powder into "fresh milk" and put it into clean bottles. Then I asked him about the missing animals.

"The game? Why these mountains are crawling with game," he said. "Problem is, you guys are making so much noise, it scares everything away. Why, I can hear you up here some days when the wind blows just right." He turned to the boss and said, "You know, McKenzie, you're putting me out of business. When you've finished pulling everything down, there won't be any reason for keeping this place open. I just may have to go back to civilization." He rolled his eyes up to the ceiling. "What a horrible thought!"

A few days later, we received good news. A company executive had been into the store, and the storekeeper had told him about us college students working down the valley. The executive decided it would be good public relations to take us on a guided tour of the giant, hidden power station that provided the electricity for the aluminum smelter.

Next morning, the aforementioned executive, who had spent the night at the store and would be our guide, was waiting for us at the dock. There was a thick, gray fog and it was cold, but we crowded into the boat. We went slowly, which was fortunate because at the mouth of the fiord, the fog turned into a great steel wall rising out of the water and towering over our heads. It was decorated with hundreds of portholes, however, and we soon realized that a cruise liner taking the Inner Passage had stopped and was waiting for the fog to lift, not just for safety, but to also allow the tourists to gaze at the extraordinary mountain scenery.

Soon we turned down a smaller fiord and came to a large concrete dock with almost no buildings around it. Nearby was a wide road in very good condition, so we walked along it until we came to a pair of massive doors built into the face of the mountain. Our guide led us in through a small door at one side, and we next found ourselves in a very large tunnel.

"It has to be big enough to get the machinery in and out," he explained. "Turbines are rather big."

We walked for what must have been a mile deep into the heart of the mountain and came to a two-story office building, which looked rather out of place deep underground.

My first impression was that it must be Sunday. Instead of clerks and secretaries bustling around, there were just one or two people working quietly in their offices.

"Everything is automated," our guide explained as he led us into the central control room. This was a huge room with all the walls covered in dials and meters. In the center was a big curved table with phones and more meters. The two or three men sitting relaxed in their swivel chairs waved to us as we came in.

"As I said," our guide repeated, "everything is automated. In an emergency, this whole complex could be run by one man."

After we had strolled around, staring at the mysterious machinery and dials, he took us down a passage and out onto an underground balcony. We found ourselves high up the side of an immense cavern carved out of the solid rock deep in the heart of the mountain. The bare and uneven rock curved high over our heads, and down below was a row of half a dozen gigantic generators humming quietly and dwarfing the one or two men working near them. We stood there with our mouths open. It was just too big to take in all at once.

"One of the generators is down for servicing," our guide said, "so maybe we can go down and see its bits and pieces." He led the way back to an elevator, which took us down to the cavern floor.

Close up, the generators were even bigger than we thought, and the roof seemed to have disappeared into the heights. We walked to what looked like a huge ship propeller with many cup-shaped blades that a gang of men were smoothing with large grinders. The men stopped to look at us.

"This is what actually turns the generator," our guide said. "The falling water hits it and spins it. Quite simple, really." He ran his hand over a gold-colored blade. "Only problem is, the water hits it with such force that it eats away at the metal. We have to keep resurfacing them and polishing them smooth. The experts keep producing tougher metals." He paused. "I think this little baby is a special bronze alloy. Don't really know, though. It's not my field."

Then he took us over to the wall and pointed to the row of generators. "Actually, you're looking at the tops of the generators. All the action is going on under our feet. That's where the falling water hits the blades."

And as we stood there in that great cavern, he explained that there were two "penstocks," or water pipes, about ten feet across in vertical shafts that had been drilled thousands of feet down through the heart of the mountain, "Rather like a dentist doing a root canal," he joked. The penstocks were lined, and their surfaces were smooth as glass, but the immense volume of water falling that great distance rapidly wore away at the sides. No rocks or even tiny stones could be allowed to enter the turbines under our feet, so every now and then one of the penstocks was drained, and men with powerful lights were lowered down from the top on a platform to check every inch of the wall for the slightest defect.

"I went down once," he said. "Once was quite enough. Now I know how to spell 'claustrophobia.'" He turned and added, "Now let's go and see where the water ends up."

At the end of a low tunnel that seemed to be a mile long, we came to a locked door that he unlocked, then ushered us out onto a narrow concrete ledge overlooking a wide canal of fast-moving water. The lighting was poor, so all we could see was the dark water pouring out of the mountain through a massive iron grill.

"This is where the water goes into the sea," he said. "But take a careful look into the water." And he turned on a powerful hand-held lamp.

It was eerie. The clear water was a solid mass of fish, all facing upstream. They were almost stationary with just their tails moving to keep them in position. Deep into the water, as far as the light would penetrate, all grey or brown in the dark, there were fish of every size, from trophy fish over two feet long to little two inch specimens, all of them waiting patiently for the solid iron gates to open.

In the boat, on the way back, our guide explained that to get the amount of water needed to provide the electricity for the smelter, the entire river and lake system of part of British Columbia (an area bigger than some European countries) had been dammed to create a 350-square-mile reservoir of rivers and lakes that all flowed backward and into a ten mile tunnel drilled into the heart of the mountain to the penstocks. At the time, in the 1950s, it had been one of the largest and most difficult engineering feats in the world.

After six or seven weeks, we students had reduced the ghost town to neat stacks of panels and scattered rubble. Now we started piling the panels onto McKenzie's truck and taking them down to the wharf. It was a tricky job because the boss wanted them piled high and the road was very rough, so we threw ropes over the wobbling stacks and walked alongside to keep each load from crashing to the ground.

Then one morning, we woke to find a little freighter at the dock. It was a tiny thing, old and battered, and it seemed to have a crew consisting only of a captain and an engineer. It had a donkey engine and a boom, and with a lot of swearing from the crew and helpful advice from the boss at our clumsy efforts—"Don't any of you stupid bastards ever take a summer job on the docks. You won't last ten minutes!"—we got the old tramp loaded. The panels were stacked so high I could only pray she would have the calmest possible weather on her trip back to Vancouver. Next day, we carefully closed the door of our house, which, like McKenzie's house, we left standing, and scrambled into the boat for the ride back to Kitimat, where the boss stopped at the bank and paid us all off.

Although I still had some summer holiday left, I decided to go with him back to Vancouver. We set off towing a small two-wheeled trailer carrying all the tools. As before, he drove like a maniac, and as the road was even more pot-holed and broken up than before, the ride was very uncomfortable. When we stopped for the night, we discovered that the little trailer had bounced so much that it had fallen to pieces. Somewhere along the road were little bits of trailer and all the tools. All we had left were an axle and two wheels. McKenzie swore, then shrugged his shoulders. "I'll claim it on my income tax," he said. "Let's have a beer."

It had been a very good summer. I had made a nice sum of money, the work had not been too hard, I had seen a bit of western Canada, and I had been to a fascinating place few people would ever see. The university courses were going to be hard, I could see problems there, but summer had been fun. I was going to like being a student.

That was the first of my summer jobs. The many summers during my university days that I spent looking for work have all blended together in my memory. I often took notes on the jobs in the form of diaries or letters to relatives, but I kept no dates and today, try as I may, I can't put all the jobs I found into chronological order.

Chapter 16
Dish Washing

The summer was hot, it had not rained for months, everything was tinder dry, and the authorities were eventually forced to shut down all forest operations. Naturally, if the loggers could not work, neither could the sawmills...and I had just landed a job that paid well in a large sawmill. It shut down the day I signed on.

I really needed that job so I decided to hang around until the weather changed, but I was almost broke. Living on one meal a day and sleeping in the park was no fun so one evening I walked to a busy all-night restaurant on the edge of town and asked for the manager. He soon appeared and he was obviously worried that I was a customer with a complaint, so I came right to the point.

"I'll wash dishes for a square meal."

The worried frown on his face changed instantly to a smile. "You'll wash dishes?" Without waiting for a reply, he grabbed my arm and led me into the kitchen, where the air was filled with the delightful smell of food.

I learned very quickly that it can be difficult getting staff for a busy, all-night restaurant, and the manager and his wife had been doing most of the dishwashing for the past week. A batch of dishes had just been washed and there was a lull, so I was led to a table, where the manager himself served me a marvelously tender steak with all the trimmings. He even popped the top off a bottle of cold beer for me.

As the middle child in a large family, I had had plenty of experience washing dishes, so the giant black pots and greasy pans the cook tossed my way were no problem. (The glass and the chinaware were washed in the commercial dishwasher, along with almost all the cutlery.) I was kept busy, but every now and then the manager would appear with a pastry or a small sandwich or sometimes a fresh beer and assure me that if there was anything that I wanted to eat, no matter how expensive, all I had to do was tell the chef. I took him at his word and very soon my belt was comfortably tight.

I could hardly believe my good fortune. I had somewhere warm to spend the night and all the food that I could possibly eat. The manager could hardly believe his good fortune. He had a dishwasher who would work enthusiastically for nothing more than food and a few beers.

At dawn after my first night, when the sun started to peek over the surrounding mountains, the manager, anxious to make sure that I would return next night, offered to drive me back into town. He also took the opportunity to slip me a generous tip. After he had driven away, I strolled down to the park for a good day's sleep. This went on for about a week and I did such a good job that the manager increased the size of my morning tip.

Then, at long last, it rained. It wasn't much of a storm, but it was enough to lift the ban on forest operations, so I phoned the restaurant and left a message for the manager. Then I got a lift out to the sawmill. It had been an interesting experience and—as far as food was concerned—altogether enjoyable.

That was not the first time I had washed dishes for a living. When my advertising job in London was not producing much money, and what little I made went on rent and other basics. I had cut down on food, but it was no fun being hungry while living over a bakery in Soho, an area of London that is packed with every type of cafe and restaurant, so I looked for an evening job and found one in a hotel only a short bus ride north of Marble Arch.

The hotel was one of those old Victorian relics, crammed with brass and polished mahogany with animal heads and ancient paintings of the Scottish Highlands on the walls. It was very popular and always crowded The customers seemed to be race track types, many of them bookies, and they all dressed and talked loudly and smoked cheap cigars and drank like fish. It was obvious that the hotel made its money from the bar and that the food was of secondary importance. However, the menu did have a few over-priced continental dishes for those lucky winners who wished to splurge or show off to their girlfriends. There were also a few rooms available, but the only guests were customers who were too drunk to get back home.

The kitchen, which was upstairs over the bar, was dominated by a huge, antique, black range that must have been as old as the hotel. The dishes were sent down on the dumbwaiter, and we could also hear much of the conversation at the bar echoing up at us through it. The chef was a bald headed, arrogant little man who affected a French accent when he deigned to talk to us, which he rarely did. He was assisted by a short, fat, elderly woman who was the cook. When the chef went off duty at seven, the cook was in charge for the rest of the evening, so there were only two of us there.

There was surprisingly little for us in the kitchen to do except sit around waiting for somebody downstairs to decide to eat, although on important race days we were often swamped with orders sent up by the big winners. As soon as the chef was safely out of the building, the cook would march to the freezer and survey the contents before choosing our supper. She took delight in selecting from the best available. "Got to put some meat on your bones," she always said. "That old bat won't notice." The old bat was the hotel manager's wife.

While our supper was being prepared, the cook invariably pressed some money into my hand and said, "Just pop downstairs and get me a couple of stouts, there's a good boy." Several times during the evening I would "pop down" and bring back a couple of bottles of the dark brew and watch in fascination as she emptied both bottles in record time. It was a few days before it dawned on me that although she was never actually drunk, she was never fully sober, either.

The only fly in the ointment was the old bat. She was over forty but striving to look under thirty and wore tight skirts, tight blouses, and tight shoes. Even her hair was in tight little curls. She had a bad temper, a sharp voice, and was constantly complaining about waste. At least twice an evening, she would make her appearance and dash around the kitchen, peering into every pot and pan and criticizing everybody and everything. Then she dashed back down to the bar. Fortunately, when she was in the bar, she often stood close to the dumbwaiter, so we could hear everything she said, and she talked non-stop. When her voice stopped booming up the shaft, we knew it was time to take our positions, the cook posed over the massive range and I standing over the sink, waiting nervously until she burst through the door.

The old bat always stopped at the garbage can and peered in. If there was a dinner roll that was untouched, she would wipe off the cigarette ash and put it back with the other rolls. If there was a stem of asparagus that still looked edible, she would wipe it clean and put it with the others. If there was a shrimp or an untouched pat of butter, back it went into the freezer. I was horrified, but I kept my mouth shut.

The cutlery was massive antique silver, or at least that's what it looked like. Actually, it was base metal with the thinnest of silver plating, and the old bat constantly warned me not to use a scouring pad or even scouring powder on "the silver." She insisted that I use only a soft sponge, but some hardened foods can be quite stubborn and I made good use of the scouring pad whenever I needed to.

One of the dishes on the menu was scampi. It was horribly overpriced, but quite popular with the big winners. We had strict instructions to place exactly six shrimps on each plate. One night the manager's wife appeared in the door waving a shrimp and yelling, "Seven! Seven! Some fool put seven on that last order. What are you trying to do? Drive me to the poor house?" And she marched over to the cook, threw the now somewhat bedraggled shrimp back into the bowl of scampi on the table, and marched back downstairs… where we could hear her voice echoing up the dumbwaiter shaft as she expressed her feelings about her kitchen staff.

After I had been working there for about a month, she caught us unawares one night. The cook was sitting with her feet up, drinking from a bottle, and I was at the big sink with one of her precious "silver" forks in one hand and a heavy duty scouring pad in the other. The tantrum she threw was a marvel to behold. It ended with the old cook crying and scuttling downstairs for another couple of stouts and me putting on my jacket and heading for the door. The kitchen served no more meals that night.

Another time I was actually refused the job of dishwasher. I was hitchhiking on the Continent and found myself in Milan, which is a very large city. I was temporarily out of money, wandering through the streets with just a few lira in my pocket and feeling very hungry, especially as it was evening and every door I passed seemed to be a restaurant.

Finally, I stopped at a medium-sized restaurant and asked the lady at the door if I could wash dishes for a square meal. She didn't understand my poor Italian, so she called her little daughter, who was studying English in school, to translate. By this time, the whole family had gathered around, and when they understood my request, there was a flurry of questions. Was I a Catholic? Had I been to Rome? Had I seen the pope? When I replied yes to these vital questions, there was general agreement: no good Catholic who had been blessed by *Il Papa* should wash dishes for a meal, even if he was a foreigner. They seated me down at once and bustled about, bringing soup and pasta and fish, all with a glass of wine, and a delicious desert followed by black coffee. Everybody seemed to bring something else, and I was soon more than full.

When they were satisfied with their efforts, they escorted me to the door, gave me the address of the municipal poor house where I could get a bed for the night, and even told me which tram to take and where to get off. Then they all stood at the door and waved as I walked off down the street.

Chapter 17
The Cement Factory

After spending long months in musty lecture halls and seeing my bank account rapidly shrinking, I needed an outside job that paid well. I had bought a car for a few hundred dollars and found work as a dispatcher at a cement factory on the river, south of Vancouver. Up to that time I knew absolutely nothing about cement and even less about dispatching, but the manager assured me that it was a very simple job and one that I would be able to handle quite easily.

The cement factory was a large plant that stood isolated on the river bank, surrounded by strawberry fields. The main office was at the factory itself, but I was stationed in the ugly concrete weigh station at the gates. It was a strictly functional office with a couple of desks, one swivel chair, four phones, and an electric typewriter. Over everything loomed the large white face of the weigh scale. The previous dispatcher, who was quitting, tried to explain the job to me as he worked, and the more he talked, the further my heart sank. Inexperienced as I was, as dispatcher, I would be responsible for all the raw material that came into the factory and all the cement that went out. This included the big round trucks carrying wet cement, the trucks carrying dry cement either in bulk or in sacks, the barges that tied up at the river dock, and the rail cars on the rail spur behind the plant. I was expected to be there at seven in the morning and to stay until the last truck returned. There was no lunch break and nobody to relieve me. Fortunately, there was a toilet.

I found lodgings with a lady who lived a few miles away and when I arrived at work bright and early the next morning, I found trucks already lined up at the scales, their drivers standing around, smoking. It was the truck drivers who actually taught me my job. With a few exceptions, they were cheerful and friendly and only too eager to crowd into the little hut and show me which forms to use and where to type in the weight and where to sign the various copies. The summer building season had started, so the stream of trucks seemed endless. Hardly had one truck disappeared in a cloud of dust than another would drive up, wheels locked and skidding and ending exactly on the weigh scale, which raised even more dust.

The dust was everywhere. Vancouver's notoriously heavy rain-fall should have kept everything sparkling clean, but it had been a dry spring and the dust covered every surface of every building and lay thick on the road. Worse, it also drifted across the strawberry fields and enraged the local farmers who, I learned later, were constantly suing the cement company. So much for fresh air.

Cement is made from limestone and other minerals that have to be crushed to a powder, which is mixed into a slurry and then cooked. It is then crushed again. The grinding and crushing of thousands of tons of rock and cement produce a lot of dust. I was never tempted to tour the plant, even if I had had the time, but I did manage to climb up to see the ovens one day. The ovens were two huge, revolving pipes about ten feet wide and well over 200 feet long. Their floors sloped slightly so the slurry that was fed in at one end slowly worked its way downstream as it was cooked into cement.

During my visit, the operator opened an observation window and let me peer through the foot-thick pane of smoked glass. Immediately over my head a nozzle was squirting an enormously powerful jet of gas deep into the long oven, where everything quivered white hot and eerie. "That's about 2,000 degrees Fahrenheit," the operator boasted. "Hotter than inside a volcano." For a lad who had heard many a priest describe the Fires of Hell, it was an impressive sight.

Along with the trucks carrying wet cement, there were also trucks loaded with bulk cement and more trucks with bagged cement, and each needed weighing in a special way and had its special forms that I had to fill out.

Meanwhile, the four telephones were constantly ringing. They were ringing before I got there in the morning and all four of them were still ringing when I left in the evening. There were calls from impatient customers asking all manner of questions and giving instructions. There were calls from the main office, calls from the railroads, calls intended for other departments, wrong numbers, and even the occasional little old lady who wanted the correct time. I became quite skilled at answering two phones at once while simultaneously typing a bill of lading and jotting down the weight of the truck currently on the scales. One day, however, I received a call that really flummoxed me. It was the police reporting that one of our wet cement trucks had rolled over on a busy highway. They wanted to know how long it would take before the cement hardened and what I was going to do about it. I passed that call up to the main office.

I had to fit lunch in while working, and I rolled the office chair from one desk to the other so many times and so violently that within a month the wheels were worn out and the main office had to find me a new chair. I was so busy that the days sped by and so exhausted in the evening that I never went out to spend the money

I was earning. But the weather was good that summer and it was delightful to spend the evening just lazing in a deck chair with a book and occasionally looking up to enjoy the flowers.

The lady from whom I rented my room was very nice and attentive. She was Ukrainian and still wore a headscarf and kept a beautifully gilded icon in the living room. Her children had grown up and moved away, so I was her surrogate son for the summer. I often think that I would have quit that job had it not been for her cheerful mothering, her cooking, and her big, flower-filled garden near the river. She loved to cook and was convinced that I needed fattening up. "Too skinny," she would say and shake her head. She had shares in a nearby strawberry farm and during the season I had strawberries with fresh cream for breakfast and a homemade strawberry pie in my lunch. After supper, the desert was strawberries in whipped cream, and when I went into the garden to relax in the deck chair and enjoy the long northern evening, she could hardly wait to bring me an enormous slice of freshly made strawberry cake.

One day her sister arrived from the prairies and they took the ferry over to Vancouver Island, where they had heard of a little cove that was supposed to be just covered with oysters. Indeed, they came home that evening loaded with oysters. They had filled the station wagon with the biggest oysters they could find. We immediately sat down at the kitchen table and stuffed ourselves. Even after they had given most of the oysters away to friends and neighbors, there were still a lot of them, and they had to be eaten quickly before they spoiled. For nearly a week, therefore, I had oysters for breakfast, oysters in my lunch, and oysters for supper, as well as a little oyster snack before going to bed. I never did get tired of them because my landlady prepared them in so many different ways. Each little morsel was a delight.

It took some effort, but I eventually got my work down to a routine so that the finished product left the factory quickly and fairly smoothly. But the incoming raw material was another matter. The limestone came by barge from somewhere up the coast, the great steel hulks appearing mysteriously during the night. The other minerals came by rail. While I had little to do with ordering the raw materials, I was responsible for the rail cars and spent a great deal of time on the phone to the railways, tracking down loaded cars and trying to get rid of the empty ones.

One evening, just as I was about to leave, I was ordered to the rail spur to move some empty cars that were blocking access to the barges. There were only four of us, and I stood there wondering how on earth four men could possibly push half a dozen huge monsters down the track and out of the way, a job usually handled by a large diesel engine. Somebody handed out long poles with wedge shaped chunks of steel on the ends. We jammed these between the wheels and the rails. Then, on a given signal, we all strained on our poles. Miraculously, the rail car rolled forward about a foot. Our next effort moved it even further and I felt a slightly ridiculous sense of power at having moved a huge rail car, even if it was empty. Two hours later, after we had moved all the rail cars a hundred yards down the track, I did not feel quite so exhilarated.

Toward the end of summer, when I saw that my bank balance had greatly improved, I decided I had breathed in quite enough dust. I started to look for something less hectic to occupy my days. When I gave my notice, the factory manager tried to persuade me to stay. He even said that he was sorry to see me go. I smiled at the compliment, which was something I had rarely heard, but I left the cement factory anyway.

Chapter 18
The Fish Cannery

Prince Rupert, which is the northernmost Canadian seaport on the Pacific, lies about 100 miles south of Ketchikan, Alaska. While the Alaskan city is a popular tourist attraction where the cruise ships always stop, Prince Rupert is a working city. The work is logging or fishing; when I arrived there looking for a job, since I had neither logging boots nor rain gear, I ended up in a fish cannery.

My first morning, I was given rubber boots, a huge yellow waterproof apron, and a pair of cotton gloves. Then I was led to a long metal trough filled with water and dead fish, where I joined a group of women, mostly Indians from the region. (I found out later that they made more money during the fishing season than their husbands made all year.) One of the women gave me a bent spoon and showed me how to scrape the sea lice and other unwelcome parasites off the fish. It looked easy, so I plunged my hands into the water and grabbed a fish. The shock of the icy water was almost too much to bear. The women were busy working, however, and chatting as if they were washing the supper dishes in warm water, so, filled with masculine pride, I gritted my teeth, clenched my frozen fingers around the fish, and scraped away. The cotton gloves helped me hold the slippery fish and, surprisingly, also seemed to help keep my hands slightly warmer than absolute zero.

By the time lunch break came around, I had become so used to the cold water that I hardly noticed it. As I followed the women to a sandwich shack on the docks, one of them told me of a boarding house close by that had vacant rooms.

For the next few days, I spent my time cleaning the outsides of a steady stream of fish, which were then moved to another area, where the experts, with their wickedly sharp knives, cleaned the insides.

I seemed to have passed some kind of test at the cleaning tank because, one morning, the boss sent me to work with the men on the table. When the boats arrived with their loads of fish, the crew would pile the catch into a huge net, which was then hoisted up onto the dock and suspended over a large wooden table with drain holes in it. One man would climb up onto the table, reach under the dripping net, and pull a rope which released a great cascade of fish. The trick was to get out of the way really fast, not easy to do in clumsy rubber boots on a slippery surface. The fishermen would then hurry to reload the net, and we would hurry to sort out the fish and slide them into the proper bins. I learned to tell one kind of fish from another, but, fortunately, they were mostly salmon that were sorted by size only. To handle the fish, we used sharp hooks, and I was warned to hook the fish only by the gills, never in the body. With a dozen men working furiously, it was hard to avoid getting stabbed or, worse, sinking my hook into somebody else's hand.

Salmon fishing is strictly limited and the fishermen had just a few weeks in which to work. They went out in all kinds of weathers with great boxes of sandwiches and huge containers of sweetened coffee. They worked twenty-four hours a day, non-stop, until the hold was full of iced fish, then raced back to the canneries, unloaded as fast as they could, took on fresh ice (and sandwiches and coffee) and hurried back out again. They would go for days without sleep, which may explain why they always seemed haggard and filthy, with bloodshot eyes and extremely bad tempers. The slightest delay in unloading the catch or delivering ice would bring forth an astounding stream of extraordinarily expressive language.

After being sorted, the fish were stacked in bays, where they were covered with ice. There they waited for cleaning and processing while the dock was hosed down for the next fishing boat. The boss was a fanatic about cleanliness, so whenever there was no catch to unload, I was ordered to drag the heavy-duty hose around washing down everything that didn't get out of my way. Everything was hosed into the sea, where the crabs and other bottom feeding creatures must have dined extremely well.

We used a lot of ice. While much of it was dumped over the waiting fish, a great amount slithered down a chute into the holds of the waiting fishing boats. One morning, when the fishermen began to complain that the ice was not moving fast enough, I was sent up to the huge ice making machine high up near the roof to find out why. The machine dropped its load into a big hopper, where it sat until the loading chute opened. An unusually large number of boats arriving in just a few days had almost emptied the hopper, except for the large chunks frozen into the corners. The boss solved the problem by handing me a shovel. "Get that damn ice moving!" For the rest of the day, I slithered and slid in my rubber boots, bashing at the chunks of ice so that they wouldn't clog the chute and shoveling ice as fast as I could. Meanwhile, the ice machine was raining a steady and unceasing flow of ice on my head. It came down in bits the size of a silver dollar and was more irritating than painful, especially when it slid down my neck or got into my boots. I also had to keep from sliding into the chute. Working in the hopper, I had constant visions of being stuck half way down the chute and being buried under tons of ice. The room was well insulated and I should have been frozen, but there was no let-up and I had to keep moving. Whenever the river of ice slowed, I got an earful from some angry fisherman yelling up the chute. By then, instead of freezing, I was sweating. I did not relish spending another day in the hopper; fortunately, the machine was left on overnight and next day it was filled.

The cleaned fish were next packed into cardboard boxes and wheeled into the freezer room, where the temperature was so low they were soon as hard as iron. My efforts in the ice hopper must have pleased the boss because, next day, he gave me the comparatively easy job of pushing the loaded racks of fish in and out of the freezer room. Unfortunately, however, I wore glasses, and so the instant I pushed through the hanging rubber strips that blocked the door, my glasses fogged up. It only took a minute or two to unfog them, but when I left the room my glasses instantly steamed up in the slightly warmer air outside and I had to stop to wipe them again. This went on for about an hour. Loaded racks began to pile up on both sides of the door. Soon the boss arrived. After watching my antics for several minutes, he shook his head and said, "Get back on the table."

When the salmon season ended, the fishermen began to bring in halibut. Much of the catch consisted of fish no more than two feet long. The men called them "chicken halibut" and said they would end up in the supermarkets, whereas the larger fish were destined for restaurants and banquet rooms. Now and then a boat would bring in a giant fish. Half a dozen times while I was there, I watched with open mouth as one of those great flat monsters, sometimes well over six feet long, was winched out of a boat by a chain around his tail. Salmon were left whole, but halibut had their heads cut off on the table. This was done by experts with razor sharp machetes. My job was to turn the fish so that the white side was uppermost, which enabled the men with the knives to chop the head off. Flipping over a large, flat, very slippery fish was not easy, especially on a table cluttered with fish heads and slimy with blood. Chopping the head off one of the giant halibut took three or more powerful strokes and, as I write this, I shudder to think of the times one of those machetes came a little too close for comfort. .

About once a week, a neatly dressed elderly lady carrying an old fashioned shopping basket came up to the table. After removing a pair of white cotton gloves, a small knife, and some clean newspaper, and completely ignoring us, she would slip on the gloves, pick up halibut heads, carefully slice out the chunks of flesh from just below the eyes, and place them on the newspaper. When she had a nice package of about two pounds, she would carefully remove her gloves, put the package in her basket and walk back down the dock. I learned that she had been collecting halibut cheeks for years. They are an expensive item in the better seafood restaurants. What fascinated me was the almost magical way in which she avoided being splattered by blood, guts, or dirty water. She never seemed to get a speck on her.

At this time, I roomed in an old wooden hotel that catered to men only. There was a bottle opener screwed to the door jamb of my room and there were a dozen huge ash trays scattered around. It was not exactly the Ritz, but it was clean and cheap, and all I needed were a bed and a shower with an endless supply of hot water. Even fresh fish have a smell, and the first few days, after I left the cannery, I would stand under the shower and try to scrub the smell away. In time, however, it ceased to bother me, and then

I didn't notice any smell at all, probably because the whole town smelled of fish. It was only after I had left Prince Rupert and was many miles away from the coast that I realized that my hair, my skin, and every article of my clothing had a slightly fishy smell. For the next few weeks, until I was altogether sure that it had gone, I was extra generous with the aftershave lotion.

Now and then a few odd fish appeared on the table. They were usually just kicked into the ocean, but once we all stopped to admire a large sturgeon about four feet long. The prehistoric fish lay there, gleaming blue, green, and silver, with its long jaw and wickedly efficient teeth. Compared to the sleek salmon, it was probably quite ugly, but I thought it was a beautiful fish. So did the plant manager, who soon appeared and quickly wrapped it up for his supper.

It was the busy season and the boats never stopped coming. Some evenings, we would have hosed everything down and iced the fish and have our aprons off when another boat would appear through the mist. It was unforgivable to let it sit there overnight. The fish had to be unloaded and iced down and the fishermen had to have their fresh ice. Without complaining, we would don our gear and get right back to work. That far north, it stays light long into the evening, and sometimes we would be busy until almost midnight.

The main reason we were happy to get the work was the pay. Base pay was reasonably good, and we got time and a half for overtime and double-time for extra hours. We also got time and a half for working Saturday, with overtime pay for more than eight hours. Sunday was all double time with overtime paid accordingly. Since I had nothing else to do, I worked every day of the week and, like the rest of the crew, grabbed as much overtime as I could. There is always a shortage of labor during the season in that isolated region. The Indian women flocked to the canneries, but their husbands and sons were too busy working the inlets and rivers, trying to catch enough salmon to last through the long winter. For them, a fat paycheck could not equal a shed full of smoked salmon.

The town itself was not very interesting except for the way it had grown over the steep and rocky peninsula. Everything was up or down a flight of steps, and some of the roads were in two sections, one side hacked out of the rock, the other side resting on wooden piles. Despite the rocky soil, there was vegetation everywhere. This was because everything was damp. Weeds sprouted furiously from every crack in the roads and bright green moss grew on the roof shingles of the older houses and, although it was pleasantly warm and the sky often seemed sunny and bright, I never once actually saw the sun all the time I was there.

Being wet myself most of the time, I hardly noticed when it rained. But I did notice the lack of sunshine. Sometimes there was a heavy fog, sometimes just a light mist. Sometimes the clouds dropped down almost to sea level, and at other times the sky was just a bright white ceiling that looked like the sun was about to shine through. But it never did. There are islands all around the peninsula, but I couldn't see them because they remained hidden in the mist. This lack of a horizon, coupled with the permanent overcast, created a weird isolated and boxed-in feeling. Slowly but surely, I began to hate the permanently gray sky and the lack of sunshine. Toward the end of summer, as the work slackened off a bit, I looked at my bank balance. I had a nice sum, and there was still a bit of summer to enjoy, so I hung up my yellow apron, said goodbye to the fish cannery, and…smelling ever so faintly of fish…hitched a ride out of town.

The next year, when I had to start looking for another summer job that paid well, I thought of all the money I had made in Prince Rupert. There was a large cannery quite close to Vancouver and, with my experience, I was soon hired. Unfortunately, the cannery was a large, modern, highly mechanized, food processing factory with a two-shift system that allowed no overtime for anybody. When I arrived for work, I was sent to the animal feed shed, where the foreman showed me to a machine. My job was to slip plastic-lined bags up onto its nozzle. When I asked what it did, he said, "It fills the bags with animal feed. You don't have to weigh them, the machine does that, and you don't have to seal the bags, either. That's done automatically. Just dump them on the pallet behind you and keep them coming." He demonstrated the process for a few minutes.

Whatever was going into the bags was wet and heavy, and the bags felt squashy, rather like bags of jelly. "What's in them?" I asked.

"Mink food." he said. "Very expensive feed for mink farmers. Don't damage the bags." And with that, he disappeared.

The work was boringly simple. Half way through my first morning, when an older workman came by sweeping the floors with a wide broom, I asked him what went into the expensive mink food.

"All the odds and ends," he said with a laugh. "Ain't nothing wasted here. They collect the fish guts and the heads and tails and anything else that's not good enough to can or turn into cat food, and it all gets crushed up." He shook his head and added, "God, what a stinking mess it is! But the mink farmers like it. They say it gives a real shine to the fur."

I felt as if I were doomed to spend the summer stuck in front of a machine that poured into neat and brightly labeled packages all the offal I had hosed into the sea a year before. It was a job, but not a well paying one, and I knew I would never save enough for next year's tuition and living expenses. What was worse, it was dreadfully boring. At lunch time, I quit.

Chapter 19
Picking Fruit

One summer, when I was hitchhiking through the lovely valleys of southern British Columbia and looking for work in construction or the sawmills, I found myself in a large fruit-growing region. It was the cherry season and many of the farms had *Pickers Wanted* signs on their gates. The trees were black with ripe cherries and the weather was perfect. How difficult, I wondered, would it be to pick fruit?

I found out the hard way.

Being new to the game, I mistakenly picked a farm where the trees had not been pruned for many years. The trees should have been compact and low, but these were big and the branches were wide and almost touching each other. The farmer took my name, handed me a basket, pointed to a stack of ladders and a pile of fruit flats, and quoted a price per flat that seemed quite good.

I set to work. The ladders were big and heavy, so I seemed to spend a great deal of my time dragging my ladder around and positioning it where I could climb up and reach the most cherries. Filling the basket was quite easy. I would climb down the ladder with my basket and fill the flats that I had brought along. Then I would climb back up the ladder. It didn't take me long to realize that my leg muscles were not used to climbing ladders, so I tried walking the branches. But I was wearing the wrong kind of shoes and nearly slipped a couple of times. That's when I decided to pick just the fruit I could reach easily.

Soon, unfortunately, the farmer came up to me. "You have to clean the whole tree," he said in a very sour voice. "Don't leave any ripe fruit behind."

After a few hours, the ladder seemed to have doubled in weight and I was spending more time positioning it than picking fruit. Nevertheless, my pile of filled flats was growing quite nicely.

There were a few other pickers scattered throughout the orchard. Near me was a pair of young girls wearing white head scarves and full skirts. They were Doukhobors, a Russian religious sect, and they chatted away in Russian as they worked, scampering up their ladders and filling their flats at a pace that made me look like a lay-about. I tried to copy them, but they had years of practice and they didn't stop to munch on a handful of delicious cherries every few minutes. I had not had breakfast, and the cherries were big, juicy, and tastier than any that I had ever had before or since.

By noon, my leg muscles were beginning to cramp and my back muscles were aching from handling the ladder, so I carried my flats over to the packing shed. The farmer grabbed each flat and shook and banged it violently until the cherries settled and compacted down. Next, he topped up each flat and shook the cherries down again until there were almost as many empty boxes as full ones. Then, without a word, he reached into his pocket and pulled out a few bills and paid me.

For a long, hard morning's work, I had made barely enough to buy one square meal. But then, I reminded myself, I didn't need to buy lunch because my belly was already full of those delicious cherries.

Chapter 20
The Airline

Edmonton is the northernmost major city in Canada. I arrived there one summer with the vague idea that I would find work in the Canadian Arctic, but it was too late in the season and I had to look elsewhere. At the airport, where I went inquiring after baggage-handling work, I was told that there was nothing available in Winnipeg, but they needed another baggage handler in Fort St. John, a small town further north. There was an oil-drilling boom in the region and traffic at the airport there had increased enormously. I could have the position if I was ready to leave immediately. An hour later, I was on the plane and astonished at my luck since I had less than a dollar in my pocket.

The airport at Fort St. John was quite small, consisting of just a few hangars and a minuscule terminal surrounded by open fields. I noticed that the runway had a very obvious dip half way down its length.

A man whom I presumed to be the manager was at his desk trying to fill out the manifest while at the same time answering the constantly ringing phone and fielding questions from passengers. There was also a young man at the desk making out three or four tickets at once while answering a stream of questions, and two other young men were labeling luggage and stacking it on a cart and arguing with the owners of the luggage while a much older man was trying to help the incoming passengers with their luggage, answering their questions, and trying to check off the incoming freight. Taxi drivers squeezed through the crowd looking for customers and the teleprinter rattled away in the background. The noise was almost deafening.

I needed no instructions but pitched right in and helped pile the outgoing luggage onto a trolley and wheeled it out to the plane, where I crouched in the cargo space in the belly of the plane for the next ten minutes and stacked the mixed luggage and freight that somebody else passed up through the hatch. When all was secured, I crawled out of the belly of the plane and stood by the passenger stairs with another loader. There was a long pause while bored passengers peered out of the small windows and an impatient stewardess stood tapping her foot by the open door. Eventually, the manager hurried out with the manifest, the doors were slammed shut, the engines began to roar, and the plane crept to the runway. A few minutes after the plane disappeared in the far distance, a wonderful silence descended on the little airport. As if by magic, the crowd had vanished and we all went into the terminal and relaxed in the plastic chairs.

I soon found that what I had just experienced was the regular routine. There were only three planes a day—the southbound plane, the northbound plane, and the Vancouver-bound plane—and they were scheduled to make only a very short stop at Port St. John. Somehow, the traffic experts at the airline's head office had not taken into account the work involved when any plane arrives at any airport and loads or unloads passengers, luggage, and freight. Our days consisted of long hours of boredom broken by minutes of utter chaos.

When the last taxi into town had vanished in a cloud of white dust, I was finally introduced to my coworkers and told that I would bunk in with them in a little house they had rented because, thanks to the oil boom, housing was scarce and prices were high. My housemates proved to be a lively bunch.

When I asked the manager the next day what exactly I was hired to do, I got no direct answer and quickly found out that nobody had any training or specialized in anything. We were just supposed to help with anything and everything. But there was one thing we had to concentrate on. No matter when the plane arrived, *it had to leave on time*. Fifty years ago, the planes were much smaller and lighter than they are today, so the weight of the passengers and the cargo and the way that weight was distributed throughout the plane were all very important. It was all recorded on a manifest, and the pilot could not take off without that piece of paper. Making out the manifest involved subtracting the weight of incoming passengers and freight and adding the estimated weight of the outgoing passengers and freight. These calculations took time. Consequently, very few of the departures from our little airport were ever on time and somebody always had to sit down at the teletype machine and explain why.

Most of the flights were from Edmonton to Whitehorse in the Yukon, with stops at half a dozen isolated towns, including Fort St. John, in between. There was another flight a couple of times a week that stopped at Fort St. John on its way to Vancouver. The airports were all connected by the same teletype machine, so any message typed onto the machine would print out on all the other terminals. Almost daily we had to concoct a reason for a flight delay, and our wonderfully imaginative excuses were the source of quite a few jokes. Sometimes we said it was a bear on the runway…or maybe it was a stray dog or a moose. Quite often, it was a late passenger or a pregnant lady or (now and then) a leaking or broken container in the freight.

Part of my job was to help invent the day's excuse and type it out. I suspect that the other teletype machine operators sat waiting eagerly each day to see what new, weird excuse we came up with. The other operators added anonymous comments that we all saw, and there were days when the teletype printout read like a short story by James Thurber. One operator, who refused to identify himself, loved to remind us when we had last used the same excuse. He would write comments like "Is that the same flock of geese you had last Wednesday? Strange. It isn't the migratory season."

The manifest was a very important document but it was impossible to complete it in advance because we were never sure until the last minute exactly what would be loaded onto the plane and what would be unloaded. The passengers and their luggage were easy to calculate, but when an urgent shipment of the heavy oil drilling bits arrived or when boxes of drilling cores were shipped out, the change in weight had to be calculated. In the plane, this weight had to be evenly distributed and often I found myself kneeling in the cramped cargo space pushing and dragging sacks and boxes back and forth until both the manager and the captain were satisfied that balance had been achieved. One time, an impatient pilot simply ordered all the passengers to move to the tail section until the plane was airborne, at which time they were permitted to take their assigned seats until it was time to land, when they all crowded back into the rear again.

If things went smoothly, the manifest would be handed to the stewardess as she closed the doors, but all too often the pilot would taxi to the end of the runway and sit there, fuming, as one of us raced out to the plane in the pickup truck with the manager standing in the back holding a long pole, which he would use to hand the paper up to the copilot.

The only place to buy a ticket was at the terminal. As this entailed an expensive taxi ride out of town, many passengers waited until the last minute to buy their tickets. Fortunately, the planes were rarely full, but the last minute hassle with baggage and tickets only added to the confusion. A lot of trouble came from passengers who wanted to carry a bulky or awkward object on the plane with them. We had to deal with pool cues, skis, freshly caught trophy trout, a genuine Inuit harpoon, and even a tiny but nasty looking baby wolverine.

Sometimes drunken oil rig workers would stagger in and demand a direct flight to somewhere the airline did not go. If they really insisted, we would sell them tickets to Vancouver, knowing that they probably would not turn up for the flight. One man who insisted on a direct flight to Chicago pulled a huge wad of money out of his pocket, slammed it on the counter, then proceeded to produce equally large rolls of currency from every other pocket. It took two of us to shove his money back into his pockets and steer him to a waiting taxi. We never saw him again.

The men who worked on the drilling rigs were making very good money, but there was almost nowhere to spend it except in Fort St. John, which at that time boasted just two hotels and no licensed restaurant. So they gambled. One evening, some of us from the airport drove out to see the drilling and dropped by the mess hall. Almost all the tables in the room were crowded with men smoking huge cigars and playing poker. Every table seemed to be covered with stacks of money, and the smallest bill on the tables was $20. I had never seen that much money in one place before in all my life.

Fort St. John is in the Peace River region of northern Canada.

Today, it is probably a respectable little town, but in the middle of the 20th century, it was just a few stores, two hotels, and a Chinese restaurant that had sardine cans on the tables for ashtrays. Small, plain, unpainted houses were scattered across the bare countryside and the town also had wooden sidewalks and two or three hitching rails, all of which gave the place a western frontier atmosphere. Now and then an Indian family would come into town with all the children riding bareback on one horse.

The Peace River region is the northernmost limit of the prairies. It is a wild and beautiful land with rolling fertile plains, swift rivers, and forested mountains toward the west. It is blessed with long, warm, summer days when the sun never seems to set, although true summer, alas, lasts only ninety days. The town lies on the Alaska Highway, also called the Alcan Highway, which was constructed during the Second World War and is the only land route from the contiguous forty-eight states through Canada to Alaska. It is a very busy road, especially during the summer. It's about 1,500 miles long, and a thousand miles of it was, at that time, unpaved gravel, making it not only a rough ride but a very dusty ride. Much of the traffic consisted of huge trucks that raised blinding clouds of dust and threw large stones into the air, making it also an extremely dangerous road. Two or three times, we had to load accident victims onto the plane, sometimes unbolting seats to make room for stretchers. Today, the road has been properly surfaced.

Toward the end of summer, when I was starting to think about returning to the university, we received a teletype message informing us that the head of the airline was flying up to the Yukon. It was not exactly an official inspection, but we were advised to be on our toes. Also, no flight delays would be tolerated. Even though the VIP was not going to stay overnight, we were determined to look good, so we scrubbed and polished the terminal from top to bottom, sent our overalls to be washed until they were spotlessly white, and even raked the gravel parking lot. But for some reason the VIP's flight was delayed and did not arrive until after dark. Since there was almost no passenger transfer and little freight that late, everything went smoothly. There was even a chance that the flight would leave a fraction of a minute early. I closed and secured the luggage compartment, ducked under the belly of the plane, grabbed the passenger loading steps and, when I heard the cabin door slam shut above me, I put my shoulder to the metal and pushed it away from the plane.

Unfortunately, I was pushing directly into the glare of the floodlights. The correct place to leave the ramp was against the terminal building, slightly ahead of where the plane was parked, which meant that I would have to walk under the wing tip. I had done this many times before, but in the excitement and the glare of the lights, I miscalculated. There was a loud bang from over my head. The ramp stopped dead. I looked up. The top hand rail was jammed firmly into the space between the wing and the left wing flap. For what seemed like a very long time, I stood there in the floodlights as the faces peering at me from the plane and the small crowd around the terminal doors gaped in silent horror.

And then, suddenly, all hell broke loose. The passenger door flew open and the entire aircrew stood glaring down. The terminal door swung wide, and a large crowd poured out. Somebody shoved me out of the way, and I dashed into the washroom, where I shed my white overalls, shoved them into the trash can, put on my civilian clothes, and quietly joined the crowd of spectators. The second ramp had been brought up by then, and the pilot and copilot were surveying the damage. Standing with them was a short man in a business suit who was probably the VIP. They carefully pulled the offending ramp away and stared at the damage. The wing seemed to be fine, but the end of the flap was slightly warped and a few rivets had popped. Somebody worked the flap, and there was a distinct noise. The copilot was cheerfully optimistic and suggested that if the passengers were unloaded, they could give it a little test flight, but the captain, an older and more serious man, ignored the suggestion. That plane was going nowhere.

I spent the whole night hiding in an empty hangar or peering through the window, afraid that at any moment somebody would recognize me and haul me off for an instant lynching. The aircrew clustered around the teletype machine, typing out a long and detailed report and obviously trying to estimate the damage. The manager, now white with anxiety, hustled about, pouring coffee for the VIP and making dozens of phone calls. The VIP, to everybody's surprise, was taking it all very calmly. No tantrums or angry accusations. No demands for somebody's head. He didn't even raise his voice. He sat quietly in the manager's chair, sipping coffee and letting the manager and crew get on with their jobs and solve the problem.

The problem was that we had a plane full of passengers and there was not a hotel room available for a hundred miles in any direction, much less any buses to transport them. Much to the disgust of the stewardesses, the passengers had to spend the night on the plane. The manager's wife arrived and took the VIP off to sleep in the manager's house, but the aircrew spent the night slouched in uncomfortable waiting room chairs, where, since they were still on duty, they could only drink coffee. While I cowered outside, everybody else tried to look busy. It was a very long night

At dawn, two planes arrived. One took away the unfortunate passengers and the still amiable VIP, while the other brought a new flap and a crew of mechanics. They worked quickly, and by noon both planes roared off. Everybody was very quiet that day. I sat

hunched over the keyboard, reading the string of messages, reply-
ing to some and ignoring the sarcastic comments from operators
further up the line. Nobody spoke to me.

That night I packed my bag, and next day I was back at the
machine, writing a report and waiting for the axe to fall. The Vancouver plane had just arrived when the machine coldly informed
me that my services were no longer required. I made out a one-way
ticket for myself, shook hands with the manager, and boarded the
plane, thankful that at least I would not have to hitchhike back to
Vancouver.

The plane stopped at Prince George, over 300 miles from
Vancouver, where several passengers boarded. There was only one
seat left when the airport manager called me in to the terminal,
where there was a pretty little stewardess also trying to get a seat.
He solved the problem quite efficiently. "Why are you going to
Vancouver?" he asked the girl. "I'm going to get married." she said
with a happy giggle. He turned to me. "Why are you going?" With
a sinking feeling I answered, "I've been fired." I hitchhiked back to
Vancouver.

A few weeks later, I was at a party where most of the women
were airline stewardesses. With little skill and a lot of booze, I managed to corner a particularly pretty one and was doing quite nicely
when a friend of hers interrupted and started complaining about
the way her holiday had been ruined. It seems that her boyfriend
was copilot on the Whitehorse run and, "Some damn fool up in
Fort St. John went and smashed the plane! We had to wait three
days for another seat to Hawaii." She clenched her fists. "I'd just love
to get my hands on that idiot!" She was still describing in detail just
what she would do to her victim as I quietly slunk away.

Chapter 21
Danger in the Forest

I was often turned down for a job that I had applied for, usually with no explanation. One time, however, the boss took the trouble to show me why. This happened when I was still in the Canadian Rockies and desperately looking for a summer job in the logging industry, where good money could be made. The company needed a "whistle punk," and I had a good pair of caulked logging boots and rain gear so I applied for the job. The boss looked me up and down and said, "No way."

The whistle punk, he explained, has the lowest job in the forest. It is he who drags the heavy logging chains around and fastens them to the logs so the tractor can haul them out onto the road or, in mountain country, the donkey man can lift them high in the air and swing them away to a truck loading dock. It's noisy, and the men often cannot see each other, so all signals are made with whistles, which means the whistle punk had better get the signals right and securely fasten the chains because a giant log running wild is a very dangerous thing. Since everybody is paid on the number of logs cut, the whistle punk also has to move fast. If you include the rain and/or the heat, plus the mosquitoes and the black flies, the whistle punk's job is a very nasty one. But it pays well.

When I insisted that, despite having no experience whatsoever,

I could handle the job; the boss stood up from his desk and said, "I have to go out that way for a minute. Come along, and I'll show you why I won't give you the job."

We drove a few miles in his pickup, then he stopped and led me into the forest. "This is all virgin timber," he said, "and we're cutting just selected trees. No clear cutting here!" We scrambled deeper into the forest, clambering over a sea of ancient, fallen tree trunks and a tangle of vegetation.

"There hasn't been a big fire through here for fifty years," the boss said as we scrambled up a particularly steep hill. "That log you're standing on is just the top of a pile of deadwood that goes down more than ten feet. And it's all locked together. You pull one, and all the others will move." He swung his arm around, "All this could shift, and I don't care how good your caulks are, you'd have to move like a monkey to get out of the way."

I looked at the great tangle of logs and branches and imagined trying to haul a bunch of heavy chains through it for ten hours a day, slipping on the damp logs and swatting black flies.

He looked at me, tall and skinny and wearing glasses. "We'd be carting you off with a broken leg on the very first day. And our insurance rates would go sky high."

We started back to his pickup where he flagged down a passing truck for me and said, "Stick to the sawmills. The pay's not bad, and it's a damn sight safer."

Even seemingly safe jobs in the forest can have their dangers. One summer I picked up a job clearing brush and small trees out of the power company's right-of-way through the forest. I had seen these arrow-straight lines from the air and often wondered who had the job of keeping them clear. It was healthy, open air work, but the pay was miserable. I had only taken the work till I found something better.

There were six of us in the gang and all we had to do was cut anything higher than a couple of feet and leave it on the ground. For the first few days, the work went smoothly. The weather was perfect, with a breeze that kept away the mosquitoes and black flies, the air was sweet, and the forest silence was broken only by the sporadic conversation of the other men along with the sounds of our axes.

After a few days, our team reached a very damp spot on a hillside. Water was seeping down the slope, which had not been properly cleared for years and was heavily overgrown with very tall saplings, mostly poplars. It was axe work, and I was hacking away enthusiastically when one of the guys came up and said, "Watch out you don't fall one across the power line." He pointed up. Just where I was working, the power lines came quite close to the ground, and some of the trees were dangerously close to the wires. I played it safe and cut down only those that were lower than the wires, leaving the bigger ones for somebody else to cut.

During our lunch break, the leader said to me, "You know that you were hired to take the place of a man who was killed?" I must have looked surprised because everybody laughed. "Yeah," one of them said. "Electrocuted himself when he dropped a tree against a wire and tried to push it off with his hands." There was general laughter, and he added, "These poplars are wet with sap," after which somebody else said cheerfully, "He jumped like a frog and then dropped down dead." He paused. "Well, he won't do anything that stupid again, will he?"

When we went back to work, the leader said, "Here, I'll show you," and with a few swift cuts, he dropped a tall, slim poplar sideways between the lines. "Now this is the way *not* to do it," he said as he started on one a little higher up the slope. It fell toward the power lines.

I stood well back and watched as the tip of the tree brushed against one of the lines. There was a short crackling sound and blue lines danced around the tip of the tree, then it slipped free and crashed to the ground. We scrambled down the slope to the butt end of the tree, and he pointed to a faint black streak that had not been there before.

"Feel it," he said, and I gingerly put out my hand. It was quite warm. "You could end up fried like a piece of bacon if you're careless," he said. Then he went back to the area he was clearing.

Actually, the biggest danger I faced on that job was the possibility that the axe might slip and slice open my leg or the heavy machete would take off a toe or two. I worked carefully and was very glad that I had invested in sturdy boots.

A couple of days later, I heard about a possible job in a town further north and handed in my axe and machete.

Chapter 22
Forest Firefighter

One summer when I was looking for work in a small town quite far north, I met a couple of other students also looking for work so we stepped into a beer parlor to compare notes in comfort. We had just finished a round when a Mountie came through the front door and stationed himself just inside, with his legs apart and his arms folded. The big room was filled with men, who all immediately rose and headed for the back door, only to find that door blocked by a forest ranger holding a clipboard.

We had been "volunteered" to fight a forest fire. The ranger quickly weeded out the old and infirm and the gainfully employed among us, and within minutes we were seated in a big yellow school bus racing down a secondary road where, about half an hour later, we were transferred to the back of a less comfortable pickup truck that bounced down a rough trail through the forest.

After what seemed a very long time, we jolted to a halt in the fire camp. The trees and brush had been bulldozed back to form a wide clearing, and I saw a long row of small, four-man tents and a large open tent with crude wooden tables and benches in it. Nearby were a couple of stoves and a canvas shack partly covering boxes of food and cooking utensils. The place was empty except for a cook and another ranger, who quickly assigned us tents, gave us blankets, and showed us where the coffee pot was.

The cook, a skinny, talkative little guy, told us the fire had been burning for weeks and there was another fire camp a few miles away. "The timber here isn't worth much," he added, "and it's too far from the road to log. But the fire might spread to more valuable timber. You guys are here to keep it under control."

When one of us asked when they estimated that the fire would be put out, the cook laughed. "Put this one out? Nah! It's a ghost fire. It's just too far away from everything to worry about. Just have to keep an eye on it till it rains."

At sunset trucks loaded with men bounced into the clearing, then two or three bulldozers rumbled out of the forest and parked at the edge of the camp. For a ghost fire that nobody was worried about, this seemed to be a lot of men and equipment. The food was plain but plentiful and well cooked, and everybody started eating before they even bothered to wash at the tin buckets near the portable water tank. There was just one lamp, and it hung in the kitchen part of the big tent, so after we had eaten we went straight to bed. The camp bed was reasonably comfortable, at least after I had bundled my clothes into a crude pillow. It was better than sleeping on the ground.

Everybody was up at dawn. The communal toilet was simply a peeled sapling that had been fastened between two trees over a trench. Toilet paper was stuck on stakes, and there was a large tub of a white powder that I think was lime. When we finished our business, we sprinkled a handful of it to keep down the flies. Washing was done at the tin pails in cold water, but a large green towel had been included with the blankets and there were also plenty of bars of soap. Breakfast was as much fried eggs, sausage, and hash-browns as we could eat. Each man grabbed a bag of sandwiches as he headed for the trucks. We newcomers were assigned to various trucks, and very soon we were bouncing off into the woods. Up to that point, I had not seen the fire, nor had I seen any smoke or smelled any burning.

After a mile or two we came around a bend. There in front of us was a great wall of dirty white smoke. The breeze was blowing it away from us, and I could see that it spread a mile or two in both directions. But I could not see any flames, just smoldering brush and trees.

The straw boss, or acting foreman of our gang, handed out long-handled shovels to most of us, but also gave backpack water pumps to the four biggest men. "Your job is to put out all these little fires still burning," he said as he pointed at smoldering patches. "If the wind changes, we don't want them to start up again. Do a good job. Bury them with dirt. Then we'll have a good firebreak." And he hurried off to another truck.

It was dirty work. I was lucky that I had been wearing good boots and tough blue jeans when we were picked up because in places the ash was ankle deep and every movement brought up a cloud of hot smoke and stinging little sparks. Finding the hot spots was easy, but finding enough dirt to throw on them was not so easy because the ground had been burned down to the rock in many places.

We set to work and slowly worked our way along, killing all the little fires, digging out hot spots, and squirting water on burning twigs. It was a fine day and we had all eaten a good breakfast, so we worked enthusiastically and cheerfully and the time passed quickly. When somebody eventually called a lunch break, I was surprised at just how much ground we had neutralized. Scrambling up and down ridges and gullies and swinging the shovels was hot work and used a lot of energy, so we made short work of the sandwiches and almost drained the tank of fresh water on the truck.

After an hour the truck drove off to find more water and we went back to work. By late afternoon we were ready for a square meal. We piled back into the truck, which bounced us back to the fire camp, where we stuffed ourselves, splashed some water on our faces, and wriggled into our blankets.

The work was the same for three or four days, and we fell into a routine. But inevitably the wind changed, and our easy routine was disrupted. By this time, we had reached a large hollow where the trees were much bigger and closer together. The fire was roaring through the forest, and the bulldozers were busy trying to make a firebreak, but burning sparks kept blowing over the machines. We were hurried in to stamp out all the little fires.

Right in the middle of the hollow was a marshy spot. Sure enough, one of the huge machines got mired in the black ooze, and we were then kept busy dragging steel cables through the brush and wrapping them around suitable trees so the driver could winch his machine free. Unfortunately, because of the soft ground and the weight of the bulldozer, the trees were soon uprooted and we had to drag the cables to more trees. Meanwhile, the fire was creeping closer. It looked as if we were about to lose a bulldozer when another, bigger, machine arrived and was hitched to the cables. There followed a great deal of noise from the huge diesel engines as both monsters skidded about in the mud, trying to get a firm grip as the fire came so close we had to hold up our shovels to protect our faces from the heat. For a while, it looked like we were going to lose both machines, but after a struggle and a lot more noise, they both emerged from the mud and the smoke and, as soon as we had removed the tow, turned immediately toward the flames, pushing burning trees over and into the fire, making a slim but effective fire break.

It was not only blowing sparks that spread the flames. Sometimes it was the heat itself. One time, three or four of us had stopped for a breather in an open space some distance from the fire. About fifty meters in front of us stood a handsome fir with heavy branches. It stood alone, some distance from the flames. As we watched, the side of the tree facing the flames began to smolder then, with an incredible *whoosh!* the entire tree exploded in a great cloud of sparks and flames that shot into the sky and left behind an utterly naked trunk. In a few seconds the whole tree had been stripped bare. Now it stood there, black and smoking and very dead.

"That's what they call a candle tree," somebody remarked.

We did not go back to camp that night, but kept working until it was too dark to see well. When the sun went down, the breeze stopped and the fire died away to a surly red glow. After a long day in the hot sun and too close to the blistering fire, we found the ground to be delightfully cool, so we roughed out a camp in a hollow left over by a fallen tree. But the temperature continued to fall and the ground was damp, and after about an hour, we were cold and shivering. That's when somebody went over and brought back some red embers on a shovel. We all scratched around and found bits of wood, and soon we had a nice cozy fire. "Silly, isn't it?" somebody said. "We spend all day putting out the fire, then have to start one to keep warm."

It was a miserable night. At dawn, a truck arrived with food and hot coffee and we were soon back at work. The wind changed again, and so we widened the fire break. Next we were sent to another hot spot, then on to another. It was a long day.

We also saw our first sign of animal life. The fire and the noise of the machinery had long since driven off most of the game in the area, all but one stubborn creature. I was about to push through some bushes when I heard a hiss. My first thought was to look down for a snake, but the sound came again, and it was coming from a tree branch directly in front of me, not two meters away. I looked more carefully. What I saw was a mink. The little creature's coat was tangled and matted, and she had obviously come too close to the fire. Poor thing, she didn't look a bit like the glossy pelts one sees in the expensive stores. I guessed that it was a female and that she was protecting her babies, because she sat up on the branch and challenged me to come any closer. When other members of the crew arrived, she stood her ground and bared wickedly sharp teeth at all of us, still glaring menacingly and obviously quite prepared to fight. The oldest member of the crew said, "I'd rather tackle a bear than a mink. They're vicious little bastards. Leave her alone." And so we did.

A couple days later, the straw boss drove some of us out to a small lake, hardly more than a pond, where we could get a decent wash, although the water was too cold to actually swim. Since we had only the clothes we'd been wearing when we arrived, we had begun to stink. While we were at the lake, we noticed some small trout that seemed to have no fear of people. In fact, they swam right to the surface and looked us over.

"I doubt that anybody has ever fished this lake," the straw boss said. "They'd probably bite on anything." We all immediately had the same idea and began to search for loose lengths of thread and tiny bits of metal to make hooks. Somebody rigged up a crude line. We twisted a bit of aluminum foil on the hook, then watched as the angler lowered it into the clear green water. For about five minutes the fish pushed and shoved each other for the dubious honor of taking the wonderfully gleaming bait and being instantly jerked out of the water. But even fish have brains, and they soon vanished.

We took half a dozen little trout back to camp and fried them immediately, and they were delicious.

A few days later, the truck I was riding did not go to the fire, but instead went to the other fire camp. When we arrived, we saw a sorry sight. The entire camp had been burned to the ground. Just a few ridge poles from the cook tent remained. All the rest was just ashes. The camp had been set up on top of a hill, and it was clear what had happened. A tongue of the fire had reached the foot of the hill, and the updraft had sent it roaring up the slope and directly into the camp. Seeing what was coming, the men had all piled into the trucks and raced to safety. Seconds later, the inferno crested the hill and devoured the camp. There was not much for us to salvage, and as the fire had been put out, we returned to our camp.

Back at the camp, when I jumped down from the truck, I twisted my ankle on a rock. The ankle swelled up so quickly I could hardly get my boot off. When I'd finally pulled it off, I soaked my entire foot and ankle in cold water for an hour, but that didn't do much good. After carefully inspecting my ankle, the ranger told me to keep off my feet for a day or two and stay in camp. My first thought was that I was going to be terribly bored for the next few days.

The next morning, after the trucks and bulldozers had left, I sat in the shade of the cook tent, dozing in the sudden deep silence. In the tents closest to me about a dozen men were still sleeping. These were the experienced fire fighters who served on the night crew and had come in at dawn.

Suddenly, the cook jabbed my arm and whispered, "Will you look at that!" He pointed at one of the tents. I sat up and stared in astonishment. A large black bear had come in out of the bush and was sniffing around the tents. As we watched, it walked into one of the tents where some men were sleeping. There were no guns in the camp, so the best we could do was to grab some pots and pans to bang together in hopes of scaring the animal away. We sat quietly, waiting to see what would happen. The bear merely sauntered out of the tent and entered the next one. Again we waited for a horrible uproar, but again nothing happened. The bear strolled out and entered the next tent. While we watched, fascinated, the bear systematically inspected every single tent in the row. Obviously disappointed, it turned toward the cook tent. Fortunately, the bear saw us standing there, clasping our pots and pans. It had second thoughts and wheeled around and quickly vanished into the brush.

For the rest of the day, the cook and I sat there and discussed what we would have done if we had woken up to find a bear sniffing around inside the tent. We also debated whether or not to tell the men when they woke up. In the end, we decided not to tell them. "They have a rough job," the cook said. "Why add to their worries?" I agreed with him. It remained our little secret.

The cook had a little secret of his own. Between the two stoves he kept a large enamel pot covered by a white cloth. He called it his "teapot," but he wasn't drinking tea. He had been making a fine brew of raisins and sugar and whatever else moonshiners use. I had wondered why, when he was not working, he was always sipping tea from his dented enamel mug. That night, he produced supper for the crew when they returned, then, when I had gone to bed, he started some serious tea drinking.

Next morning I was awakened by a lot of shouting. I limped out of my tent to find a ranger and some other men hurriedly trying to fix breakfast for the entire crew while a Mountie and six men were trying to get the cook into a pickup truck. The skinny little man had turned into an arm-waving, bundle of energy that was leaping on and off the truck and alternately trying to either hug his captors or punch them, all the time shouting nonsense at the top of his voice.

It took a while, but eventually the vehicle drove off with our cook. We lined up for a makeshift breakfast. After the other men had left to fight the fire, I helped to clear away and wash everything up.

The ranger turned to me. "Where the hell did he get the booze?" he yelled.

I pointed to the pot of "tea." "I think he was making his own."

The ranger dipped a mug into the brew and sniffed it, then sipped it and spat it out. "Christ! He was drinking that?" Picking up the pot by its two handles, he carried it over to some bushes and poured it all out. Then he turned and glared at me. It was obvious that he thought me partly to blame for the cooking fiasco.

"Well," he said, "you're the cook until we can find a new one." Then he stomped off to his truck.

I stood there horrified. I could just barely walk, and I had to make a hearty supper for a fire crew when I didn't even know how many hungry men would be lining up at sunset. I couldn't even boil water without burning it. For half an hour, I sat there in a daze, hoping that they could get the drunken cook to town, find another cook, and get back before sunset. But that didn't seem possible. So I next set about inspecting the cooking supplies. All I could make out was that there was a huge supply of sliced bread and plenty of stuff to make sandwiches. Everything else was things that I had not the slightest idea how to cook. I set to work making sandwiches. Lots and lots of sandwiches.

Toward noon, the truck drivers began to arrive to pick up lunch for the men. The cook had been too drunk to make any lunches, but, fortunately, I had a nice stack of sandwiches waiting, and we tossed in packets of raisins as well. A couple of the drivers returned later to give me a hand, and together we eventually had a nice supply of various types of sandwiches and two large coffee urns full and waiting. About an hour before sunset, the Mounties truck roared into the camp and, with a sigh of relief, I watched as a tall Chinese cook, complete with white apron, stepped out. He surveyed our work and said with a smile, "Hey, not bad for a bunch of amateurs. Any of you guys want a job some time, just look me up." Then he set to work and had a huge pot of hot soup ready to serve along with the sandwiches just as the fire crew started to arrive and the bulldozers roared into the clearing.

Two days later it rained. The weather changed almost over-night and the rain came down in sheets that soaked everything and turned the crude trails into rivers of mud.

Getting out of the camp turned into a major operation. As each truckload of men and equipment drove off down the trail, the mud got more liquid and the ruts got deeper and finally the road got impassable. I was in the last group of men to leave, about ten of us on the clean-up crew. Pretty soon, somebody said, "I have a horrible feeling that we're going to have to walk out."

As we stood there feeling miserable, one of the bulldozers re-turned with a passenger clutching a chainsaw and another clutching some wire cable. They set to at once and made a simple but strong sled out of logs the chainsaw man cut to length. We pushed the logs into position so the man with the cable could tie them together. This took less than an hour. Though the finished sled was rough and there was nothing to sit on, it was solid and there was enough room for all of us if we stood in a tight group holding each other up. The chainsaw man and his pal climbed up onto the bulldozer and leaned against the warm engine.

It was a miserable trip. Huddled under sheets of dripping wet plastic, we clung together in a group, struggling to keep upright as the heavy sled plowed slowly through the mud behind the roaring bulldozer. At times the sled became a raft and floated smoothly with little waves of yellow mud lapping over the sides and over our boots, but then we would slide over a rock or other obstacle and the mud would squirt up between the logs as the raft pitched crazily and we slithered around trying not to fall off. Within ten minutes I was not only wet, cold and spattered with mud from head to toe, but my leg muscles ached from constantly trying to keep my balance. Nobody was in any mood to make jokes, so it was a long miserable couple of hours before we reached the road, where we staggered off our craft and onto the waiting yellow buses.

When we arrived back in town, the rain had stopped and the ranger who had recruited us was waiting with his clipboard and a wad of pay checks. He smiled and said, "Thank you, boys," and other nice things as he checked our names off. We all tried our best to be polite.

The money was not very much, but it was better than nothing, and I kept telling myself what a very interesting experience it had been as I hurried as fast as I could to the hotel with its huge, old fashioned bathtubs and lots and lots of very hot water.

To my surprise, I found myself fire fighting again the next summer, but that time I was asked if I wanted to go. I had wandered into a small town in cattle country near the U.S border. The fire was up in the hills where there were some huge ranches. Since there was no work in the little town and, as usual, I was short on cash, I signed up.

The fire camp, which was high in the hills at the edge of a wide meadow, was big and well organized, unlike the hastily thrown-up camp in which I'd worked the year before. Instead of useless bush, this was valuable ranch property, and the authorities were taking the fire seriously with six bulldozers, a couple of water-tank trucks, carefully planned and constructed trails, and a full crew of firefighters.

I arrived at sunset along with a few other men. We had a light supper in the cook tent (which was more efficient than the tent I'd seen the year before) and then went to sleep on camp beds with warm woolen blankets. Next morning, we ate an excellent breakfast with pancakes and scrambled eggs.

Then we boarded a truck. It was a beautiful land of rolling hills under a wide blue sky. Much of the forest was Ponderosa pines, some of them quite ancient. As we climbed higher, the trees were clustered in groves, which thinned out as the bush gave way to huge meadows where the grass was already yellowing in the summer sun. Here and there a few healthy-looking cattle lounged in the shade, but most of the herds had already been moved to safety. We saw no wildlife except for the occasional rabbit and the high-gliding hawks.

We unskilled laborers were given shovels and backpack water pumps and set to work putting out anything that smoldered. This was what I'd done before. The difference was that last year's fire had burned the bush and trees and rapidly moved on, whereas this year's fire was a slower fire and had burned itself deep into the soil, much of which consisted of thousands of years of partly decomposed vegetation. In places it had been burned away down to the underlying rock, leaving great ugly scars on the landscape.

Finding and eradicating all the little fires was not easy. A little wisp of smoke might indicate nothing more than a twig, but it might also indicate a large underground fire that needed plenty of water to put out. Many times I poked my shovel at a suspicious puff of smoke and saw the blade of the shovel vanish into a miniature inferno. The men with the water learned to stand well back as they pumped because they were almost always greeted by a tall geyser of dirty white steam. It was hot work, and very dusty, but the weather was perfect, the scenery was beautiful, and it was good to be out in the country, high in the hills.

We made good progress day by day, and as the straw boss moved us over the burned-out land, we never actually saw the main fire. One day I asked where it was, and he said, "The main fire's out. We're just building more fire breaks and making sure it won't start up again." I learned that we were on one of the huge ranches and the owners had persuaded the authorities to go to extra lengths to protect their valuable property. Those wealthy ranchers explained the comparative luxury we enjoyed.

Although not exactly the Ritz, the fire camp was well stocked and even had a portable shower, chemical toilets and plenty of clean towels. The kitchen had two cooks and the food, which was served on heavy china plates with real knives and forks, was excellent and varied. Some evenings we had thick juicy steaks, and other evenings we had all the broiled chicken that we could eat. Milk and bread were brought in daily, and the lunches were always tasty. Nobody complained about the food.

Mornings were cool and bright, and I was always fascinated by the sight of the bulldozers heading off to work. They climbed the winding trail in line, snorting and roaring like so many bright yellow dinosaurs, alive and ready for battle with the elements, their breath floating in white clouds in the still air. We followed behind them in the trucks.

The rangers were still trying to work out the cause of the fire. By this time, they were fairly certain it had been set, so we were asked to keep a lookout as we worked for anything suspicious.

One night the fire broke out again in an area far from the original blaze. It was soon put down, but the next day we were kept in camp and a Mountie interrogated us all and checked the soles of our boots against a photograph. He was efficient but quite friendly. "It could just be some pyromaniac getting his thrills," he explained, "or it could be somebody paid to cause trouble for some reason. We may never know." He shook his head and added, "Then, again, some of these ranchers still believe in burning off the grass to bring on new growth. Just keep your eyes open."

My work group was a cheerful bunch of young men, some of them college students like me, who never lost an opportunity to amuse themselves. One day somebody hauled the chain saw off the truck and demonstrated his skill by trimming four or five blackened tree stumps to the same height. They stood in a rough circle, so somebody else tried his hand at cutting them into the shape of armchairs. Everybody tried their hands at it, and between us we eventually had a tidy circle of uncomfortable, high-backed chairs. In the middle, we placed a circle of the biggest rocks we could carry. "That should give the archeologists something to get excited about," the ringleader said. "Yeah," somebody else said. "One day this will be a Sacred Indian Site. Probably a historic monument with a sign post and everything."

Our lunches arrived in cardboard boxes, which the cooks asked us to return in good condition and which we always did. During lunch break, we almost always saw at least one blue jay hopping about and looking for scraps. They were beautiful birds, and quite fearless, coming almost to our feet to snatch a crumb or two. One day we rigged a crude trap with a box on a stick and a string and put plenty of bait under the box. A particularly large blue jay immediately dashed under the box and was trapped. We carefully secured the lid and placed the box on the truck with the other empties. Late that evening, we heard a yell from the kitchen, a loud flapping noise, and a roar of laughter from one of the tents.

Another time we were crossing a wide meadow when we spotted an enormous bull standing in the shade and glaring at us. When our driver drove the little truck closer to the beast, it began to scoop dirt with its front hoof and toss its head. Just then somebody at the back of the vehicle pushed somebody else off the truck. As the bull started toward the poor man, we all began screaming with laughter as the unfortunate victim ran madly after the truck, waving his arms and yelling to the driver. Fortunately, the bull changed his mind and went back into the shade.

These were just childish pranks, rather juvenile, in fact, but one day we met some real men. Three cowboys on horseback came by. They weren't just farmhands wearing big hats. They were real, working cowboys. They rode down the hill in single file, their horses skirting the edge of the burned area and walking slowly with their heads down. The riders were sitting relaxed, their hands resting on their pommels and their eyes on the fire damage. They didn't speak to each other and completely ignored us as they passed. Soon they disappeared silently down the hill.

What I noticed first was their boots. They were expensive boots with beautifully carved leatherwork, but they were also well worn and well oiled and looked very comfortable. The cowboys wore blunt spurs. I also noticed their hats. They weren't the white Stetsons that every Texan seems obliged to wear, nor the ridiculous things that urban wannabes wear. They were dark, high crowned hats, cool and sensible, with brims curled just enough to deflect the rain. They, too, looked well worn.

Next day another group of cowboys came by. Though they stopped to chat a little, they didn't say much. They seemed rather shy, in fact, and didn't get off their horses. They all wore checked shirts and blue jeans and had the regulation bandanas around their necks with the knot at the back. Almost all of them wore leather gloves, too, although some had the fingertips cut off. Most of them wore vests, and each one had a heavy belt with a fancy buckle that looked suspiciously like real silver. But none of them carried a pistol or had a rifle. Each saddle had a lariat of braided leather looped around the horn, but there were no silver decorations of any kind. These were well made, expensive working saddles with rain gear rolled tightly around a blanket lashed behind the rider.

While I was looking, one of the cowboys pulled a small bag of tobacco out of a vest pocket, found a cigarette paper, and, using just one hand and his teeth, rolled a cigarette. I had never seen this done before. Then he lit it with a heavy steel, flip-top lighter. When he had finished smoking, he carefully shredded the remains of the cigarette.

I had been staring at them for quite a while before it dawned on me that almost all the cowboys were Indians. The man who seemed to be foreman was obviously Anglo-Saxon, but the others—short, dark haired and sunburned—were clearly Indians. The one exception was a tall, blue-eyed, yellow-haired youngster who was badly sunburned. When he spoke, I immediately recognized his German accent. During my travels in Germany, I had always been surprised at just how much the Germans were fascinated by the American West and the cowboy mythology. Here in Canada, a young German was living his dream and obviously enjoying it.

A few days later, the crew was told that we would no longer be needed. The ranger assured us that we had done a good job and thanked us as he handed out checks and we climbed onto a school bus for the ride back to town. The pay wasn't much, but it really didn't matter; I had enough to get to another town and find a well-paid job. It had been an interesting interlude, and perhaps I had learned something (though I'm not sure what).

Chapter 23
Surveyor

There was a very good employment agency on the university campus, and one day the clerk told me that a company needed a survey crew to work "up the coast." Like most people, I had seen surveyors working with their striped poles and little gadgets on tripods, and as this sounded like interesting work, I phoned and made an appointment. I also went into the library and looked up surveying and learned that the math involved seemed to be mostly triangulation. It seemed to be a bit beyond my skills, so I went over to the science building and tracked down a professor and asked him a few questions.

He smiled and said, "So, you have found a summer job surveying and you haven't the faintest idea what it's all about, eh?"

I replied that he was right, and he took me into a storeroom and patiently explained what all the various bits of equipment were for. The surveyor's compass and the transit looked like something I could handle, so with a friendly "Best of luck!" from the professor, I headed off down town where, with my little bit of knowledge, I convinced the interviewer that I knew something about surveying and got the job.

I was to start the next day. "Be here at seven with all your gear," said my interviewer. "You'll go up the coast with another guy, then fly in. There's a camp all set up."

And with those very brief instructions and no other information whatsoever, he ushered me out of his office. It was obvious that we would be in tents somewhere along the mountainous coast north of Vancouver, so I dashed around to various friends and scrounged a sleeping bag and some rain gear, which I shoved into my duffel bag along with my own pair of very good boots.

Next morning, I joined another student and we climbed into a heavily-loaded station wagon driven by a stranger who spoke very little. We took the ferry across to Vancouver Island, then drove north to the little town of Campbell River, where we stopped at a shed near a patch of shallow water. "You'll fly in from here," our driver said as he piled all of the contents of the station wagon at the edge of the water. That done, he drove off.

There were three or four small planes sitting on large pontoons floating in the little patch of water. The pilot of one of them started his engine and coasted over to us. It looked very small and the pilot looked very young, but I said nothing and we began to load the plane. I was surprised to see how much stuff we managed to squeeze into that little plane and still leave room for three passengers. Some extra long bits of cargo we lashed to the pontoon struts, and a bulky package we wrapped in plastic and fastened to the struts of the other pontoon. Then we sat down to wait for the third passenger.

It was a woman. Outside Vancouver and Victoria, the standard dress for a female of any age, summer or winter, was at that time a pair of blue jeans, a checked shirt, and a parka. This woman was a lady who was dressed in a well-cut suit in bright pink with a rather tight skirt, nylons, and high heels. She was young and very attractive, and we hurried to help her board the plane. This wasn't easy, however, because she had to climb down a muddy slope and step across to the wet and slippery pontoon and clamber up into the cabin, all in her tight skirt and high heels. These maneuvers took some time, and a couple of times I thought she was heading for a dip in the muddy inlet. The pilot frowned anxiously at her, but she remained happy and excited, and when we were all safely seated, she explained that she was from Seattle and had met a handsome logger. There had been a whirlwind courtship and marriage, and now she was heading into the wilderness…to a logging camp, in fact, where she would set up house with her handsome husband. It was all very romantic, but I hoped she had not been reading too many novels or watching too much TV.

I expected the pilot to taxi the plane out into more open water, but he simply edged his way past a few small boats, aimed the plane toward the open water, and roared across the tiny patch of wetness. We were airborne in seconds. The flight, which was very smooth, lasted about half an hour and we flew quite low. When we reached the mainland, the mountains loomed high and massive, and I felt a strange sensation as we flew between the peaks rather than over them. At times, we came, it seemed to me, rather close to rocky walls and skimmed low over hilly crests, but the pilot seemed relaxed and the lady sat with her nose pressed to the window, exclaiming happily at everything she saw, especially the great patches of snow near the 10,000-foot peaks and the glint of a glacier in the far distance.

Knight Inlet, our destination, is a great fiord that cuts deeply into the coastal mountain range. The logging camp was at the head of the fiord at the mouth of the Klinaklini River. From the air, we could see that the camp was a very big operation with lots of buildings and at least six giant log rafts waiting in the water. The mountains were bare and scarred with logging roads, and as we dropped lower, the pilot said, "Clear cutting! The bastards cut everything down to the ground, and then there's one good rain and the soil gets washed away down to the bare rock. They keep promising to replant it, but I've never seen any replanting. Soon there won't be any soil to plant in."

The landing was smooth. We all helped get the lady out of the plane and onto the wooden float where her husband, whose name we learned was Andrew, was waiting for her. I could see why she had fallen for him. He was a big man, quite handsome, with a generous smile and a deep voice. He had a message for us. We were to stay overnight in the company bunkhouse while the plane went on up to the camp with supplies. Meanwhile, his wife insisted that we were to come up to their house and have a real home-cooked supper.

After we dumped our bags in the bunkhouse and washed up, we made our way along the narrow wooden paths raised about three feet above the mud and weeds until we found their house, also raised on stilts.

"It can get pretty wet here at times," Andrew said as he greeted us at the door. "In fact," he said with a laugh, "I believe we have the highest rainfall in Canada."

That made me have second thoughts about living in a tent for the next month or two. I didn't find the prospect very funny.

We were led into a comfortable little company house, and while the wife, who had changed into more practical clothing, prepared an excellent supper, she told us that she had been born in Seattle and her only experience of anything out of the urban area was a couple of camping trips in the summer and some boating in Puget Sound. This—she pointed to her husband and the house— was all an exciting new adventure to her, and she was enjoying every minute. Her excitement and curiosity were infectious, but

I couldn't help but wonder how she would feel after six months of primitive conditions and what she would think when the rainy season started.

Andrew was a logging truck driver, and he amused us by telling us some of the hair-raising experiences he had had. Logging truck drivers are highly paid, but it is definitely one of the most dangerous jobs in a dangerous profession. Eventually, our conversation drifted to, of all things, philosophy. Andrew was a country boy who had not even finished high school, but his hobby was reading the great philosophers. He compared and contrasted various philosophies and philosophers as eagerly and as easily as many men discuss their favorite ball teams. He was mostly interested in the German philosophers and rattled off names like Nietzsche, Schopenhauer, and Kant that I barely recognized and theories that I had never seriously studied. He had quite a good library of books, and it was obvious that his was not just casual interest. In my opinion, he could have been teaching philosophy at the university instead of driving a logging truck in the wilderness.

Back at the bunk house, it was cold and damp, and the mist did not clear until noon the next day, when the plane arrived and we flew up the valley. In less than half an hour, we were in a region of dense forest with here and there a small, pale blue lake. There were no roads or even rough trails, and the mountains were steep on every side. Suddenly the pilot dived down toward what seemed a tiny lake with immensely tall trees growing right to its edges. I clutched my seat and held my breath, but he put the plane down lightly and taxied to a clearing on the shore, where we could see two or three tents. We were greeted by three other young men, who helped us unload the plane. It immediately roared off, just skimming the trees.

The camp was small and primitive, with two sleeping tents

and one for the provisions. Two of the young men were students like me, and one was a French-Canadian named Maurice, who was a now-and-then student who had some experience in surveying. After we put the cargo away, Maurice produced mugs of coffee and explained what we were doing.

"This is an advance survey," he said. "The company wants to know if they can push a logging road through here and what kind of timber is further up the valley." He smiled and added, "We've been here a couple of weeks, and it looks to me like it would be too damn expensive. This is wicked country. Anyway, Dutchie is in charge, and he says to keep at it." When I asked who Dutchie was, he said, "Forestry degree and surveyor's license. He likes to climb mountains in his spare time." He laughed again. "Don't you just hate fitness freaks?"

When Dutchie turned up, he was a big, blonde man with a slight Dutch accent. He didn't bother to introduce himself. "Can you cook?" he asked. When I said I had minimal culinary skills, he scowled and said, "We all take turns. Everybody gets to cook. One week each." Then he looked me up and down and said, "Tomorrow I'll show you how to be a chain man."

I took a machete and cut a pile of fir twigs to put under my sleeping bag for the night. Next morning, after a simple breakfast, Dutchie gave orders to the others. Then he tossed me a loaded backpack, and I followed him as he shouldered the transit and set off at a rapid pace for the northern side of the lake. It was rough going through the forest with thick bushes and tangles of fallen trees and swampy patches. But it was worse when we reached the slide area. Almost the entire northern side of the lake was one gigantic rockslide. For centuries, rain and snow and winter ice had been eating at the mountainside, sending huge quantities of rock tumbling down into the narrow valley. The boulders ranged from the size of a house down to tiny pebbles, and it was all loose. The slope was so steep that every step we took disturbed rocks that rattled down the slope and sometimes started small landslides. It was very difficult going, and Dutchie didn't help much when he said, "Watch your step. Last year we had a man break his leg just about here. It took a couple of days before we could get a helicopter to take him out."

When we reached our destination on the slide overlooking the lake, Dutchie passed me a long yellow canvas measuring tape and pointed in the direction he wanted me to pull it. "That's called the chain," he said, pointing at the tape. "It should be metal, but I prefer a lighter one for a job like this."

My job was to measure off the full length of the tape, a distanced called a "chain" (about sixty-six feet), place the striped pole on the exact point, then watch for his hand signals. When the pole was in the precise spot he wanted, I had to poke a stick with a piece of orange plastic tied to it into the ground. The problem was that we were working on bare rock, so there was no earth to place his transit in. That meant I had to scramble around to find enough stones to build a small cairn with, then tie the plastic ribbon onto a rock in just the right position. The cairn could not be too high, as he would have to place his transit directly over it when he reached it. He worked quickly, and it was obvious that he thought I was too slow. But I just could not leap from rock to rock the way he did. The last thing I wanted was a broken leg.

During our lunch break he opened his record book and showed me how to record the measurements. Although he also allowed me to peer through his surveyor's compass, he would not let me touch his transit.

As the day wore on, he became more and more frustrated with me and found fault in everything I did. Even the size of the little rock cairns and the length of the orange marker tape were wrong.

This situation lasted for three or four days until the evening when we returned to camp. After we had all eaten supper, he slammed his notebook to the ground and exclaimed, "I'm just wasting time! Nobody could build a road across that slide. We'll just have to try the other side of the lake."

"I told you so," Maurice said. "That's the most unstable bit of mountainside in this whole damn valley. You've been wasting your time, for sure." The other students had blazed a trail on the south side of the lake and had cleared a rough opening through the trees that was good enough to survey, so he was obviously needling Dutchie. But it didn't work. Dutchie just picked up his notebook and went into his tent.

Cooking at this primitive camp was done on a table-top, two-burner, kerosene camp stove with a sheet of plastic on sticks above it in case it rained. So far we had been lucky and had seen no rain. The lake provided icy cold water and the forest was our toilet. The only sign of civilization there was the radio antenna, which was tied to the top of a large fir that overhung the lake and had been stripped of all its branches. We were supposed to call in every evening, but reception was often poor. One night the man operating the radio had a really bad time. He happened to be a Hungarian student from Sopron, Hungary, where the entire faculty and student body of the forestry department of the University of Sopron had simply walked across the border into Austria to escape the Russians. In an extraordinarily magnanimous gesture, the University of British Columbia, which has an important forestry department, took in the entire faculty and student body. That night, he was swearing wonderfully in Hungarian when suddenly a voice answered in Hungarian and politely asked him to moderate his language. His tirade had been picked up by a fishing boat far out in the

Pacific. The other Hungarian just happened to be one of his professors.

One evening when I was in the storage tent, I saw half a dozen rifles. They were old British Lee-Enfield .303 rifles with their stocks cut down to lighten them. One of those rifles could have been the one I had marched around with during my military service.

"Oh," someone said, "we're supposed to carry those things when we're out in the woods. But they're too heavy. We carry tin cans instead." I must have looked puzzled because he explained, "Get an empty can, put in some stones, tie the thing on your pack and hit it now and then with your elbow so it makes a noise. Bears don't like that noise. They'll leave you alone."

One thing I did *not* want to run across was a bear, so I quickly found a can and some pebbles and made my "bear scarer."

Some of us were better cooks than the others, some were worse. I was the very worst. When it was my turn to cook (of course), the rains came. I had to drag myself out of my warm but slightly damp sleeping bag in the predawn dark and pump up the kerosene stove. Next I mixed oatmeal porridge, then I fried bacon and made scrambled eggs from powdered eggs. I also had to make lots of coffee, all on two burners while the rain dripped down from the plastic overhead. The first morning I almost screamed in frustration when the porridge came out lumpy, the bacon turned into congealed rubber, the powdered eggs refused to mix, and the coffee tasted like weak water. Fortunately, I had made all the sandwiches for lunch the previous evening.

When the rest of the crew started breakfast, nobody said one word of criticism, not because they didn't want to hurt my feelings—quite the contrary—but because they all remembered the cardinal rule of camping: "He that complains about the cooking becomes the cook."

Even with all the practice I got—my efforts each morning and my carefully prepared suppers in the evening—I barely improved. There was a general sigh of relief when the end of the week came and somebody else took over in the kitchen.

One of the cook's jobs was to stay in camp all day and make as much noise as he could. This was to keep the bears away from our food supply. The plane came only once a week, and a hungry bear can make short work of a food tent. What it doesn't eat, it ruins.

The region swarmed with bears. A couple of weeks before I got there, a full-grown bear had been caught red-handed entering the supply tent in broad daylight. It was chased away, but it soon returned, so the cook shot it and the carcass was dragged into the woods. Some days later the smell of the rotting bear carcass became too much to bear, so Dutchie ordered the crew to drag it farther into the woods. It was a messy job. They had to pile dead wood over the decomposing remains and set fire to it. After the carcass was well and truly roasted, other bears turned up to enjoy the barbecue. The south side of the lake was heavy forest mixed with thick bush and broken by swampy patches covered in skunk cabbage, which is a big-leafed plant that smells like skunk when squashed. The bears liked to dig it up and eat the roots.

Dutchie was pleased with his progress on this new route on the south side of the lake and kept me on as chain man, but he was still extremely annoyed at my complete lack of knowledge of forestry. To me, a tree was a tree and when he yelled, "Over toward the Douglas fir," or "Back up to that cedar," I just stood there like a dummy. Once, in frustration, he tore twigs off some trees, shoved them under my nose, and yelled, "That's fir! That's pine!" In time I learned to recognize most of the trees from the texture of their bark.

My backpack now contained a machete, which I kept nice

and sharp. As I dragged the chain through the brush, I had to hack away everything that was in the way, especially anything that would block the view through the transit. I became quite proud of my skill with the gleaming blade and began imagining myself a modern-day Hiram Bingham uncovering the ruins of Machu Picchu.

But one fatal day I took a swipe and sliced through the yellow canvas chain. If it had been metal, there would have been no damage, but we were using a canvas tape and as soon as I cut it, I realized the disaster I'd caused. Dutchie stood there, holding the two ends and swearing in a mixture of English, German, and Dutch while I quietly packed our equipment. We would not be doing any more surveying that day.

Back at the camp, we spent the rest of the day and worked late into the night, trying a variety of ways to repair the vital chain. We tried stitching it, but the cotton thread broke through the canvas. We tried taping it together, but the tape would not hold. We tried gluing the ends to a wooden splint, but the only glue we had was pine sap, which stuck to our hands but would not stick to the chain. Eventually we tied a knot in it, but the knot kept snagging on the brush. We needed one that would not snag. Before we could knot the ends together, Dutchie had to make an accurate measurement of the exact number of inches that would thus be deleted from the chain. Every single measurement he made from now on had to be recalculated to take the missing inches into account. He was not happy with me.

Next day, another student became chain man. I was sent off with the rough survey crew, whose job was to work our way up the valley, find a possible route for a logging road, hack out a rough trail, and clear the brush for the surveyor. This team of three men had been working hard and was already a couple of miles beyond the head of the lake, so we had quite a distance to hike each morning before we could start to work. It was difficult, dirty work and by evening we were usually exhausted.

But I liked it. The forest was wonderfully quiet. The immense trees shaded the ground under them so that there was little undergrowth around the trees, but in the sunlight where the trees were thinner, there were large areas of thick bush. Here and there, a small creek tumbled down the mountain, and there were swampy patches where a variety of strange plants grew, though I saw no flowers or berries except some blueberries. Our boots made no noise on the soft dirt, and so the only sound we usually heard was our own breathing as we struggled up and down the rough trail. There were practically no birds there except for an occasional woodpecker or a curious blue jay, and there was no outside noise whatsoever. Not even a high flying airplane disturbed the silence around us.

The Hungarian forestry student spent his time studying the trees and noting their types and sizes. He had a notebook and kept rough notes, especially his estimates as to the amount of prime timber we came across. While it was a wonderfully beautiful forest to me, it was just hard cash to the logging company.

My job was to clear the blazed trail just enough for the surveyor to use it. The other two men on the team were more interested in pushing ahead up the valley, clambering up and down to find the best route for a logging road, and they also seemed to spend quite a bit of time just exploring. That meant I was often quite alone. I liked working alone, and it was impossible to get lost in the narrow valley, especially if I followed the blazes on the trees.

"Blazing" a trail simply means making some permanent mark on the tree trunks. One of the crew carried a small axe, which he used to slash a mark in the bark of a tree at eye level and within viewing distance of the last mark. The cut was just deep enough to expose the white trunk, and the flap of bark was left hanging.

Properly done, the blaze would not damage the tree, but it left a clear trail of white patches against dark tree trunks. The blazes thus stood out so sharply in the gloom that even I could follow them.

It was not unexplored forest, however. The Indians had traveled it for years, making their way down from the interior to the ocean. Prospectors had been there during the various gold rushes, and it had been looked at, though with little enthusiasm, by the early railway builders. A few hardy hunters came into the forest occasionally, but we never saw one, nor did we see any Indians. We never, in fact, came across the slightest sign that humans had ever set foot in the valley until the day we found the ravine.

It was not a very wide ravine, just a good stone's throw, but it was deep. The ravine ran from high in the mountains down to the river, and the rushing water we could clearly hear far below had cut a sharp-edged slice through earth and rock. The ravine was so deep, we had to lie on our bellies to peer cautiously over the edge. And it completely blocked our path. As we worked our way up and down the edge, looking for a way across, we came upon the remains of a suspension bridge. It was the oddest thing to find in that wilderness, and for a while we just stood there and stared.

Sometime in the past, somebody had gone to a great deal of trouble to find four trees in just the right positions, then to haul in four lengths of steel cable and a load of shackles. The trail to the bridge was long overgrown now, and the boards that had been shackled to the cables were all rotted away, but the cables themselves were still in good shape, although the ends were almost absorbed into the bark of the trees. When Dutchie came the next day to inspect the bridge, he decided we would rebuild it, as it looked like the only way to cross the ravine. He talked to someone back at headquarters on the radio, and the next time the plane brought us supplies, there were a box of shiny steel U-bolts and shackles, a load of roughly cut planks, and a hand drill.

We began rebuilding the bridge. I do not have a very good head for heights, but Dutchie, who never lost an opportunity to show us how fit and healthy he was, more than once walked across the ravine on a lower cable using the upper cable as handholds. Nobody else tried to do this. I helped drill holes in the slabs of wood, and the other crew members fastened the wood to the two lower cables with the hardware. This meant that whoever was doing the work had to lie on the narrow bridge with half his body hanging out into space and reach underneath to fasten the bolts in each plank. To add to the adventure, the bridge would swing at the slightest excuse...and the constant roar of the water kept reminding us of the long drop to the bottom of the ravine. I tried to take my turn working on the bridge, but just could not make myself go more than a dozen steps. I had to crawl back on my hands and knees, carefully avoiding looking over the edge. Maurice thought this was hilariously funny, Dutchie was simply disgusted, and I was sent back to clearing a new trail. They finished the bridge without me, and I never did walk across it.

There was usually a slight breeze coming up from the ocean, but when it stopped, the mosquitoes and black flies descended on us in swarms. We had cans of fly spray and ointment, but they were almost useless, and when I found that the plastic frames of my glasses had become soft, I quit using the spray. Anything that could melt plastic was not going into my lungs. There were days when work was impossible. We just stood there, swatting and scratching, unable to hold a compass steady or even swing a machete. Using the transit was out of the question. We would go back to camp, light a wood fire, and throw damp green twigs on it to make as much smoke as possible. Then we sat there in the smoke and prayed for a strong breeze. Or even rain.

We worked a six day week, then had the seventh day off. If it was sunny, we aired out our sleeping bags, washed our clothes, and tried to get ourselves clean. Dutchie invariably set off on his own to climb the mountain and returned late in the evening to find us greasing our boots. Somehow, he always managed to keep himself very neat and clean. He never looked grubby like us, and his kit was always in perfect condition. This was very annoying. Since the lake was icy cold, the best we could do was stand in the shallows and hurriedly splash water over our bodies. One day, I saw Maurice standing alone, quite naked, washing himself. He was a weird sight because his body was pasty white, but from the neck up and from his elbows down he was almost black from suntan and wood smoke. As I watched, a small duck popped up out of the water right in front of him, sat staring in amazement at this bi-colored monster for a few seconds, then took off down the lake, running on the water and shrieking its fool head off while Maurice stood there shouting, "What did I say? Hey, girl. What did I say? So go ahead and tell your daddy!"

The lake, which was a pale milky green, was astonishingly clear. It was fed by streams that tumbled down from the melting snow high in the mountains. There must have been fish in the lake, but we never saw any.

What we did see was a loon. I had never seen a loon before and had never heard one, either. The loon is a curious duck that can barely walk on land but can swim deeper and faster than any other water bird. It has a strangely mournful call that echoes through the silent forest late in the evening. The bird wears a white feather necklace around its dark neck, and the Indians have various legends that explain why the gods gave it this ornament. We had a small rubber boat in the supply tent and one day after we saw the loon, we inflated the boat and I set off after the bird. Whenever I got close, it would dive. I could see it flash through the clear water as swiftly as a fish. Then it would vanish, and minutes later popped up far away across the lake. Some years later, when Canada issued a new dollar coin, it had a loon on it and was instantly called a "loonie." When the two-dollar coin was issued, it inevitably became a "toonie."

Bush pilots are a special breed. One day I asked our pilot just how small a lake had to be before he refused to try to land on it. He smiled and said, "I just drink a lot of American beer, then open the door and take a good long pee. That usually gives me enough to land on."

One evening after a hot day when I was sweaty and filthy and the water looked so inviting, I staggered down the hill, dropped my pack, stripped off all my clothes, and edged out to the end of a fallen tree where the water was deep. Without stopping, I plunged into the crystal waters. All I remember was the extraordinary shock of ice-cold water followed by a glimpse of the bottom of the lake, which was covered with bits of weeds and branches in that clear, green water. Then I was standing on another tree trunk about twenty feet away. I don't remember swimming or even moving my body. All I could remember was the icy shock.

"Boy," somebody remarked, "you should've seen yourself. Half a second after you hit the water, you came zooming out like a rocket. Straight up and out and onto that log without moving a muscle. Bet you couldn't do that again." I didn't take the bet. I never tried to swim in the lake again.

On another evening, I was returning to camp alone through an area of fairly open forest. I had been banging my "bear scarer" every now and then, but because we used the trail every day, I didn't think that there would be any bears around. Then I looked up. A bear! We had cut the trail along a steep hill so there was a bank about shoulder-height on one side and a sharp drop-off on the other. The bear was standing on the bank about twenty feet from me. It was staring down at me. I stopped, reached for the "bear scarer," and gave it a vigorous shake. I shouted at the bear. The bear kept staring at me. I reached for my machete, but then I remembered that I had tucked it away in the pack. As the bear lifted its nose and sniffed the air, I froze. Then I took a closer look at it. It was a young bear, maybe two years old, and it had obviously never seen a man before. Well, I wasn't going to take any chances. I was *not* going to walk under that bear. That meant I had two choices: (1) I could go back up the trail and find another route back to camp, or (2) I could tumble down the bank into the gully below. I was sure, however, that no matter what I did, the bear might get excited and come after me. I decided to wait it out.

We stood there, eyeing each other, for about five minutes. The bear was obviously puzzled. I refused to back up even one step. I rattled the tin can every minute or so and shouted at the bear. Eventually, it turned and walked a short way up the hill. I grabbed the opportunity and scurried down the hill and leapt onto the fallen log we were using as a bridge across a creek. Halfway across, I turned. The bear was following me. This looked like a good place to stand and make a fight of it, so I reared up and waved my arms in the air, yelling like a madman and banging my bear scarer like a rabid sports fan.

Looking puzzled, the bear stopped and stood up. After a minute, it dropped on all fours and slouched away, but only a couple feet past the end of the log. I took this to mean that I'd won and hurried on my way, all the while making as much noise as I could. Every time I looked back, there was that dark figure still watching me.

When I told my tale to the other surveyors, Maurice asked, "Black bear or grizzly?" I assured him that it was only a black bear, but then he said he had spent the day working on the trail downriver from the camp and had seen a grizzly. Not only was it very obviously a grizzly, but it was a female with a cub. Fortunately for him, she was on the far side of a wide and very rocky stretch of the river. Just to be safe, he had jumped behind a tree. "Old Mama Grizzly," he concluded, "she put her nose in the air and she smell me. Sure as hell she did. But she don't know where I am, and I put my belly to the ground and I get out of there pretty damn fast, that's for sure."

Dutchie joined the conversation. A year earlier, he had been exploring farther down the valley and had come across a man living in a cabin deep in the forest. He had spent a day chatting with the recluse and learned that he was a well educated man who had decided to retreat from civilization and had, all unknowing, built his tidy little cabin right in the middle of what is probably the heaviest concentration of grizzly bears in Canada. The man had become quite used to the creatures wandering around his cabin and had eventually written a book about them. He became famous among bear experts and scientists and, whether he liked it or not, civilization came knocking on his door by way of the post office and the float plane and the occasional hiker.

Our last experience with a bear was the funniest. We were all sitting around one evening enjoying a rest when a fat young bear suddenly wandered out of the forest and headed straight for the supply tent. We all jumped up and ran yelling toward the intruder, who turned and ran back into the forest. But not very far. Each time we charged him, he retreated, but then he turned and stared at us. When we went back to camp, he followed us. Dutchie brought out one of the rifles, but he didn't want to shoot the bear, so he waited until it got too close to the tents and fired three or four shots into the air. The idea was to give the bear such a fright that he would never come back. It worked, more or less. The bear ran through the camp and up the tree from which our radio antenna was hanging. This tree overlooked the lake.

We were standing around the tree, staring up into it while the bear peered down at us when Maurice suddenly had an idea. He dashed into the supply tent and came out waving one of the large signal flares we kept for emergencies. "This baby will do the job," he said. "I'll give him such a scare he won't stop running for two days. How do you light this thing?" Somebody showed him how to pull the tab, then he climbed up the tree until he was right below the unhappy bear. He pulled the tab and held the flare high. There was a huge burst of orange light, a cloud of smoke, and a yell of triumph…which suddenly turned to a scream of anger. The flare dropped down into the lake, and when the smoke cleared we saw the bear still clinging to the top of the tree. And Maurice? He was madly scrubbing at his hair and face. The bear had indeed been frightened, so frightened it had emptied its bowels all over Maurice. The bear had been gorging on blueberries.

We couldn't resist laughing. In fact, we all stood under the tree roaring with laughter. Even the normally humorless Dutchie thought it was hilarious. But Maurice saw no humor in the situation. Swearing loudly in French, he slid down the tree, marched into the supply tent, came out with our big double-headed axe and proceeded to chop down the tree, complete with radio antenna and bear. The tree fell into the lake, and the bear took off swimming. Within minutes, it was just a tiny speck in the distance, and Maurice was standing naked in the icy water.

"Somebody pass me the soap," he yelled. "It's going to take a week to get this damn bear shit out of my hair. And," he added,

"I don't want any of you clowns telling anybody about this. You hear? It's embarrassing! Don't go shooting your big mouths off to anybody. Especially girls." We all solemnly promised never to say a word.

A few days later, we were informed that the company had all the information it needed and there was nothing more for us to do. We packed up and left. I was assigned to the clean up crew. We took everything of value and left what we did not want in a neat stack by the lake where the bears and the winter weather would soon dispose of it. It took two plane trips to get everything out.

At first, I was eager to get out of the forest and all the dirt and discomfort. I couldn't wait to get back to civilization and hot water. As I worked at cleaning up our campsite and shoving odds and ends into the plane, however, I looked up at the towering mountains and the dark forest and across the lovely lake where the loon lived. The summer, I thought, had certainly not been a holiday, but it had been an extraordinary experience and maybe I had learned something.

When we stopped at the logging camp for the night, I asked how Andrew's new wife was getting along. The foreman looked at me for a moment, then said, "I guess you haven't heard. Andy was killed. His truck rolled with a full load. His wife went back to Seattle." He sighed. "Yeah, I liked Andy. He was a nice guy." It was a sober trip back to Vancouver.

Chapter 24
The Grain Elevator

One summer I decided to stay in Vancouver. But I didn't want an office job or a factory job. I wanted to be out in the open, far from overheated lecture halls and stuffy libraries, under blue skies where I could breathe fresh air. Where I ended up was on the docks. It is usually impossible for a non-union worker with no connections to get a job on the docks, but, as luck would have it, there had recently been a huge surge in the demand for Canadian wheat, and the grain elevators were hiring any temporary labor they could find, with or without experience. I got a job in a grain elevator.

The heart of any grain elevator is the silo. These unique structures, which are dominant features of the prairie states and can be seen for miles, often tell the traveler what kind of town lies ahead. If there is only one old, rectangular, wooden elevator in need of paint, this usually indicates a tiny settlement that may or may not have a motel and a decent restaurant. Two elevators indicate a small town with a choice of places to eat. And if the elevators are modern, gleaming, circular, concrete towers, the traveler has reached a major city. I had seen them countless times between Winnipeg and Calgary, but I had never been up close to one before.

The university employment office sent me to a very large

dockside grain elevator dominated by ten enormous concrete silos. As I crossed the railway tracks and dodged the trucks on the
roads near the tracks, I could see that the complex not only loaded
ships, but it also processed a variety of animal feeds and probably
supplied grain to the local breweries. At the office, I was sent to the
main building. My first impression was the smell. The cavernous
grain warehouse, partly filled with great stacks of burlap sacks and
paper bags full of grain, and all the area around it (and even the
docks outside), were saturated with that strong but pleasant smell
of grain found in barns and feed stores. My second impression was
the dust. Everything was covered in a thick layer of grain dust. The
floor was soft with it, the fork-lifts were coated with it, and dust
dripped from the huge wooden rafters like yellow icicles. Grain in
bulk is extremely dusty, and that building had seen thousands of
tons of grain in its time. Grain dust is also highly flammable, and
the *No Smoking* signs were also covered in yellow dust.

But I had no time to stand and stare. A large, red-faced man
asked me my name and scribbled it on a clipboard. Then he said,
"You're up top," and pointed into the corner. There were no stairs
in the corner, not even a wooden ladder. All I could see was a
vertical leather conveyor belt rising from a hole in the floor and
disappearing through a hole in the ceiling, which was high above.
Every few feet there were bits of wood fastened to the belt. While
I stood gaping, somebody shoved me aside, stepped up to the belt,
and was magically wafted up to the ceiling, where he disappeared.

I stood there horrified. I never have had much of a head for
heights and feel slightly queasy even driving over high bridges, so
the thought of trusting my life to that contraption was almost too
much to consider. But, typically, I was more afraid of the embarrassment I would suffer if I refused to use the belt-elevator. Like a
small child hesitating on the edge of the swimming pool, I stood

there, plucking up my courage, and when a line started to form behind me, I reached out, grabbed one wooden bar, and stepped quickly onto another. Never have I clung to anything the way I clung to that piece of two-by-four. With my heart beating loud enough to be heard by the men waiting behind me and my nose pressed tight against the belt, I felt myself rising through the air. No solid elevator walls, no safety belt, no comforting hand rails. Just two skinny bits of wood between me and a horrible death.

Through half closed eyes, I saw that I had risen to the ceiling and was passing through a dark hole…and the belt was still going up! That's when I began to wonder when I should get off. And how to get off. Because there was absolutely nothing to indicate where I was or how high I was, although, in my state of near panic, I seemed to have risen very high indeed. Well, I told myself, I had been told to go to the top. I clung to my perch with sweaty hands. It seemed like hours later, but suddenly I popped out into what had to be the top floor because I could see the belt flapping its way around a huge overhead roller. It was either get off or head back down. Upside down. It took all the willpower I had to persuade my fingers to unclench themselves from the wooden bar. My first thought was how I would get back down again.

At lunch time, rather than ride the conveyor belt down and up again, I remained "up top" and ate the sandwich I had stuffed into my pocket that morning. The only other exit was the fire escape, which consisted of bare iron rungs on the outside of the silo. I stuck my head out the door, looked down, and shuddered. Even an experienced fireman would hesitate to make that descent. And so, at the end of the day, I waited while the others stepped casually to the conveyor belt, gripping the nearest wooden bar nonchalantly with one hand and disappeared through the floor. My turn. Teeth tightly clenched and eyes almost shut, I followed them down. Going down was less traumatic than going up, and by the time I was half way down I had my eyes completely open. Before the week was over, I, too, could step casually onto the conveyor and nonchalantly hold on with just one hand. But I must admit that I maintained a grip that must have left dents in the wood.

When I stepped off the belt the first time, I found myself in a wide room with a dozen or so huge, stainless steel pipes sloping off in various directions. Although all the windows were wide open, the air was thick with dust, and there were pigeons everywhere. To my right there was a long, covered gallery that, I guessed, ran along the tops of the ten enormous, concrete grain silos.

There were a foreman and three or four of us laborers, and although we were kept busy, the work was not hard. Our job was to make sure that the various grains ended up in the correct storage silos. It was vital not to mix the various types of wheat and corn and oats and barley. When it was needed, the grain was extracted from the silos by giant augurs buried in the ground far below us. Each delivery pipe was color coded and numbered. The grain was pumped up to us in the pipes and then distributed to each silo by conveyor belts under the floor. These were fed by the giant pipes which had wheels on their ends and could be pushed and pulled into position over holes in the floor. Somebody in the office far below kept track where the grain was. All we had to do was listen for the phone, then follow the instructions carefully and drag the appropriate feed pipe across the floor to the correct hole. Now and then one of us would walk along the gallery above the silos and check that there were no problems. Spilled grain was supposed to be swept down a special pipe, but that rarely happened thanks to the flocks of pigeons that made their home in the rafters high over our heads.

Up to then, I had never realized that pigeons came in such a wide variety of colors, shapes, and sizes. They ranged from pure white beauties that could have won prizes in bird shows to battered old multi-colored veterans that a cat would decline to chase. When they weren't stuffing themselves, they were mating and defecating. Good Canadian winter wheat must contain a powerful bird aphrodisiac. The pigeons didn't waste much energy building nests; they just laid their eggs on any handy surface. Unfortunately, these handy surfaces happened to include the flexible canvas connections to the overhead feed pipes, which we had to push or pull into place. Almost every day, somebody would put his shoulder to a pipe, give it a healthy shove, and find his energy rewarded in a particularly sticky way. I was christened on my very first day.

One day we had our revenge on the pigeons. A youngish man in overalls and tennis shoes with a cloth bag slung over his shoulder popped up through the floor and immediately started climbing up into the rafters. He was the squab collector. With astonishing speed and agility, he swung himself from rafter to rafter, reaching into the dark corners and running his hands along every surface, looking for baby pigeons, which he killed with an expert flick of his wrist and tucked quickly into his bag. In minutes, he had cleaned out the room and was swinging gracefully along the silo gallery to the next silo. I got the impression that he was Italian, but he wasted no time in conversation and only smiled a giant smile when he completed his search and, with his now bulging bag, vanished down the hole. Later, we caught glimpses of him working his way swiftly across the roofs and under the eaves and even among the wooden pilings of the docks. After watching his acrobatics, I found the conveyor belt elevator much less frightening.

The view from the top of the silo was fantastic. When we had a spare minute or two we could stick our heads out through the open windows, enjoy the breeze, and pick out landmarks. Vancouver, with its rain-washed air, is undoubtedly the most beautiful city in Canada, and the view, which extended from the mountains, which still had a little snow on them, across the harbor to the ocean, with the rolling green city with its many parks in between, was magnificent. On exceptionally clear days, we could just glimpse the top of Mt. Baker, across the U.S. border in Washington State. Directly below us, the harbor was packed with ships waiting to load grain

One day the dispatcher phoned and reported a problem in one of the silos. We opened the inspection hatch and lowered a light on an extension cord. Through the haze of grain dust, we could make out a huge clump of grain clinging to the wall about half way down. Some damp grain had slipped by the inspector and was now blocking the flow from the silo. For half an hour, we tried to dislodge it by dropping a weight on a rope and by swinging the weight against it, but it was stuck quite firmly. Eventually, the foreman wheeled a metal contraption over the hole. It consisted of a hand-operated winch and a steel cable holding a suspended metal chair. Somebody would have to be lowered into the silo and use a long iron bar to pry the blockage loose. As the youngest man there and as the newest employee, I was the one they all turned and looked at.

And there I stood, looking down the hole at the blockage so far below it was just barely visible in the yellow dust. Then I looked at the flimsy iron contraption on which my life would depend. And then I looked at the little group of men who stood with barely disguised smiles on their faces, calculating whether or not this newcomer had any guts. Although somebody handed me a face mask to keep the dust out of my lungs, it wasn't the dust that worried me. My first thought was the horrifying idea of swinging over a hundred feet down inside that silo, suspended on a thin cable being driven by men who might or might not be reliable and who might just attempt a practical joke. Then there was the grain at the bottom. Men have drowned in grain, and I knew that a loosened chunk of damp grain could easily knock me out of the seat to plummet hundreds of feet down into the loose grain below. Apart from the auger at the bottom of the silo, the inspection hatch was the only exit from the silo. And finally there was the air. There was absolutely no ventilation in the silo. It didn't take a college degree to know that what little air there was in that silo was barely fit to breathe. A dust mask was insufficient. Whoever went down there should be wearing an oxygen mask.

All these considerations whirling through my head, I stepped back from the hole and said, "No way. I'm not going down there!"

I could tell immediately by the looks on their faces that I had failed the test. I was no longer one of the crew.

Without a word, the foreman stepped into the chair and adjusted the dust mask over his face. With the minimum of wasted effort, they lowered him down into the silo, along with a light on an immensely long extension cord. Then they lowered a long steel rod. For about twenty minutes we watched him knocking loose chunks off the blockage until the dust got so thick he disappeared. For a few minutes, we listened for the clang of the metal rod striking the concrete wall or for his voice swearing at the grain, but there was no sound.

With two strong men on the windlass, we brought him up very quickly. When he came out of the hole, he was slumped forward against the safety chain and quite still. But he was still breathing, so we dragged him over to the nearest window and shoved his head out into the stiff breeze as one of the men pounded him on the back. After a few minutes, he coughed and swore and stood up. There was a general sigh of relief and a few crude jokes. When we all went back to work, somebody handed me the broom, and I silently swept the floors for the rest of the shift.

Next morning, the warehouse manager (the large, red-faced man who had sent me up top) was waiting for me. I expected to be fired, but, instead, he took me down some stairs to the windowless basement and into a large area where there were half a dozen machines. It was poorly lit, the ceiling was low, and there was a thick layer of dust over everything.

"Need a man down here," he said, and walked quickly from machine to machine, rattling off a stream of instructions. Then he was gone. I stood staring into the gloom with mixed feelings. I had really come down in the world, but at least I hadn't been fired.

The work "down there" was too easy. All I had to do was keep an eye on the machines and clean them now and then. I soon worked out that most of them were grain cleaning machines in which loads of grain were moved rapidly on a conveyor belt under a long magnet and then dropped through a mesh filter designed to catch bits of wood or glass. In its long journey from the fields to the railroads and then to the docks, grain can pick up quite a bit of trash. Grain to be exported was simply poured into the ships' holds, but if it was for domestic use or was going to be made into animal feed, it had to be clean. The grain passing through the machines, I guessed, was nearly all destined to be rabbit or chicken feed.

There were rags on a bench and a large barrel for the trash, so I spent the first hour or two busily wiping bits of iron and steel off the magnets and cleaning the filters. It was fascinating to see how much junk and what a strange variety of metal parts could get into a load of grain. I could have set up a hardware store with the nails and screws alone.

But the novelty soon faded. With nobody to talk to and no window to look out, I was soon horribly bored…and then I found myself polishing not just the magnet but the whole machine. They were not big machines, and they had few moving parts, so I got a little pleasure shining up the chrome and stainless steel. It was, after all, better than sitting on the bench and staring into space. Within a few days, therefore, all the machines were gleaming like new.

Next, I found a broom in the corner and swept the floor around the machines. Very soon I had swept the entire floor. When I found odd bits of wood and abandoned machinery against the far wall, having nothing better to do, I began to tidy them up, too. A cute little mouse ran behind a sheet of plywood, so I dashed to the other end and crouched there, ready to catch him, but suddenly the biggest rat I have ever seen dashed out from behind the plywood and ran across my feet. I jumped so far back I fell on the floor and banged my head on the concrete. As I sat there rubbing my aching skull, I finally realized that the basement, especially the dark tunnel that led off under the silos, was swarming with rats—and they were *big* It was only my constant cleaning and sweeping that had kept them back in the shadows so far.

There were half a dozen weigh scales in the room that I thought had been abandoned, but one morning I arrived to find a man working at the scales. I introduced myself, and he explained that he only came down when all the upstairs scales were busy. He was a bagger, a job that has now been eliminated by automatic bagging machines. With obvious pride, he showed me how he hooked a sack on two nails and pulled a lever that allowed the grain to flow into the sack while he watched the scales until the big red hand was exactly on fifty pounds, at which point, and with astonishing speed, he ran a large needle with sacking thread along the top, sealing the bag perfectly tight and leaving two tufts of sacking just large enough for somebody to get hold of.

"Rabbit ears," he said proudly. "I make the best rabbit ears in the whole company." Then, with a quick jerk, he grasped the rabbit ears and swung the sack neatly onto a pallet ready for the forklift.

Turning back to me, he tapped a small pin on his chest which, when I peered at it, said that he had worked for the company for fifteen years. He explained, with undisguised pride, that he had been bagging grain eight hours a day, five days a week, for nearly seventeen years and had never taken a day off work, and he was faster and neater than any two other men. "Here, you try it," he said.

And I did. I took the long curved needle and tackled a full sack just the way I had seen him do. What he had done in about ten seconds took me nearly two minutes, and when I grasped the rabbit ears to toss the sack onto the pallet, the whole business gave way and spilled chicken feed on the floor.

He smiled sympathetically. "Takes time," he said. "Takes time."

He was the last of the old-time baggers. Today, almost all the bagging is done by machine.

I had been in this basement purgatory for about two weeks when the foreman came down again. He stood in the middle of the room and looked around at the machines and the floor, his hands on his hips and his mouth half open. "Never seen this place so clean," he said. "Go up to the rail cars. They need extra hands." I left him still standing in the middle of the spotless floor.

Because of the extraordinary demand for grain that year, the railways were pressing into service every boxcar they could find, even old wooden wrecks that had been retired years before. Much of the grain arrived at the silos in giant tank cars that were pushed over a grid, where they dumped their load, but most of the older grain cars were pushed into a revolving cage that tilted the car on its side and allowed the grain to flow in a great, golden flood through the doors and down the grill, where it would be pumped up into the silos. The whole operation took only minutes and could be handled easily by a couple of men. That day, however, we had received a consignment of a dozen old, wooden boxcars that the manager deemed too fragile to be handled by the machine. They would have to be emptied the old fashioned way. With shovels.

I was part of a six-man crew. Our first job was to open the doors, which seemed to have been nailed shut and reinforced with a sheet of plywood on the inside. This done, we stood back as the golden tide flowed out and through the grid, but the doors were narrow, so only about a third of the grain actually moved. The rest we had to shovel out. So, carrying our wide, aluminum snow shovels, we climbed inside the boxcar. It looked like easy work, but walking in the grain was as tiring as walking in thick mud, and the grain was much heavier than it looked. In addition, it was a hot summer day and the boxcar was like an oven. The air in the car was also thick with dust, and whenever we stopped for a minute of rest, the head dispatcher glared at us and looked anxiously at his watch. Working flat-out, we took nearly half an hour to empty one car. We were exhausted. Eleven more cars were waiting for us.

It was close to sunset when we finished emptying all the boxcars, but we had been on overtime for some time, a fact that helped take the ache out of our muscles. I was so tired, and every muscle and bone in my body ached so much, that I was actually looking forward to returning to the peace and quiet of the purgatorial basement. But it was not to be. The foreman pointed a finger at me and said, "I want you on the loading dock tomorrow."

Loading the grain into the ships was simply a matter of guiding a huge pipe over the ship's hold and letting the grain pour in like water. Loading the trucks, on the other hand, was muscle work. Three of us stood around a slowly revolving table at the foot of a wide chute. Down the chute came a steady flow of hundred-pound sacks of grain twice the size of the sacks I had previously handled. Somewhere on each sack there was a label indicating its contents. Our job was to drag the sacks off the table and stack them neatly on the appropriate pallets.

I am not and never have been much of an athlete, and my body will never grace the pages of a muscle magazine. Tall and skinny is probably the best description. After long months of sitting in lecture halls and library chairs, I thought those hundred-pound sacks weighed a ton. I struggled all morning to keep up, dragging the sacks off the table and setting them on my shoulder, then staggering to the pallets, where I dropped them in a heap. The fork lift operators immediately explained, in not very polite ways, just how they wanted them arranged.

At lunchtime, I just sat somewhere and rested, too tired to even eat my sandwich. All too soon, the hour was up and more sacks began sliding down the chute. I don't remember how I got through the afternoon. What I remember is soaking my aching body in a hot bath for at least an hour before tumbling into bed.

Some people pay to go to a gym and work long, monotonous hours on exercise machines. They have the option of stopping whenever they feel like it. They don't have a chute crammed with hundred-pound sacks and half a dozen impatient truck drivers standing staring at them.

For the first few days, I switched off my mind and dragged my aching body to and from work, sustained only by the thought that the pay was very good and the hourly pay rate on the loading dock was higher than what I had been getting before. I ate like a horse and drank gallons of water. After a week or so, I found that the sacks no longer weighed a ton. Somehow they had shrunk to only two hundred pounds, and soon they had mysteriously shrunk to barely ninety pounds. Now and then, when there was the chance of a little overtime, I found myself volunteering. I no longer dragged the sacks across the table and staggered under them to the pallets;

now I tugged them by their rabbit ears and swung them gracefully through the air to land exactly where the forklift drivers wanted them. One day I was astonished to find that my shirts had become too tight across the shoulders and that I actually had small, but quite hard, biceps. For a week or two, I reveled in the fact that I was as fit as I had ever been in my life. I swung the sacks effortlessly and handled them as if they were feather pillows. The sun shone in a blue sky, my paychecks fattened, and life should have been good. But it was boring.

We were too busy, and it was too noisy, to carry on any conversations, so one of the men had brought a cheap portable radio, which he turned up as loud as possible. His choice of music—mostly country—was execrable. Even blasting from a small and very cheap speaker, it was barely more than noise, but it was a type of noise that I particularly disliked. Once I tried turning the radio to a different station, but I was loudly and rudely told to leave it alone. I suffered in silence.

What with the monotony of the job and the irritation of the radio, and backed by the fact that I had a nice little sum in the bank and the summer was more than half over, I soon decided that, muscles or no muscles, it was time to leave. I have never worked on the docks or in a grain elevator since then, but whenever I walk into a feed store to get a few pounds of rabbit or chicken feed, I stop and sniff the air and remember. I also have to have the clerk carry the sack for me. Those muscles are long gone.

Chapter 25
On the Pipeline

One summer as soon as exams were over I hitchhiked out of Vancouver and headed for Alberta to try my luck in the oil fields. My money ran out in a little town in the north, where I heard that they were laying a gas pipeline somewhere nearby. Oil and gas companies always pay well, so I took a gamble and walked out to the site. I saw a lot of equipment and plenty of activity, but when I got to the hiring shack I was abruptly told that there was no work. I would normally have walked away, but I had nowhere to go that afternoon, so I sat down on the step of the hiring shack and waited. Now and then during the day other men came up looking for work, but I warned them all off with, "If you ain't in the union, you're just wasting your time." I had not the faintest idea whether or not there was a union, but it served to scare off any competition.

Every morning for three days, I walked up to the shack, clutching an apple for lunch. I sat on that step until the sun went down. Finally, on the fourth morning, a man came out. "Hey, you," he said. "Come with me. I need a man on the ditch crew." Thus was I hired.

Laying a pipeline means digging a ditch, but not by hand. A giant mechanical wheel with huge scoops works its way slowly across the land, but every now and then the router cuts through a patch of sand or loose gravel, and the sides of the ditch collapse.

"Here," somebody said. "Grab a shovel and get to work." I soon found myself down in the ditch with five other students. The ditch was two feet wide and about five feet deep, so tossing the dirt high and wide enough to clear the ditch out required strenuous effort. Within the first hour, I discovered back muscles that I had not used in ages. All day long, as we followed the monster machine, we grabbed a short break only when it passed through good, hard clay. Although I was exhausted by late afternoon, we didn't stop until the sun began to set.

"We work all the hours that the sun shines," said one of the other students. He gave a happy grin. "Lots of nice overtime on this job." Another student added, "Just hope it doesn't rain. Nobody works if the pipe gets wet."

It had been hot and dry for days, and the thought of nice, cooling rain had crossed my mind, but when I heard that, I glared at the blue sky and dared it to produce even one little rain cloud.

After a clerk from the hiring shack took my name and details, I reminded myself to bring not just a lunch but a supper too, and for the next few days I got some good exercise working from dawn to dusk. In the summer, the northern days are very long, so I got quite a lot of good exercise.

When we had covered a good distance, we were set to work throwing wooden planks across the ditch. The crane came along behind us and set lengths of pipe on the planks. The pipe was about eighteen inches wide, and we had to push it into position so that the ends touched, but just barely.

Next, the welder appeared. He was a highly skilled—and highly paid—specialist who was paid by the number of welds he did in an hour; our job was to make sure that nothing interfered with his work. If he wanted a pipe moved, we moved it, if he wanted a drink of water, we all dashed to fetch it. The pipeline depended on his skill, and it was a marvel to watch him at work. He had two assistants, one to handle his wires and tanks and the electric generator on his truck, the other to keep new welding rods coming and keep sliding fresh tinted glass into his safety visor. This team worked smoothly and moved quickly along the pipe, leaving a trail of perfectly welded joints behind them.

When the welder had finished about half a mile of pipe, we helped move the "pig" into place. The pig was a large metal plug that fit exactly into the pipe and was sent hurtling down the pipe by a blast of compressed air to clean off any bits of welding that might have dripped inside the pipe. It also cleaned out any debris in the pipe. "You'd better stand back," one of the gang said. "Onetime I saw a pig rip through the pipe and fly into the air. It was a weak section of pipe. That pig really messed things up." He grinned and added, "All the more overtime for us."

After being reamed out by the pig, the pipe had to be pressure-tested. We were sent on ahead to continue cleaning out the ditch, and then our dirty work began. The pipe had to be coated with a special thick, black tar before it could be lowered into the ground and buried. The tar was in a metal box that lay on top of the pipe and folded around it, and there were rubber gaskets that allowed it to spread evenly over the pipe. On the sides of the tar box were handles by which four of us dragged it slowly along the pipe. Because of the nature of the thing, the box leaked, and very soon not only was the pipe covered in tar but so were we. Tar dripped everywhere, on our hands and arms, on our shirts and boots, and especially on our jeans. The other two men in the gang took turns with us, but their job was no better. They had to pour the hot tar out of a large can to keep the box filled, and they were constantly leaning across the ditch, opening the lid, and pouring the tar in. Some of us wore heavy work gloves, but they were soon so caked with tar they were worse than useless.

It was filthy work. The box was about two feet long, and when it was full, it was very heavy, so we had to strain to get it to slide clumsily along the pipe. By late evening, we were all covered in tar, but we hardly had the energy to find the drum of paint thinner and wipe some of the foul stuff off our hands and faces. It was useless trying to get it off our clothes, so we just cleaned our boots. We were all staying at the same cheap hotel, and when we were working with the tar box we went back to the hotel and left our filthy clothes outside the back door, sure that nobody would steal them. When we put them on the next morning, they were so stiff we felt like knights putting on their armor. Fortunately, we all had at least one change of clothing. One of the students had an old car, and we usually commuted to the job site in it, but when we were covered in tar we walked all the way. The long hours and our exhaustion cancelled any social life we might dream of. None of us even saw the inside of the beer parlor for the length of the job.

All this activity inevitably caused the side of the ditch to collapse from time to time, so we were also busy cleaning it out until the time when the planks were removed and the pipe lowered into the ditch. At this point, the laziest and richest student on the ditch crew woke up. All the time we were working, from dawn to dusk, this young man sat on a small tractor with a blade in front and a cheerful sunshade on top. He just sat there with his feet on the dashboard and his cap pulled well down over his eyes. We couldn't see if he was sleeping or not.

One day he descended from his throne and deigned to speak to us. "It's my father's tractor," he said. "I rent it from him by the day.

I have the contract to fill in the ditch after you guys have finished fooling around."

"But you just sit there all day," somebody said. "Are you getting paid for that?"

He smiled. "Yep. You get laborer's wages, I get machine operator's wages, and my hours are the same as yours. In fact, mine are longer because I can't fill in until you guys have all gone home. Sometimes I have to work till midnight." He smiled again. "Oh, I forgot—the company also pays for the tractor. At an hourly rate! You guys should take a couple of courses in economics." And he strolled back to his tractor. That evening, we watched him switch on his headlights and begin filling the ditch with dirt. We could just see the dollars filling his pockets.

A dark cloud over our work was a small, sharp faced man in a white suit and a panama hat. He had a horrible southern accent and dropped by without warning at infrequent intervals and stood nearby (but out of range of the tar) and watched us work. Almost always, he had some kind of criticism to make, and he never lost an opportunity to make sarcastic comments about Canada and all things Canadian. He was an arrogant and sadistic little man, and, one day, just to show his power, he turned to a laborer just walking by and said, "You! You're not needed 'round here no more. Go collect yer pay."

There was a rumor that the man was the brother-in-law of the engineer in charge and had been given the job of overseer because he was useless at anything else. We both hated and feared him and spent many hours discussing what we would do to him when the job was over.

"We get the bastard and pour a bucket of tar all over him and his white suit," somebody said. Whenever he came to harass us, we smiled secretly at the thought of what we had planned once we got those paychecks safely in our hands. But the day when we were actually paid off, he was not around. Either he had guessed our plans or he was very lucky.

When the pipeline came close to the town, we had to use jackhammers to cut a narrow trench across a paved road. When it was my turn to use the jackhammer, I confidently jabbed the blade into the road's surface, switched it on, and hung on tightly to the madly vibrating machine. Which promptly dug deeply into the road and stuck there. The more I struggled to free it, the deeper it buried itself. It took somebody with another jackhammer to free my blade. The little crowd of people who had gathered to watch was not impressed by my skill and I have never operated a jackhammer since that day.

Sometimes the crowd of watchers was quite large, and little children came close and asked questions. The youngest member of our crew always replied with his own question: "Have you got a big sister?" One day, a little loudmouth shouted back, "Yeah, and she's real pretty. Only she had to go visit my grandparents in Winnipeg." Then he added, "Daddy got mad because she got fat." There was a deadly silence in the crowd and we went back to sliding the tar box.

The student who always asked about sisters was studying psychology. He pretended to see sex in everything we did. He referred to the pipe as a phallus and said we were creating an enormous erection in the biggest vagina in Canada, and when we coated the pipe with tar, he claimed we were rolling on a really big condom. Whenever the pig was sent hurtling down the pipe, he roared, "Oh, man! Now that's what you call an ejaculation!"

One day it rained. It was just a short shower, but the man from the hiring shack came over and told us to quit work for the day. Our pay would start again when the pipe was bone dry. We had nothing better to do, so we sat down under a shelter and began praying that the sun would come out soon. One of the engineers came along, a young Canadian graduate who asked us how much we were making. One of the crew had been keeping a detailed record of our hours in a notebook, so we told him how much.

"Holy cow!" the engineer said, "You guys are making more than me!" Half an hour later, he returned with a pile of old rags on his truck and told us to wipe the pipe dry so we could get back to work. We jumped into the ditch and polished away, and soon the pipe was dry enough to please the head engineer. As we were rubbing with our makeshift towels, the young psychology student couldn't resist making a new joke about masturbating the pipe.

We did not carry on planting our pipeline clear across Canada. This company had contracted to do just one section, and after about six weeks of digging and sliding the tar box, all under the eyes of the man in the white suit, we were called over to the hiring shack and handed our paychecks. We stood there, amazed, counting the zeros, and then, with one accord, we all piled into the car and bounced off down to the beer parlor. Next morning, slightly hung over, we ceremoniously dumped our ruined work clothes into the garbage and headed off, on our separate ways.

Back at school, I had enough money to buy an old car. I joined three other students, who had rented a house just off the campus. It had a huge basement cellar where we brewed our own beer. Between us, we even had enough to pay a lady to come in and cook a decent dinner for us five days a week. It felt good to be rich.

Chapter 26
On the Green Chain

The lowest job in a sawmill is on the green chain. This is work that requires plenty of muscle and very little brain, hard, monotonous work with no let up. But for an unskilled worker, it pays well. The logs arrive at the mill and are sliced into planks of various sizes, which then run along a conveyor belt called the green chain. They are sorted according to size by the workers. It's called the green chain because the lumber is still fresh and green and very heavy. The cut lumber has to sit and dry out before it can go any further.

I was hired in town, got a lift out to the mill on the supply truck, and arrived in time to grab a cup of coffee and a slice of pie in the cookhouse and find a bunk in the large bunkhouse. It was a big outfit and was obviously both a mill and a logging camp. At dawn the next morning, I ate a hasty breakfast, then joined a crew of about half a dozen men and walked between tall stacks of drying lumber and past the towering, black, trash burner to the green chain at the base of the sawmill. As soon as we arrived, the wide belt began to move and the straw boss pointed to a space and said, "Twelve-inch boards there. Put four spacers in each row and keep the stack straight!" That was all the instruction I got. I had to learn everything else the hard way.

The efficiency of a mill depends on the skill of the sawyer. When a log is clamped down onto its mobile carriage, the sawyer has just seconds to decide how he can cut it to make the greatest profit. It is not like slicing bacon or cheese. There are many factors to consider. Good, clear heartwood, for example, brings a better price than knotty wood. Thick, wide support beams bring a better price than regular construction lumber. The sawyer also has to ask himself if the mill is overstocked with one type when there may be a demand for another. Is there a split in the log or an awkward bend? A skilled sawyer can cut a wide variety of sizes from one log and do it so well that there is very little waste.

After the rough cut lumber is edged and trimmed, it slides onto the belt, at the end of which the green chain gang has the problem of sorting everything out. My job was to spot the twelve inch planks, pull them off the chain, and stack them behind me for the forklift operator to take away. Each layer was separated by thin strips of wood for better air circulation between the planks.

The problem was that the planks did not come in an orderly fashion. There might be a gap, then five or six all together. The chain never stopped. It moved at a relentless walking pace, so I had to haul each advancing plank off, drag it to the stack, align it, and turn to grab the next plank before it got past me. Along with each layer, I had to grab four spacers, reach (and crawl) on the stack to place them exactly, and then get back to the chain to meet the next twelve-inch plank. And those planks were not short. The mill seemed to produce nothing under twelve feet in length, and green lumber can weigh as much as fifty percent more than cured lumber. Before the first hour ended, I was sweating and aching all over.

The green chain was out in the open, where the sun beat down remorselessly from a bright summer sky, and there I was, pulling and heaving planks as fast as they came at me, peering anxiously along the conveyor belt to see how many more were coming.

Inevitably, a plank slipped past me. I ran along, trying to catch it, but the man working a few feet away shouted, "Leave it! Pick it up later." So I left it to ride to the end, where it fell on the ground. The rule was simple. Any lumber that slipped by had to be picked up and stacked properly during our short breaks. And nobody helped me. After two hours of grabbing and stacking heavy twelve-inch planks, I staggered to the end of the green chain and recovered the lumber I had lost...and so lost my sorely needed break. The other men just sat and stared at me.

The lumber kept coming, and by lunchtime, I was too exhausted to eat the sandwiches and pie that a pickup truck delivered. I just sat on the ground and drank as much water as I could hold from the huge cooler.

By quitting time, I was completely exhausted. I had forced myself to keep working right until the mill whistle shrieked its welcome sound, but then my body had switched off. When the other men walked back to the bunkhouse, I just sat on the wooden catwalk, unable to move, and watched them disappear. Every muscle ached. I was too tired to give a damn.

Now I began to reconsider how I had persuaded the personnel manager to give me the job. He had looked at my rather skinny, 165-pound frame and my glasses. He had listened to my English accent and seen my untanned arms and clean hands. "You don't know what you're asking," he said. "This is not the type of job you can handle. One day, maybe two, and you'll be shot." He leaned back in his chair. "Yeah. I know the money's good and you need it for college. I was in your shoes once. Frankly, I really don't think you'll last very long on the green chain."

But I had talked like a door-to-door salesman, and I got the job. And now, after only one day, I was indeed well and truly shot. But I had my pride and I needed the money. Just a few weeks, I told myself, survive just a few weeks, and I'll be back in Vancouver with money in my pockets. The only problem was how to get back to the bunkhouse.

That problem was solved a few minutes later when the straw boss appeared in a Volkswagen and helped me into the front seat. He was silent until he dropped me off at the bunkhouse. "Hot shower," he said. "Lots of hot water." I thanked him for the ride, ignored his excellent advice, staggered to my bunk, and fell asleep fully clothed. Next morning, I woke so stiff I had to roll out of the bunk sideways. I walked so slowly to the cookhouse that I only had time for a cup of coffee and a slice of apple pie before it was time to leave. Despite all the water I had drunk the previous day, I did not need to urinate. As I walked with the others down to the green chain, my muscles stretched and relaxed a little, and when the chain started, I gritted my teeth and went to work.

It was bad, but not as bad as the first day. The company supplied us with strong leather gloves that protected our hands from the rough lumber, but as tough as the leather was, those gloves only lasted five or six days. There was a large box of new gloves near the water cooler. Also next to the cooler was a barrel filled with water. In those rare intervals when we had a minute, we took off our T shirts, soaked them in the water, and put them back on soaking wet. They were soon as dry as a bone, but then they were quickly soaked with sweat. Well, putting them in the barrel was a nice break. The salt content of that barrel must have been quite high from our sweat-soaked shirts.

As I got into the swing of things and learned little tricks by watching the other men, pulling the heavy lumber became slightly less difficult and I lost only a few planks. By noon, I was ravenous and ate every scrap of my lunch.

After lunch, I found out the hard way just how high the stack had to be. The lifting machine looked exactly like a giant yellow spider, with wheels at the bottoms of eight-foot-tall legs. The operator, perched up high, was constantly shouting down at me to make the stacks taller. That afternoon, he drove to my stack, but now it was too high. The top couple of layers were knocked off and went flying everywhere. The mess was too much for me to handle alone, so a couple of the men quit pulling their planks to give me a hand, which led to a pile-up on the chain.

The straw boss immediately hit the button, which stopped the chain, but this made the sawyer look out his window high overhead and start screaming down at us. Despite the confusion, though, everybody worked quickly and efficiently, and soon the mess was cleared up, the chain was emptied, and the lifting machine operator went away with his load. No angry manager or administrator had appeared, and with one last rude comment, the sawyer went back to work. I, too, was glad to get back to work.

I had been seriously worried that I would be fired for incompetence, but the opposite happened. The other men on the chain crew had seemed to barely tolerate me. They had not included me in their conversation and treated me like an intruder. But after the minor catastrophe that afternoon, their attitude changed. I had ignored the screaming sawyer and the sarcastic comments of the lifting machine driver and had helped to clean up the mess without fuss or comment. I had also not uttered one word of complaint about the miserably hard work under the broiling sun. I was now one of them.

They were an interesting bunch. Three of them were pure Neanderthals with huge arms and shoulders and conversation restricted to a grunt or two. They worked, ate, and slept and rarely showed any expression or feeling. The fourth man, Eddy, was quite the opposite. He was a big man who never wore a hat or a shirt and talked a lot as he dragged his lumber, making crude jokes, making up stories of his sexual exploits, and usually just talking to himself. The straw boss was a small man, all sinews and tight muscles, his skin almost black from the sun. He was an intelligent man who had never finished high school and seemed to regret it. He was quite surprised that a college student would take a job on the green chain and asked me a lot of questions about the expense of an education and the other jobs I had had. I learned later that he lived in town and drove home almost every night to his family. I got along quite well with everybody, including big Eddy, who was constantly picking at pimples on his skin. Whenever he had a short break, he began searching his skin for something to pick at, rather like a huge, smooth-skinned monkey. For some strange reason, this irritated me, but I kept my mouth shut.

As far as the work was concerned, there was a strict pecking order. Last man in got the heaviest lumber. I was the last man. The straw boss got the large support timbers, which were heavier, but there were few of these, and he could go for quite some time waiting for something to pull. Eddy got the two by fours, and there were plenty of them, but they were the lightest and easiest to handle. He could flip them around like matchsticks. The Neanderthals pulled the one-inch planks of various widths, and I got the two inch monsters. It was hard, non-stop work, but it was work, and the days out in the sunny valley between the dark forested hills passed quickly.

Near the mill was the burner, a thirty-foot-tall, black metal cone in which the odds and ends and much of the sawdust were burned. All day and all night, a conveyor belt carried the trash to the burner and dumped it into the smoldering fire, whose smoke drifted down the valley for miles, polluting the air and stinking up the countryside. Now and then it also drifted across us as we worked and left us coated in fine grey ash. In those days you could tell by the smell when you were approaching a mill town, but today nothing is wasted, and the old burners stand rusting and empty and the sky is clear again.

The food at the mill was not just good and plentiful; it was excellent. Loggers are notoriously famous for the amount of food they can scarf down, and the mill workers had equally hearty appetites. Since the mill worked on two shifts, there was a small army of cooks and helpers, and food was available at all hours, day or night, and there was no skimping on either quality or variety. The first evening that I wasn't too exhausted to be aware of my surroundings, I stared with astonishment at the range of food on the serving counter. It was mostly beef in huge portions and cooked in every way, but there were also chicken and stews, along with soups and salads to tempt any appetite. A cook stood ready to serve it up just the way you wanted. On the long tables there were always pies of every variety, and the cooks were constantly bringing fresh pies hot from the oven. There was no alcohol allowed anywhere on the mill grounds, but there was an endless flood of rich black coffee and real cream.

The loggers were astonishing eaters. One evening I sat and watched, wide eyed, as the man in front of me, who was quite small, polished off two giant steaks with baked potatoes and all the trimmings and then started on the pies. The whole pies were sliced into quarters, and he reached for another giant slice almost as quickly as he stuffed one slice into his mouth. In minutes he had polished off two large pies. And he didn't even belch.

Like my mother, the cooks believed that a man should start the day with a good breakfast. They served not just oatmeal porridge and pancakes but also eggs cooked in every known way, plus bacon or ham and fried potatoes or corn mush and, of course, more pie straight from the oven. It was not rare to see a man tackle a stack of pancakes six inches high and dripping with real Canadian maple syrup, then start on half a dozen fried eggs with three or four rashers of ham and finish off with a couple of slices of pie. I ate like a pig whenever I could, but I never came close to eating what Eddy called "a decent, man-sized meal."

A manager explained to me one day that the cost of feeding the men, including wages for the cooks, was actually only a small fraction of the mill's overall costs, but since well-fed crews work harder and good food dissuades men from leaving for other outfits, any well-run logging outfit keeps a good table. There was, I later learned, a logging outfit up the coast near the Alaska border that was built entirely on huge floating rafts that could be moved from place to place. The company paid very well but tended to skimp on the food. According to scuttlebutt, the loggers eventually got, so to speak, fed up and pitched the cook out the window and into the fiord. When the next cook was no better, they threw him out the window, too. The food improved very quickly. In my opinion, our cooks were in no fear of a ducking.

After I'd put in about two weeks of intense labor, my shirt seemed to feel a bit tighter. The lumber felt a fraction lighter, too. I was now feeling quite fit and extremely proud of myself. Despite the heavy eating I was doing, I had lost any fat that I might once have had and had not put on any weight. So I was in a good mood when a man from the second shift approached me and asked if I would do half of his shift on the dry belt so he could go to town for a few beers. He promised to be back on time and said he would pay me cash. It looked like a good deal, so I agreed.

After the rough lumber is sufficiently dry, it goes to the planer mill, where it is finished off and made ready to be shipped out. I found that my beer-drinking coworker was pulling mostly one-inch boards, which were half the size I normally pulled, and they were shorter, too. The best part was that they were dry lumber and weighed much less than the green stuff. It was so easy I almost laughed. The evening passed quickly, and, since there was very little to do in the bunkhouse except read old sports magazines and sleep, I was pleased to have the work. Word got around after that, and quite a few times I did somebody a favor…for hard cash.

All logging and milling in that region had been banned twice that summer because of fire hazards, so the company was eager to make up for lost time. That meant we worked six-day weeks and spent Sundays washing clothes and doing other personal chores. The loggers, who were paid by the tree and also wanted to make up for lost time, often worked on Sundays. One Sunday, I was dozing in the shade when I was offered a lift by one of the overseers who was going up to the area where they were logging to check on something. It was a long drive up into the hills on the rough roads, and we kept having to squeeze over onto the shoulder to make way for massive logging trucks with their enormous loads.

"See those tanks over the wheels?" he said. "See they're dripping water? That's to keep the brakes cool. They get hot enough to melt on these hills."

When we reached a large open space that had obviously just been cleared, he said, "They're rigging a new spar tree, and I want to make sure it's a good one." He put on his hard hat and walked over to the middle of the clearing, where he looked at the soil and kicked at the exposed rock. One massive tree stood all alone there. He walked slowly around the tree, then came back and grunted, "Looks good."

This was the spar tree, at the foot of which a man festooned with lengths of cable and various bits of metal stood holding a chain saw. He fastened his safety belt around the tree and began to climb. As he reached each branch, he trimmed it off close to the trunk and slowly made his way up to the next branch, leaving a bare trunk behind him. When he got to the top, he slowly and very carefully began to cut off the top section.

"This is the dangerous part," my friend said. "It's got to fall away from him without kicking out and hitting him or splitting the tree."

There was complete silence on the ground until the top of the tree slowly toppled over and fell away. When it hit the ground, there was a general relaxation and somebody cheered. For the next few minutes we watched as the small figure high above us fastened a collar around what remained of the top of the tree, then hooked up a couple of pulleys and threaded cable through them.

"That's just temporary," my friend said. "The riggers will fasten up all the rest of the cables and have everything ready by tomorrow." He pointed to a large donkey engine at the edge of the clearing. "The logs are hauled out of the woods by cables fastened to the spar tree. I've never had one break on me…but you never know." Then he laughed. "The topper is Jack Mooney. I think I know what he's going to do next. Let's move back a bit."

I was getting a crick in my neck watching Jack Mooney. Since he seemed to be finished, I thought he was going to come back down, but he didn't. First, he lowered his chain saw to the ground on one of the cables. Then, very carefully, he removed his safety belt and draped it over a pulley. Once again there was silence on the ground as we all stood there, horrified, watching Jack. Nimble as a cat, he gave a push and then stood upright on the very top of the spar tree. There was not a breath of wind, nor did anybody even take a deep breath. We just watched him, standing with his hands on his hips, staring off over the trees, not moving an inch.

"God. I hope he's sober." somebody muttered.

"Nah," somebody else answered. "He's drunk as a bishop."

Then, as if he had heard the remark, Jack Mooney zipped open his jeans and peed on his audience! It was a wonderful performance. The loggers thought it was hilarious, and I giggled like a schoolgirl all the way back to the mill. I was still giggling next morning when I told the rest of the green chain gang about it. Even the Neanderthals laughed.

Eventually the summer ended, and it was time to leave. I got a lift back to town, where I picked up a fat paycheck, then caught the bus back to Vancouver. I was in excellent condition, and although it had been hard work, I had enjoyed the experience. I had also learned everything I would ever want to know about the timber industry.

Chapter 27
Geologist

I took a course in geology one winter, not because I needed it but simply out of curiosity. I found it very interesting and got a good grade, so when I heard, early in the summer, that a company in Vancouver was looking for geology students, I jumped at the chance.

The office was on a busy street, and the window was wide open to the roar of the traffic, so when the interviewer said, "I take it that you have some knowledge of geology?" I answered truthfully.

"I have taken quite a few courses in geography," I said. I just happened to put the emphasis on the "geo-" part of the word and slur over the "-graphy" part. Thanks to the noise from the street drowning out much of our conversation, he seemed quite happy with what he heard.

"Good," he said. "Be here early on Wednesday with your kit."

Early Wednesday morning, I tossed my little duffel bag into a Land Rover and squeezed in alongside a couple of men my age and an older man who was driving and who was obviously the boss. We went over the bridge to North Vancouver, then up the winding coast road until it turned into little more than a rough track. I had enough sense to keep quiet and listen to the others and soon learned that the driver was a qualified geologist and the other two were genuine geology students. As we traveled, they commented on the rock formation and other geological surveys they had been on. I very soon accumulated enough information to be sure I would not give myself away as soon as I opened my mouth.

At one particularly rough spot, we saw that the bulldozers had uncovered an enormous flat rock in the middle of the road. As we drove over it, the driver slammed on his brakes and we all jumped out to look at the rock.

"Garnets!" somebody exclaimed. Sure enough, the rock was dotted with clusters of dark red garnets, hundreds of them. The driver poured some water on one cluster, and we stood there and admired the little jewels sparkling in the sun.

"Well," he said, "there's not much we can do right now, but when we come back this way, we're going to get ourselves a few samples."

At midday, we turned off on a forest trail and ended up at a ranger station and general store with a bar attached. There, as the boss, who was also a professional geologist, explained our mission to the ranger, I learned that we would be taking soil samples from the various creeks in a side valley and that the company was looking for copper. After lunch, we drove further into the forest until we came upon a man holding the bridle of a shaggy packhorse. I had never even seen a packhorse before, but the others took it in their stride, so I gave what assistance I could and helped fasten all our gear onto the wooden rack. The horse stood patiently through it all and never complained, even when it was loaded down with what seemed an extraordinary number of bundles wrapped in ground sheets. We left some odds and ends that we wouldn't need in the Land Rover, then drove the vehicle deep into the brush and parked it. Then we set off up the track behind the horse. It was a long climb but the horse moved at its own slow pace, stopping to nibble at anything green.

"She's just a hairy pig," the wrangler told us. "I feed her better than my own kids, but she still wants to stop and eat." He tugged on the line. "Come on, Greedy Guts."

Eventually we reached a level spot on the hillside and set up the tents, unloaded the horse, and watched as horse and wrangler disappeared back down the trail.

Things went smoothly until it was time to cook supper. One of the crew had been chosen to be cook, as he actually could cook and liked cooking, too.

"Where's the can opener?" he shouted. We all started searching for the can opener, but after half an hour it became clear that the can opener had been left behind in the Land Rover. "Well," he said, "we can't do without a can opener."

The geologist started eyeing the boxes of canned food. "We can open some of the cans with a knife," he said, "but somebody will have to go down and get the can opener."

All eyes were immediately on me. In the expectant silence, I smiled and said "Oh. Okay, I'll get the can opener. Who has the keys?"

Somebody passed over the car keys and shoved a large flashlight into my hand. "Here, you'll probably need this."

The trip back down the mountain was not too difficult. When I found the Land Rover, I also found the can opener, but by the time I was half-way back up to camp, the sun had set. I went on, stumbling through the forest guided mainly by horse droppings and edging carefully along a particularly sharp cliff where the trail dropped off steeply. It was pitch dark by the time I reached the camp. A rough supper was made, and I had just enough time to make myself a crude bed before I fell asleep. During the night, the cold and damp of the bare ground told me that I needed a much better sleeping bag and that I needed to cut a whole stack of twigs to form a mattress under my sleeping bag if I wanted to survive the summer.

We were given our assignments the next morning. I was to go with an experienced team member, who would show me how to choose a good soil sample and how to make a rough sketch-map and record locations and code numbers in a notebook. We then made lunches for ourselves and set off along a faint trail until we came to a stream where we started drawing a rough map. Then we climbed down into the stream, and my partner showed me how the silt tends to collect near the downstream sides of rocks.

"If there's any metal, like copper or gold," he said, "it will settle in a spot where the water has slowed down. Most metals are heavier than sand." He picked up a handful of grey silt. "That's the idea be-hind panning for gold," he said. "Look for quiet spots behind rocks or along the bank. You'd be surprised at how many samples show trace of gold…but we're looking for copper this year." Then he put a tiny sample of the silt in a plastic bag, climbed out of the stream, and showed me how the company wanted the bags labeled and how the spot was to be identified by a code.

Although it involved a bit of scrambling up and down and my boots were soon soaked, the work was easy to do. We spent the day slowly climbing up the mountainside as we followed the stream to its source, where it was barely more than a trickle.

"If the water runs over a seam of copper," my friend said, "it will show up in samples from the bottom of the stream. These up-stream samples will help pin-point anything that's here. These hills are loaded with copper, but we've never found a good rich seam."

With our packs bulging with samples, we made our way back

to camp, where I took a machete and cut myself a nice pile of twigs to lay under my bed for insulation from the cold, cold ground.

The other men wandered in, and we had a simple supper, augmented by anything we found in a can that interested us. Our conversation was mainly on the geology of the mountain. The campsite was on a little shelf that overlooked a valley and there was a soft breeze. "Just enough to keep the black flies away," somebody said.

It was agreed that I understood what had to be done, so next morning I was to go out by myself. With my nice new pile of fir twigs under me, I slept better that night, though I still needed a better sleeping bag.

The next day I set out on my own. I found the next stream along the trail and worked my way slowly up the mountainside, taking a sample every now and then and noting locations and code numbers in the log book. The forest was extraordinarily quiet, and as I climbed higher, the heavy cover of large trees and brush thinned out to slimmer trees and occasional natural clearings. Here and there I ran across a blueberry bush, but there were no other flowering plants. Everything was so still that the only sounds I heard were my own footsteps. There were a few fallen trees covered in moss, but no signs that the area had ever been logged off or, indeed, that any man had ever been there. Occasionally I thought I heard something and wondered about bears, so I made a bit of noise now and then. When I sat down to write my notes or eat my lunch, I usually perched on a high rock or a raised stump where I could see in all directions. But I saw no sign of bear. Complete silence is very rare in our modern world, and as the days passed, I came to love the silence and soon began to believe that I was working in a primeval forest.

But one day I had a surprise. I thought I heard sounds in the forest, but they were very faint. I stopped on a game trail to listen more carefully. Suddenly a group of about half a dozen people appeared, walking single file along the trail. The group included a couple of elderly women, and they all had backpacks and were carrying woven baskets. The men wore jeans and heavy shirts, as I did, but the women wore long skirts. After a minute, I realized that they were Indians. They were as surprised to see me as I was to see them.

There was a minute of silence, which I broke. "I'm on a geological survey," I explained. "Taking soil samples."

This seemed to be enough explanation. One of them said, "We're going up to collect blueberries. We do it every year. Should be a good harvest this year."

"We've been coming up here since my grandfather's time," another one added. "It makes a nice holiday." And he turned to one of the women, "Eh, Grandma?"

I thought maybe they would stop for a rest and I would learn more about what they did with the berries, like how they dried them and what they cooked them in. Instead, they carried on walking silently up the mountainside and soon disappeared.

Another day, the stream I was following did not dwindle away. There was very little silt on its stony bottom, so I decided I was wasting time there. But I was curious, so I followed it higher and higher. Suddenly I came out of the trees and found my path blocked by a huge patch of snow. It was the last remains of the winter snowfall. It was a hot midsummer day, and the brightly glaring snow just lay there, defying the temperature as if determined to last until winter came again.

My biggest surprise was the day I came out on the top of the mountain and found a giant steel power line pylon. It was high and massive and set in solid concrete, but there was neither road nor track anywhere around. It just stood there with its cables disappearing off into the distance. I puzzled about this for the rest of the day, and when I got back to camp that evening and set my samples in the cardboard box, I told the geologist what I had found.

"How on earth," I asked, "did they build that thing way up there?"

He smiled. "They didn't. They brought the whole thing in by helicopter. Even the cement for the foundations and the riggers who finished it. All by helicopter."

"God, that must have cost a fortune," one of the others said.

But the geologist just shook his head. "Compared with the cost of building roads and trucking everything in for each pylon, it was relatively cheap. That line is hundreds of miles long. I hate to think how they would have built it without helicopters."

The thought of helicopters buzzing over what I had come to believe was a primeval forest inhabited only by a few Indians deflated my happy illusions, but it took nothing away from the beauty of the forest.

One day the breeze died away, and the black flies and mosquitoes appeared in their customary clouds. There was nothing we could do except build a smudge fire and sit in the smoke until the blessed breeze reappeared and drove off the bloodthirsty creatures tormenting us. While we were waiting for the breeze, the geologist went over my notes and studied the crude map I had drawn.

"I think you've about done that slope," he said. "Tomorrow we'll all work below the trail down to the main creek."

Next day, we scattered along the trail and worked downhill. The brush was thick and the ground was quite damp. It was steep in places, but we all got our samples and met down on the creek bed. Two of the crew had been exploring along the creek, and suddenly one shouted, "Hey! Look at this!"

There, in the water and among the rocks, lay a huge, cast-iron fly wheel. We immediately explored farther and we came across the remains of a steam engine. There was no date on anything, but it was obviously very old.

"Must be at least seventy years old," somebody said. "Probably older."

We all stood there, staring at the huge, enormously heavy machine lying in this lonely little canyon far from any road or town.

"Somebody spent good money to have this thing brought up here by ship," the geologist said. "Then they must have used a mule team to drag it through the forest to this spot." He looked all around and added, "That means they found something of value. Boys, let's take a closer look."

A lost gold mine? The mere thought set us moving. Within minutes, sure enough, we came across a low cave that was obviously manmade. We peered in. The floor was muddy with yellow and blue streaks.

The geologist needed only one look. "Copper!" He pulled the flashlight out of his pack, and we went in. About fifty yards in, the roof had collapsed.

"We can easily make a hole in that." said one of the crew, so we all began pulling chunks of rock away and sweeping away mud with our bare hands.

Suddenly there was a squirt of water and in seconds, the dam burst. I was standing on one side, so I only got soaked, but the youngest and lightest member of the crew was hit squarely by a three-foot-high tsunami of muddy water and went tumbling out of the cave. We all dashed out to pick him up and sighed with relief to find no broken bones.

"Christ! That's filthy stuff." he exclaimed as we watched the blue-tinted tide slowly dissipate. "It's been sitting there stagnant, soaking up copper for years, just so it could dump its damn self on me."

He swore energetically, but with little imagination, as the geologist splashed his way through the thick mud and studied the rest of the cave. When he came out, he reported only a small seam of low-grade copper. Our dreams of a fabulous gold mine vanished.

Surprisingly for the west coast of Canada, it only rained two of the days we were on the mountain. During those two days, there was little we could do except sit huddled in the tents and try to keep our sleeping bags dry. Meals were little more than canned beans and slabs of Spam, but everybody remained relatively cheerful. We also spent the time rubbing waterproof grease into our boots.

We had been contracted to work seven days a week for six weeks. When the end came, the wrangler reappeared with his shaggy, ever-hungry horse. He had been up a couple of times before to take down the cardboard boxes of samples and stack them in the Land Rover, but this time it was to take us down from our mountain.

It didn't take long to load the packhorse, with the wrangler doing all the lashing and tying special knots to make everything secure. Everything went smoothly until we reached the narrow part of the trail, but there the horse's greed caused a small disaster when she suddenly saw a nice, juicy clump of grass growing at the edge of the trail. She reached out to snatch at it. But the weight of the laden horse was too much for the soil, and part of the trail gave way. I was walking just behind and watched in horror as the horse slid slowly down the gravel slope and came to rest against a rock.

There was a moment of absolute silence, and then everybody burst into hysterical laughter. When she started to slip, the horse, instead of struggling frantically to save herself, stretched out her long neck and tried to take a mouthful of grass as she slid past another particularly green patch. Even though she was now caught precariously close to a drop that would kill her, she was busy looking around for something else to eat. As we watched, she stretched her head and neck toward a clump of weeds, showing her huge yellow teeth, in a vain effort to have one more snack before plunging to her doom.

Before that could happen, the wrangler produced a length of rope, and we lowered the geologist down to the horse, where he tied the rope securely around the pack saddle.

"Well," one of the guys whispered, "if the cinch breaks and that stupid horse goes over the cliff, at least we won't lose our equipment."

But the wrangler heard him. "We ain't gonna lose old Greedy Guts," he said. "She's been in worse scrapes than this." He scrambled down the slope just far enough to find the end of his lead line.

When the geologist was back up, we all strained on the two lines and soon had the horse and her cargo safely back on the trail. There was hardly a scratch on the tough old nag, and the load had not shifted an inch. An hour later, when we had everything stowed in the Land Rover, we waved goodbye to the wrangler and Greedy Guts as they ambled off up the valley.

Of course we had to stop for a cold beer at the little bar near the ranger station. We students sat at the only table, relaxed, happy and laughing about the old horse, while the geologist stood at the counter talking to the manager, who was obviously very excited about something, though we couldn't hear what he was saying.

Suddenly the geologist walked over to our table and said in a low voice, "Get the hell into the Land Rover as quick as you can!"

He went back to the counter and we gulped down our beers and piled back into our vehicle. Seconds later, the geologist hurried out of the building and dived into the driver's seat, and we raced off down the road. After about a mile, he slowed down and said, "You know that old mine we found?" We all nodded our heads. "Well, it seems that there's a fish hatchery downstream in the valley."

We were puzzled for a moment, then it dawned on us. "So all that filthy water loaded with copper flowed down the stream and into the hatchery?"

The geologist nodded. "Yep. It killed about half the baby fish before they could stop it."

"But we didn't do it on purpose!"

The geologist snorted and we were all silent for a while. Then he said, "I don't want anybody mentioning this. Don't say a word to anybody. *Ever*. They're so mad they want to arrest somebody and sue the pants off them. They're talking about pollution and vandalism and stuff like that."

One of the crew finally spoke up. "And I suppose we were the only people up there at the time, so we look guilty. Drive faster, Chief. I don't want to spend next semester in jail."

When we approached the part of the road where we had seen the garnets, we slowed down and scrambled around for geological picks and hammers. We were looking forward to taking some big specimens. But the rock was gone. While we had been up on our mountain, the road builders had laid down a beautifully wide, gleaming black stretch of new road…directly over our garnets. We didn't cheer up until late that evening, when we arrived back at the office in Vancouver to find the boss waiting with our checks.

Chapter 28
The One-Room School

I needed one more year to graduate from college, but it had not been a very profitable summer, and I was stuck in a small town in the far north, closer to the Yukon border than to Vancouver. I was sitting in the beer parlor with some other students, sketching out a rough budget for the coming year. We were all dreading the thought of taking out even more student loans, when somebody said, "I heard the local school board is looking for teachers. The pay scale's good, and there isn't anything to waste your money on up here. It could be a way to save up a bit of money."

I looked at him for a few minutes as I considered his suggestion. "Where's the school board office?" I asked.

Despite the fact that I had no teaching credential and no experience, I was hired almost instantly. This, plus the fact that nobody had told me very much except that it was a one-room school "rather far out of town," should have made me suspicious. But I was eager to start and gain some income and quite confident that I could handle the job. It looked like an interesting adventure.

The superintendent himself drove me out to the school, and as we sped for what seemed like miles through the dark forest he explained, "We had an elderly lady teaching here for years, but she suddenly decided that she couldn't go back again. She quit a few days ago. We might have had to close the school if you hadn't turned up."

Then he turned off the main road and bumped down a trail for a mile or two and stopped. There I saw a wide clearing, scattered around the edge of which were five small, unpainted houses, a tiny store, and a dilapidated service station with the usual collection of old car parts and bits of rusting machinery behind it.

"The school is over there a bit," the superintendent said.

We drove deeper into the woods to where a pair of freshly painted, small, white buildings stood on either side of a huge propane tank. The larger of the buildings was the school; the smaller, my house.

Because the superintendent was a busy man, he had only enough time to give me a quick tour and brief instructions. "You'll find everything you need there," he said as he shoved a pile of papers into my arms and handed over the keys to both school and house. "Of course," he added, "I expect you to wear a jacket and tie during working hours."

And with that, he dived into his car and raced back to town, leaving me standing with my duffel bag and staring proudly at my new home and my new job.

If I had taken careful notes, I would now be writing an entire book about my experiences that winter. It would be a best seller and would probably be made into a movie. But my diary notes are incomplete. I was too busy just trying to do the job without making too many mistakes. Needless to say, however, teaching in that one-room school was a fantastic experience that changed the whole course of my life.

My house consisted of a small living room with a propane stove and a sink in one corner, plus a table and two chairs. There was a separate bedroom with a comfortable bed and mattress and a water closet with a chemical toilet which, I gathered, had to be emptied somewhere in the forest every now and then. In the dead of winter, when the temperature plunged to thirty-five degrees below zero, that inside toilet was a godsend. It was also the only inside toilet for twenty miles around.

The only phones in the village were in the store and in the service station about 200 yards away, so my first chore was to go to the store to fill my empty cupboards and phone a friend in Vancouver to pack up all my belongings and ship them to the school board office, where somebody would bring them to me. I introduced myself to the storekeepers and noted that quite a few people had already dropped in to take a look at the new teacher. The men were all wearing blue jeans, checked shirts, and heavy boots, the women, blue jeans and light parkas. Those with children introduced themselves, while the others just stared curiously.

I needed a blanket and a few other necessities, and the storekeeper was only too eager to give me credit. As he pointed out, loud enough for all his customers to hear, "Yours will be the only reliable paycheck I'm liable to see this whole winter."

When a man stepped out of the crowd and said, "I drop off a couple of milk cans of water for you every day, one at your house and the other at the school," this was the first time I realized that there was no running water in either the school or my house. The cans were big, and they were always there bright and early, so there was no problem until the temperature dropped. In the dead of winter, the water froze very quickly. I always dragged my can in and left it near the heater while I was at the school, whereas my pupils smashed the ice with an old laundry flat iron they called a "sad iron," then scooping out water to drink or to wash their hands. I never did ask where the man got the water.

Taking a bath using lukewarm water and standing in a tiny

wash basin was no fun, so on rare occasions I arranged a trip into town on Saturday and booked a room in the hotel. After taking my clothes to a laundry, I returned to the hotel to luxuriate in a steaming hot bath for an hour. Then I had a decent restaurant meal and went back to the hotel for another long soak. It was an expensive luxury, but worth every penny.

The school room was just that—one room with about three dozen desks and chairs. It was freshly painted, but quite bare except for the stack of cartons containing school supplies that waited inside the door. The school toilets were outhouses tucked under the trees, and the playground was a rough, rock-studded clearing.

On my first day, while I was sorting out all the papers and forms spread across my desk, the door banged open and a huge man marched in and introduced himself as the owner of the service station. He was very friendly and showed me how to light the propane wall heaters and how to stand on a student desk and light the half-dozen propane lamps hanging from the ceiling.

"Lucky you," he said. "The old school had a wood-burning stove and oil lamps."

I agreed that I was indeed very lucky to have propane.

Then he produced a two-foot length of automobile fan belt and slapped it on my desk. "You'll have my boy," he said. "He's a bit big for his britches. Just don't take any nonsense from him. Use this on him. I always do."

I stared at the lethal-looking weapon and assured him that I was sure I would never need it, at the same time quietly wondering what the other children were like. The boy turned out to be one of the nicest young men in the class. Two days later, the children turned up. They proved to be a very likeable bunch. There were thirty-two of them, and they ranged in age from age six to age twelve or thirteen, that is, from one tiny first-grader to four sixth-graders. The mothers delivered the children on the first day. They stood around the door and introduced themselves and their children, and when they were gone, I got down to work.

Over the years, I have used a great many educational gadgets, ranging from the old slide and movie projectors to modern television sets and computers, but without electricity in that one-room school, we had nothing except a battery-operated radio I bought at the store. The school library was just one little shelf of well-used books, and the school supplies had to last all winter.

I started off with six neat rows for the six grade levels, but it soon became obvious that there was going to a lot of cooperative learning—and teaching—with the older students helping the younger ones. I gradually combined much of the work into one grade level that all the class could understand. Their scholastic abilities ranged from almost zero to quite good, but they were all very interested and eager to learn. Life in the backwoods with little or no contact with the outside world is not stimulating for a bright child, so school was important to them, and no matter what the subject was, nobody ever claimed that they were bored. Despite my complete lack of experience as a teacher, I believe we covered the curriculum quite well that year. One area I worked hard on was reading and writing. I was determined that when those children went to the high school in town, they would read and write as well as any other children. Perhaps better.

But, alas, I had three failures. The first was my little Jani. He was a tiny boy, very immature and permanently unhappy. I suspected that he was underage, but his parents claimed that he was old enough for first grade. One day I got a lift out to their cabin and found Jani's immigrant family, which consisted of two men and three or four women in black headscarves operating the simplest sawmill I had ever seen. They had propped their flatbed truck up on some blocks and were running the saw with a belt from one rear wheel. While the women pushed and pulled the log along a crude saw table and carried away the cut lumber, the men either stood around smoking or gave patently unnecessary orders. One of the men explained that when they had a full load, they would sell it to the planer mill, then go into the forest and find another tree to cut down and turn into lumber. He insisted that they always paid the correct stumpage (logging tax), but I suspected that whenever the ranger was not looking, a windfall or a tempting tree ended up in their crude sawmill.

This man claimed that little Jani was old enough for school, but as he could not produce a birth certificate, I had to accept his word. It was obvious to me that school was just free baby-sitting for this busy family, and for the rest of the winter the little boy trudged the long, lonely logging road to school, often in the dark, sometimes in deep snow, with his bright red, knitted wool cap pulled down over his ears, and his lunch clutched in his hand. He rarely smiled, and not once did he ever speak a word of English.

My second, and most troublesome, failure was Mike, the biggest boy in the school. Mike was about fourteen and big for his age. He was also a bully. Things went well for about a month, but then he began to make trouble in class—he became disruptive, rude, and belligerent, annoying me and the other children, and when they protested, he beat them up after school. A trained and experienced teacher would have been able to handle him, but I was neither, and many times I wished I had not thrown away that piece of fan belt the father had given me. However, I remembered the cane and the strap that I myself had suffered so many times when I was in school back in England and I tried reasoning with the boy. It didn't work. So one day I reached the limit of my patience and sent him home in the middle of the afternoon. That evening I went around to visit his parents.

The family lived a mile away in an old log cabin in the forest. Log cabins may look charming and picturesque on postcards, but in real life they are cold, damp, and gloomy. This one was worse. The bottom logs had rotted away and the walls had sunk into the ground, so I had to step down to get through the badly warped door. I could immediately smell the damp seeping up from the ancient floorboards. The cabin was partitioned into a main room and two bedrooms, and the first thing I saw was a group of adults sitting at the table, drinking cheap red wine from a large bottle. The single oil lamp hanging from the ceiling gave just enough light for me to see a stack of six or seven rifles and shotguns in the corner. They were all different, but they were in beautiful condition and looked well used and well cared for. They must have cost a small fortune. The rest of the room was a tangle of old chairs and clothing and bits of a chain saw that somebody was repairing.

I was greeted cheerfully and offered a glass of wine. The boy's father apologized for his son's behavior, but, despite his assurance that he would "beat the hell out of him when he came home," I don't think he took my complaint about his son's behavior seriously. Suddenly, when a baby began to cry, one of the women reached into a homemade cradle and lifted out a baby that was very white and terribly undernourished. But there was no milk on the stove or on the shelf near it, and only a loaf of bread and a pot of strawberry jam on the table. When the baby cried again, somebody filled a small glass with wine and the mother, still chatting with me, coaxed the baby into drinking half of it.

The trouble-making boy had a younger brother, and when I mentioned how well behaved he was in school, the parents, proudly took me to the door of the bedroom to allow me to say good night to him. I saw two mattresses pushed together on the damp and dirty floor, and, in the gloom I could just make out four or five children, all still clothed, lying under a tangle of blankets. I said good night and made my hurried excuse and left.

When I reached the store, I phoned the superintendent and explained the situation to him. He drove down the next day and arranged for the boy to be moved to another school closer to town. The father would have to provide transportation.

My third failure was equally interesting. There were three Indian boys in my class. They were shy, but friendly and well behaved and terribly poor. The other students tended to tease them a lot, and I often had to break up fights during recess.

One afternoon the eldest of the three told me that his mother wanted to speak to me. She was waiting outside the door and marched in as soon as I nodded. She was an enormous lady, but what was most striking was that one of her eyes was completely crossed, so crossed that I had difficulty talking to her without staring at the peculiar eye.

She shoved a form into my hand and said, "You have to sign this." When I asked what it was, she said, "It says my daughter has finished school."

I read the paper carefully. "No," I told her. "It says that your daughter *is attending school* regularly. But I've never seen her."

The mother snorted impatiently. "She's been too busy. Just sign it, and I can get my money."

I explained that I was not going to sign it until the girl was in my classroom and in fact attending school. The mother stomped out. Next day, the girl appeared. She was a tall, attractive girl, looking much older than what it said on the paper. She was quite mature and completely out of place in my class of little children.

The girl came for a week and did her work well. I thought she was bright enough to go on to high school almost immediately and hoped that she would, but when I complimented her on her work and explained the benefits of a high school education, she told me that she was working as a waitress in a restaurant in town. Her mother took a big chunk of her earnings and just wanted to get more money out of the government. Sure enough, the next day the mother reappeared in my classroom.

"Now you'll sign it," she said as she dropped the form on my desk again.

"Certainly I'll sign it…after your daughter has attended school regularly for…let's say three months."

The mother stomped out of the room, and I never saw her daughter again.

I never did find out where all the children in my class lived. The village was tiny, yet every morning, as if by magic, a crowd of children appeared on my doorstep. One or two were dropped off by parents in pickup trucks, but the rest seem to drift in along various trails through the trees or down the logging roads. I'm sure they lived in shacks and cabins and log houses in the forest, and almost all of them walked long distances to school through all kinds of weather, including deep snow. During the northern winter, they walked both to and from school in the pitch dark.

The students that had to travel the longest distance were a charming little family of two boys and an older sister. They turned up as regular as clockwork. Sometimes they were so early that I had to dash out of my house and let them into the school room while I shaved and had breakfast. These three were French Canadian children with beautiful manners and a lively interest in everything. During lunch break, when everybody ate in the classroom, they often told me about every wild creature that they had seen that morning on their trip to school and described in detail the hawks and blue jays, the moose, the porcupines and coyotes, the deer and rabbits, the bears, and, once or twice, the rarely-seen lynx with his tufted ears.

One afternoon I borrowed a car and gave them a lift home. We drove up the main road for a mile, then turned off on a logging road and followed that for about two miles. Finally, we came to their house in a logged-off clearing. It was extraordinary. Their father had neatly trimmed half a dozen large stumps to exactly the same height and had built a platform on them for his cabin so that it perched high and dry, two feet above the ground. During the summer it caught enough breeze to keep down the mosquitoes, and in the winter the snow built up around the base to insulate the cabin from the frozen ground. Even in spring it was not damp.

The parents were charming and quite flattered that I was paying them a visit. As the mother plied me with cups of hot, very black, sweet tea, the father told me how he made a living trapping and hunting in the winter and logging in the summer. While the children eagerly showed me how they helped prepare the pelts for market, their mother quickly baked up a batch of scones in the wood stove.

When I asked about the distance the children had to walk, their father said, "This is quite a busy road, really. Most days, the kids get a lift on a logging truck down to the main road. I would guess they know all the regular drivers by name." He smiled proudly at his tiny brood, "Anyway, they can handle themselves quite well. No silly old bear is going to scare them. Eh, kids?"

How the people who lived in the forest earned a living was a mystery to me. Only a handful of the adults were full-time loggers. The rest seemed to work when they felt like it or picked up odd jobs wherever they found them. A few had small pension checks, and more than a few did a bit of illegal hunting and fishing. There were also a couple of moonshiners who sold bottles of clear, almost flavorless, home brew. It was powerful stuff that burned all the way down the gullet…it also burned with a clear, blue flame when touched with a match.

One freezing cold night in the middle of winter when the air was absolutely still and the stars were huge and bright, I was visited by the local Mountie, who dropped in to say hello and accepted a cup of coffee. He told me he was looking for moonshiners.

When I asked him how he tracked them down, he smiled and tapped his nose. "I just drive around slowly and stick my nose out the window. If I'm lucky, somebody will be brewing up a batch." Then he pulled on his huge, fur lined gloves and said, "Thanks for the coffee. A night like this is just perfect for sniffing out the illegal manufacture of alcoholic beverages with intent to avoid lawful taxes."

He laughed as he left my house, but he caught nobody that night and although everybody else knew just who was moonshining, I never did.

In one of the houses in the little village there lived an elderly couple from Saskatchewan. They had farmed the immensely flat, lonely, and almost treeless prairie all their lives and had eventually sold everything and moved to British Columbia. Their ambition was to see the sea. After a lifetime in the very heart of the continent, they were dreaming of a cottage on the Pacific shore. But something happened along the way. Their old car broke down, and they stopped to have it fixed in our village, where everybody was so helpful and friendly that they decided they liked it there in the big woods. So they parked the car and bought a house. There were no mountains or even attractive hills near the village, in fact there was no scenery at all, just the endless forest of northern Canada. But they liked it and had been there for fifteen years. They had not yet seen the Pacific Ocean.

Next door to the elderly couple lived a German immigrant with his English wife. He was a mechanic and had met his wife twenty years earlier when he was a prisoner of war in England. They were a very friendly couple and loved gardening. Nobody else had a garden—all the other cabins were surrounded by churned-up ground and bits of abandoned odds and ends—but the German family had a white picket fence, and there was nearly always something blooming. In the fall they coaxed their flowers, from tiny violets to tall irises and bright red lilies, to keep going right up to the first bad frost, when they covered the plants with straw or sawdust and nurtured seedlings in their cabin. By spring they were ready to plant, and in the summer, their little plot was a cloud of color that everybody admired. But nobody else ever copied them.

That spring, they had a seven-feet-high wire trellis of sweet peas that was a solid wall of gorgeous color that was dazzling against the dark firs. I asked them how they did it.

The English lady laughed. "Well, the outhouse fills up eventually," she said, "so he gets to dig a new hole right next to it and we shift the loo over a bit. Then he's got the little job of cleaning out the old hole, and we use that for fertilizer for our sweet peas. Been doing it for years, and it always works a treat."

I soon learned that the nearest beer parlor was ten miles away. Occasionally some of the men of the village talked about starting a branch of the Canadian Legion. Now the Legion is supposed to be an ex-servicemen's club, but in many communities it is merely an excuse to obtain a license to sell beer and have an exclusive beer parlor. The German spoke to a few people the winter I was there. I thought it was a good idea, too. When he wrote to Legion headquarters for permission, they wanted to know just how many ex-servicemen there were in the area. We took a survey and discovered that the membership would consist entirely of one ex-RAF member and one ex-Luftwaffe member. Our application was, alas, refused.

There were quite a few odd characters in the village. One parent was the shyest man I have ever met. He used to stand at the schoolhouse door, tall and thin and stoop-shouldered. When I persuaded him to come in, he sat on the edge of a chair, twisting his hands and mumbling one-word answers to anything I said. His son was doing very well, and he was obviously proud of his little boy, but there was no way I could get him to relax and talk to me.

Except when he'd had a drink. One beer produced a magical transformation, and the painfully shy man turned into a laughing, back-slapping fellow eager for another beer. Unfortunately, the next beer and the one after that turned him into a foul mouthed, aggressive, trouble-seeker with an urge to punch somebody or anybody. Since everybody knew what this man was like at every stage of inebriation, he was usually watched carefully and quickly dragged away from fights and taken home to sleep it off. Next morning, he was always his usual shy self and had quite forgotten the night before.

About five miles away, near the river, a couple of young Englishmen had started a farm on a few acres of rich bottom land. They were "back to nature" enthusiasts and used no chemical fertilizers, and they even had a huge horse that they used instead of a tractor for plowing. They were good farmers and produced a wide variety of vegetables, both root and leaf crops, and everything they grew was bigger and better than anything available in the supermarkets in the nearest town. Unfortunately, however, they were not good businessmen. The year I was there, when they took samples of their produce into town in the fall to show to the supermarket managers, they were turned away.

"Yes," they were told, "you have excellent produce and your prices are attractively low, and, yes, the stuff we get from California is terrible by the time it reaches us. But we have contracts with our wholesalers. You can only supply us for about two months in the fall. For the rest of the year, our wholesalers will punish us by sending us only their worst stuff."

Their fields were full of first class, chemical-free vegetables that they could not sell. Their next idea was to rent a storefront and sell their produce themselves, but the supermarkets heard about their plan and persuaded the town council to refuse them a license to retail food until they had complied with a long list of health and safety regulations, many of which required expensive equipment. They next tried to set up a farmers market and got together a few other small farmers. But still under pressure from the supermarkets, the town council again refused them a permit. Eventually, rather than let their beautiful vegetables rot in the fields, they placed an ad in the local paper and sold their crops at a few dollars per car trunk-load. For a week or two, there was a steady stream of people driving up from the farm with their trunks loaded with fresh vegetables. But as winter fell, the two young farmers took their giant horse and went logging.

Meanwhile, back at the school, things were going so well that we decided to have a Halloween party. All the children brought cakes and cookies and other sticky stuff, and we spent the morning making spooky masks and decorations out of my limited art supplies. We spent the afternoon trading and eating their goodies and generally having fun. I was, of course, the school janitor as well as the teacher, so when it was time to go home I looked at the floor covered in squashed cake and cookies, I said, half to myself, "How am I going to clean up this mess?"

There was general silence, and then one little girl said, "The dogs!" The children immediately dashed out the door and into the village and came back with every one of the scruffy dogs that seemed to loiter around every cabin. Within minutes, the skinny beasts were happily licking up every crumb. They left the place spotless.

Next to the village store stood a large, partly completed building. One day I asked the storekeeper about it.

"That was supposed to be the village hall," he said. "It got started but never got finished. Just too many arguments and no cooperation. The lumber's still stacked behind my place."

At the time I was thinking about some kind of show or pageant that the children could perform for their parents, but the schoolroom was too small. After hearing about the unfinished village hall, I spoke to the service station owner and a couple other people, then we took a look at the building material. Everything was there, even the huge wood stove. The service station owner began speaking to everybody who came in for gasoline, and suddenly the hall building project took off. Within days, men carrying hammers appeared from out of nowhere, and some evenings there were six or seven of us working away. My job was to toe-nail floorboards on the diagonal, something I already knew how to do. Most of the other volunteers had built their own homes, so the simple, one-room hall went up quickly. To crown our achievement, the service station owner put in electric lights and ran a line across to his garage, where he had a small generator.

One of the mothers turned out to be a born organizer. She made sure that the hall had a small stage at the far end and that someone dug a deep hole for the toilet. She also insisted on a "two seater" so that little children would have company when doing their business. When this mother heard my plans for a Christmas concert, she took over completely and organized everything, even finding somebody with hidden artistic skill to paint a beautiful mural of Bethlehem on paper to tack to the wall. She also rehearsed the children in their carols. All the women worked enthusiastically on costumes, and, needless to say, the whole thing went off wonderfully. The children remembered their parts and sang enthusiastically, and it seemed like every adult for twenty miles around turned up to applaud.

Watching from the back of the hall, I felt a great pride in my students. That's when I began to think about becoming a teacher.

I was not just the teacher and janitor at that one-room school. I was also the school nurse. I learned to clean up a cut and slap on a band-aid quite efficiently. Fortunately, the children were so healthy that I needed no other skills.

One day a real nurse drove up to give the students a shot for something. She was a pretty, little, Japanese Canadian woman, and the children were fascinated by her. But they were leery about taking a needle. The nurse was beginning to get a bit frustrated when she had an idea. "I'll prove it doesn't hurt," she said. "Just watch Mr. Fulford. I'm going to give him his shot, and he'll smile all the time."

She glared at me until I sat up from where I was lounging in my chair and said, "Oh, sure. Yes, indeed. I bet I don't feel a thing," and rolled up my sleeve. It did hurt a little, but I smiled widely at the class. Roaring with laughter, the children immediately lined up for their shots. I forgot to ask what I'd been inoculated against.

As the teacher I was also the person in charge of any federal, provincial, or county voting. More than once, I sat alone in the empty schoolroom with a pile of ballots and the ballot box, waiting through the dark evening until exactly eight o'clock, when I carefully sealed the empty box. The only people who ever came by were those who were curious when they saw the light on so late.

I was also the best person to come to when a form needed explaining or a signature needed a witness, and, occasionally, I was asked for legal advice. Fortunately, there was nothing too complex, as most of the villagers had a better business sense than I had.

One day the superintendent turned up quite unexpectedly to see how I was getting on. He was a mild-spoken Scotsman who had strong opinions and wide experience. I had taken off my jacket during class and hung it on the back of my chair, but he said nothing until recess.

Then, "I would like you to always wear a jacket and tie during working hours," he said. "You're probably wondering why." I nodded. "Well, first, you're the only man for thirty miles who owns a jacket and tie." He smiled, then added, "If you want to work with these people, you have to have their respect, and the best way you can earn their respect is do a good job with their children. And dress properly. Out here, your jacket and tie will impress a lot of people." At the time, I found it just an irritation, but as the days went by, I found his advice to be quite sound.

Just after Easter, I went to a meeting of all the one-room-school teachers in the district. I had often had the feeling that I was all alone out there in the woods, so I was quite surprised to find that I was one of about twenty teachers. But I was also the odd one out. Almost all the others were middle-aged ladies, sturdily built and with an air of practical self-sufficiency about them, whereas I was quite the opposite. They were pleasant and cheerful and very down to earth, and most of them had taught in one room schools for years. Over coffee and cookies, we discussed many issues, but most interesting was another young man who had been placed in an extremely isolated school. The loneliness had eventually beaten him down, and he had fled to Vancouver over Easter, vowing never to come back.

Several of the ladies looked at me, and one said, "How about you, John? Got cabin fever yet?"

I was happy to assure them that I was enjoying myself and was not liable to go scampering over the hill.

When I mention the one-room school, most people immediately ask about the winter "up north." They are usually surprised to hear that deep snow was rarely a problem. During my year at the one-room school, they got more snow in Chicago in one week than we did all winter. The problem where we lived was that when it snowed, the wind blew it into high drifts that often blocked the roads and piled up around cabin doors. That's why everybody carried snow shovels in the back of their pickups.

The depressing part of winter was the dark. When the sun did not rise before ten o'clock and set about two in the afternoon, I had to keep the propane lights burning almost all day. The nights seemed—and in fact were—awfully long. For entertainment, I had only a battery-powered radio, but I ran an antenna up a tree and got some surprising results. Reception varied widely and seemed to depend on the weather, but at times I could pick up stations from immense distances away. There was a San Francisco station that came in clear as a bell and an American military station in Korea that also came in quite clearly. The BBC Foreign Service drifted in and out, and, with careful tuning, I could often pick up strange foreign stations. When the weather was wrong, of course, I was stuck with the local radio station, which played an endless stream of monotonous country music and wailing cowboy songs. Even the announcer got bored. He livened up the programming with special "news breaks" that consisted mainly of such earth-shattering announcements as "Pete Zimmerman reports a black and white cow wandering along the road near Luke Hogan's place. Luke says he don't have no cows, but he'll take care of it until the owner picks it up." Or "May Bloomberg has a nice propane fridge she'd like to donate to a worthy cause. Just phone me for the details." Fortunately, I didn't have to depend entirely on the radio. I have always been an avid reader of just about anything, and the storekeeper kept a good supply of magazines, mainly for me.

The winter cold was another matter. Most of the time, the temperature was manageable but, all too often, a cold spell came down from the north. The sky became crystal clear and the stars sparkled wickedly as the temperature plunged. After a few days at thirty below zero, everything was completely frozen. At night, I often heard the sharp snap of trees splitting as their sap froze, and off in the distance the coyotes were howling in chorus. I had bought a good parka with a hood and had fur lined gloves and thick woolen socks, but the cold still sneaked in everywhere, and I soon found that when I lost feeling in my cheeks and my boots were so frozen they no longer flexed, it was time to seek shelter. One day I was helping the English farmers water their horse at a small lake. It was frozen hard enough for the horse to walk on, so I swung an axe to crack the ice. The axe merely bounced. It took us half an hour with crowbars to punch a hole through ice two feet thick down to the water. When we hauled up a bucket of water for the horse, it began to freeze before he had drunk it all.

Those who didn't have propane had oil barrel heaters that were simply old oil drums resting horizontally on iron legs with a door at one end and a chimney at the other. There was a layer of sand on the bottom of the heater to prevent it from melting, and it was fed with the biggest chunks of wood that would fit through the door. Fancy ones had a metal ledge on top to keep the coffee pot hot, and many had a protective railing around them for safety, because they could get very hot. The rails were also a handy drying rack. Many a time I stopped at a café or store to find the barrel stove glowing bright red. When it got really cold, that red glow became a source of pride for the storekeeper. The chimney usually led through the wall into another room to spread the heat around, but where it passed through the wall, it needed a special metal insulating ring so that the wall would not catch fire. Those heaters caused many a tragic fire, but they sure were a welcome sight on a cold night.

The loggers liked the winter. The ground was hard, there were no insects, there was no danger of forest fire, and they could drive their huge vehicles across swamps and lakes with no worries. "Beautiful weather!" they always exclaimed. "And a little bit of hard work keeps you nice and warm."

Spring breakup was the worst time. When the snow melted and the ground began to thaw, the world turned into a sea of mud. All activity came to a halt and, unless they were solidly paved, all the roads turned into rivers of astonishingly deep mud. I spent the better part of each day helping my students scrape the sticky muck off their boots and piling them by the door. They loved my rule that they had to walk around my classroom in their socks.

During the winter, the logging companies painstakingly built ice roads across the lakes by constantly spraying water on the road thus created. During spring breakup, the thinner lake ice melted first, forcing the big logging trucks to abandon the ice road, which was left rather like a floating bridge. It was often tempting to make one last run across the lake instead of making a miles-long detour around it, and many a pickup truck driver made the gamble. Over the years, quite a few lost. The spring I was there, nobody was drowned, but I heard of at least two unhappy drivers who left their vehicles at the bottom of a very cold lake.

One holiday (I forget which one it was) I met somebody who

was planning a quick trip to Vancouver. It was a long way to drive, but we shared the driving and the road was well plowed. I had a wonderful time in the beautiful city with its mild climate, and the return trip was uneventful until my friend dropped me off at the side of the main road near my village. The problem was that we could not be sure that we were in the right place. I had made an educated guess. It was past midnight and pitch dark, except for a little starlight. The snowplow had banked the snow high on each side of the road, and there was almost nothing to see except mile after mile of black forest, each mile identical to the last. I stood there in the dark and yelled at the top of my voice, but no light appeared. It was bitterly cold and it could be hours before another car came along. I had to guess which way to walk.

I chose north. After about a hundred yards, I felt the soft snow harden as if a truck had run over it. I turned left and slowly groped my way west and slammed into a telephone pole. I knew we had two phones in the village, so I marched down the lane until I stumbled into a high drift of fresh snow. I was wet and miserable by the time I had waded and scrambled through the drift, but I had also worked out where I was. Soon I found my house. I guess they had had a blizzard while I was gone, because the snow was banked high against my only door. I knew that my snow shovel was inside and that all my windows were locked. If I was wet and miserable before, I was colder, wetter, and more miserable after I finished clearing a way through the drift with my gloved hands and a piece of board I somehow found. It took the rest of the night to dry out and warm up. I sat huddled on the floor in front of the heater, wrapped in my heaviest blanket and vowing to buy the biggest flashlight in the store just as soon as it was open. It was a cold welcome home to my little house.

Just after our first real blizzard, somebody decided to have a party in the new hall. I don't remember why, but nobody needed an excuse for a party. Some of the ladies got together and organized it. I arrived that evening wearing a clean shirt and a tie under my parka and found everybody dressed up in their best. The three-man orchestra consisted of a man who could do wonders with his very large accordion and never seemed to get tired, and an old but very lively fiddler, accompanied by his son who frowned seriously but also played the fiddle well. The place was packed, the electric lights were blazing, the huge barrel heater was putting out more than enough heat, and the storekeeper was selling soft drinks at a furious pace.

Outside, the snow had been shoveled back from the building into a high wall. The first thing I noticed were the dozens of little pigeon holes poked into the snow. The ladies had decreed that no alcohol could be consumed in the hall, but all the men had brought bottles, which were all stashed in the snow bank. Everybody seemed to know where his bottle was, and small groups of men stood out in the bitter cold, passing their bottles around while the women enjoyed themselves inside.

The orchestra played mostly lively country music and everybody danced. Small children danced with each other, ladies danced with each other, and, when there was a waltz, a couple of old-timers showed off their skills. Every time one of the drinkers came in to warm himself up, he was grabbed and dragged onto the dance floor. Surprisingly, many of the men turned out to be good dancers. I myself was much in demand and managed to stumble my way through plenty of dances, helped by the fact that it was so crowded that there was little room to maneuver.

What made the party a success was that it was a very rare opportunity for the women to get out of their everyday blue jeans and dress up in their best, plus a touch of makeup and plenty of jewelry.

Despite the hard drinking going on outside, there were no fights and few arguments. Some teen-age boys wrote their names in the snow, but nothing major happened until the intermission when the ladies were selling cookies and homemade cakes. Suddenly there was a wild yell and the painfully shy parent burst through the door, ran down the hall, leaped up to one of the ceiling crossbeams, and swung there, laughing like a maniac. It was quite a jump, and I was ready to applaud, but the crowd failed to appreciate his acrobatic skills. Eventually, he dropped down into the arms of a couple of large men, who took him outside to cool off in a snow bank.

My first year of teaching came to its end at last. We survived the mud of the spring break-up and tiny flowers appeared in the woods. The English lady's sweet peas blossomed in a riot of color. The three little Indian boys accompanied me on walks in the forest and showed me things that I would never have seen had I gone alone, like the giant porcupine hiding under a log and the young deer hiding in the thickets and the squirrels scuttling through the branches. The birds appeared after the long winter, and green things sprouted everywhere. I bought an old Pontiac that the service station owner assured me would run for years and explored the countryside, bouncing down logging roads and creeping along rough trails to lonely lakes, where I tried my luck fishing, with little luck but lots of pleasure. The days lengthened and soon it was almost summer.

I spent Easter doing paperwork, and all too soon the year was over and the superintendent paid me another visit. He spent some time going over my paperwork, then asked me, "How do you think you did?"

I thought for a bit. "I like teaching. I think I did a pretty good job, considering my lack of experience."

He nodded his head and said, "Well, you seem to have what it takes, but you need the training. Experience just comes with time." He paused, then added, "It was good to have you here. When you get back to UBC, you may want to consider switching to a teaching course. Maybe I'll see you back up here some day,"

We shook hands, and a few days later I drove off back to Vancouver. I have never been back to that one-room school.

That year I switched over to an education major, and even though it meant an extra year, I found that I was not only a good teacher but I also enjoyed teaching. After graduation, I taught at the high school level, but over the years I found that the elementary students were more fun and more receptive than their bigger brothers and sisters. What I was most seriously interested in was teaching English to students who spoke some other language, and so I began to specialize in ESL, English as a Second Language. I have always remembered little Jani and my failure to get him to speak even one word of English.

Chapter 29
Mountain School

After I graduated with my B.Ed. degree and planned to settle down in Vancouver, I applied to the Vancouver School District for a teaching position. I hoped to find a little house and perhaps find a pretty girl to marry. I was determined that all the wandering was behind me now. I was going to put down roots.

But it was not to be. The school district had a rule that they would not hire any teacher who did not have at least two years' experience. I had to look for a teaching job out of town.

My choice was a small town in the mountains near the source of the Columbia River. I decided on that area not because it is very beautiful country and the pay scale was attractive but because of the Doukhobors. This is a Christian religious sect that originated in Russia, an extremely fundamental group that rejects all organized religion, all civil government, and even the Bible. They were severely persecuted in Russia and about a hundred years ago, with the help of Leo Tolstoy, they migrated to Canada, where one group found fertile land in the valleys near the headwaters of the Columbia. Hoping to avoid the modern world, they settled in small, isolated communities that still spoke Russian.

But the world came to them. Roads and railroads were cut through their land, Minerals were discovered, and loggers eyed their forests as greedy land speculators brought in their lawyers. The problem was that the title to the land held by the Doukhobors was not well documented and the land was held in common by individual groups. Both federal and provincial governments refused to support the transplanted Russians because they paid almost no taxes, and, when the Doukhobors tried to use civil disobedience by taking their children out of school to bring attention to their plight, the Mounties were called in. Many Doukhobor children were placed in a prison camp.

I was very interested in studying how the Russian-speaking Doukhobors handled the English language, so I was pleased to find that I was to teach English at the junior high school level. On my first day in class, however, I was astonished to find that my entire class was Doukhobor. Somebody had dumped all of them into one class. When I discussed this situation with the other teachers, I discovered that the superintendent (a strange little man) had ordered that every student in the district be given the same IQ test. It was a cheap, four-page, badly-designed thing that the teachers considered a joke. The superintendent massaged the results into a perfect bell curve, which he proudly showed to the school board, the members of which knew absolutely nothing about IQ tests or bell-shaped curves.

"The superintendent," said the school secretary when the principal was not listening, "has decreed that the district's bell shaped graph is sacrosanct!" Then she smiled and added, "None of you teachers can give a grade this year more than one grade higher or more than one grade lower than what's on his silly graph!" And, "Right through the district, all the students are permanently stuck at their grade level."

There was a stunned silence until somebody asked, "You mean that a C student could never get an A? No matter how hard he works? And an A student could slack off the whole year and I couldn't give him lower than a B?"

She nodded her head. "You've got it right."

We were horrified, but our principal was a hopeless incompetent who was terrified of the superintendent and refused to discuss the matter. The students, who all spoke reasonably good English, knew all about the ludicrous system, too, and when I introduced myself to my new class, I was greeted by, "Hi, Mister Fulford. We're the dummies!"

Because of the way the IQ test was written, students who did not have an excellent grasp of the English language, such as my students, were at a serious disadvantage. Since their mother tongue was Russian, the Doukhobor children all scored quite low. I tried to assure them that they were as good as any other student in the district, but they didn't believe me. I concentrated, therefore, on improving their English as best I could. They all spoke English quite well in school, but among themselves and at home, they spoke a form of Russian that had been so badly degraded by isolation and lack of formal education for nearly a century that it was hard for a modern Russian speaker to understand. The local high school offered a Russian language course, and I heard that it was difficult for the Doukhobor students to adjust to correct, modern Russian.

Canada's third language, after English and French, is Ukrainian. Many Ukrainians arrived in Canada at the end of the 19th century and settled mainly on the prairies. The high school Russian teacher was a Ukrainian from northern Alberta who had had to learn modern Russian.

The students were a lively but friendly bunch. I struggled to learn all their names, twisting my tongue around Sherstobitoff and Sherstovikov and, thanks to a lot of intermarriage, sorting out one Popov from another. When they discovered that I was genuinely interested in Doukhobor history and their way of life, some of them cautiously suggested that I might want to come meet their parents. Doukhobor women nearly always wore the babushka headscarf. When the women are young, they are very attractive, with their perfect complexions and shy smiles. However, the good food that they prepared so well, like their delicious borscht, soon went to their hips, making almost all the adult women very large indeed.

Academically, it was not a good year. We teachers did our best, but we seemed to get sabotaged at every turn by the crazy super-intendent or the extraordinarily useless principal, both of whom seemed to think that they could control every little aspect of our work, even our private lives and our activities after school. I loved teaching and enjoyed my students, who made good progress that year despite being the "dummies," but I was deeply disappointed to find that teaching was not quite what I had expected. "Welcome to the real world of stupid administrators," I told myself, and then I carried on the best I could.

The school was brand new and had been built either by the lowest bidder or somebody who had a friend on the school board. Within a month, the floors started to buckle and doors to stick. The rooms lacked sufficient shelves and cupboards, and when winter set in, the building leaked heat and allowed cold air in everywhere. The worst fault was the inadequate plumbing. The students soon figured out that if they blocked the toilets first thing in the morn-ing, the principal would call the school buses and they could all go home. They did this for three days running until the superintendent shipped up a pair of portable toilets, set them right in front of the main door, and warned the students that if they blocked the sewers again they would have to use the portables.

They had built the school on the side of a hill where the road was quite steep. This was no problem…except on those days when a sheet of ice covered the road. Then the climb up was a wheel spinning adventure, and the drive down was one long slide, often sideways. Quite often, a school bus failed to make it up the hill and the students had to walk. I always carried two sacks of sand in the trunk of my car, along with a snow shovel.

There were only two places to have a beer in town. One was the beer parlor, the other, the Canadian Legion Hall. The superintendent turned up at the beer parlor one day and proclaimed, "I forbid any of you, especially the ladies, from frequenting this beer parlor. I have arranged for you to be honored guests at the Legion. That's the only place for respectable people to have a drink."

So one evening four or five of us went to the Legion Hall. We had hardly settled down when a fight erupted at a nearby table. Then beer splashed across the floor, and soon three or four drunks were trying vainly to punch each other's noses. The next time we went out, we went back to the beer parlor, where the female teachers greatly enjoyed the stares of the loggers and mill workers, and where, under the watchful eye of a huge bartender, everything was pleasantly quiet.

The little town had no library or cinema, and the TV could only pick up one or two stations that showed nothing worth watching. It was a very boring place, and if it were not for my interest in the Doukhobors and exploring the surrounding countryside, I would have gone crazy. As it was, there were times when I had to drive down to Vancouver to keep my sanity. This meant a drive up and over three major mountain passes but when the road was clear it was no problem, and I always enjoyed the fantastic scenery along the lonely road. In the fall, the deciduous trees were a blaze of color against the dark firs, in the winter the snow-covered mountainsides were right out of a holiday calendar, and in the spring the new green buds and the blossom were a delight. Once or twice in the spring, I detoured through the Okanagan Valley just to admire the acres of glorious fruit blossom and breathe in the heady scents.

When the roads were icy or the snowplows had not been by, crossing those mountains could be hazardous. More than once, I slid into the ditch and had to wait for somebody to help haul me out. I bought a set of chains, but I always waited until the last minute to put them on. Lying under the car in the snow and the dark, fiddling with cold chains with my frozen fingers, and holding a small flashlight in my mouth was not exactly fun. Inevitably, as soon as the chains were on, I would reach a clear stretch and have to take them off before they broke.

In a two-room elementary school far up the valley were two Australian teachers, neither of whom had ever seen snow. One Saturday they heard that it had snowed high up in one of the passes, so they persuaded me to drive them up to see the fascinating white stuff. For over an hour the two young women frolicked happily, throwing snowballs and taking photos. That winter was one of the worst on record, and blizzard followed blizzard for weeks on end, so that just getting to their school was a major operation for the Australian girls. One evening when we all got together at somebody's place for a little party, only one of the girls turned up.

"Where's your pal?" somebody asked.

"In bed," she replied. "When we get home in the evening, she eats, then goes right to bed and hides her head under the blankets. Says she hates snow so much she isn't going to come out until every last drop has melted." She smiled wryly, then added, "Can't say I blame her. It is bloody horrible stuff."

The snow brought many challenges to the area. The tiny local airport was often closed, so our mail had to come in by truck, which meant it was often days late. Sometimes roofs collapsed under the snow. The snow often packed up in huge lumps on the main street of the town. When this happened, the city fathers, in their wisdom, borrowed the giant snow blower from the airport and proceeded to clear the street. With disastrous results. Traffic had packed the snow into icy chunks, and the blower simply picked up the chunks of ice and slammed them through the windows of all the stores along the street. It looked like a war zone and there was a mad panic to contact insurance companies and buy plywood to cover the exposed windows.

The snow kept falling. When one of my boys mentioned snowshoes, I found that all of them had snowshoes at home, so I organized a competition in which my class challenged all the other classes. Walking on snowshoes, especially the wide "bear paw" type, is an acquired skill. My students were very skilled, of course, and won quite handily. But when it came to the teachers' race, it was a different matter. None of us had the faintest idea how to walk on snowshoes, and soon the field was a tangle of fallen bodies and flailing arms at which the students cheered and roared with laughter. The day was a great success.

One day a Mountie stopped by after school for a little chat with me. It seemed that three of my boys were often absent on different days of the week, and a pattern had emerged. They were called into the principal's office, and very soon what was happening became clear. On weekends, the trio went out searching the forest for a suitable tree in a good location. Then, during the week, one of them would take his father's chainsaw, fell the tree, cut it into lengths, and remove all the branches. Next day, another student would borrow his father's pickup truck and haul the lengths of tree out to the roadside and hide it. The third student was the ring leader. He had contacts in a local sawmill and arranged for the logs to be picked up. He received the hard cash from the truck driver and shared out the money with his two buddies. It was a smooth operation. They had been doing it for months before the school secretary noticed a pattern in their absenteeism.

After the boys had been taken away, the principal went on a sanctimonious rant about the criminal minds among the Doukhobor. But I saw it otherwise.

"You know," I told him, "that's pretty sharp for fourteen-year-old boys. Maybe we should persuade them to take lots of business classes when they get to high school. They've got real potential." The principal snorted. "That's if they ever get to high school. I'll make damn sure they never get there!" I never saw the boys again.

Whenever I had time and the weather was good, I drove around the countryside tracking down Doukhobor families and snapping pictures of their unique communal houses. I got quite passionate about the subject, and it wasn't long before people began to recognize me. The normally uncommunicative adults began to talk a little. Many of my students also invited me home, and I shared quite a few cups of sweet black tea with adults who were slightly suspicious, but extremely polite. Although they refused to talk about their religion, they were more than glad to explain all the details of the huge communal houses.

When they had first arrived in the 19th century, the settlers had built family-centered communal housing. Life was hard, and every pair of hands was valuable, so cooperation was paramount. The architecture of the houses followed a fairly rigid pattern. Two large, square, two-story, wooden houses sat slightly apart to form the back of a rectangle of attached single-story houses and storage sheds. Although there was a wide entrance facing the road or lane, the square of buildings had a medieval defensive look about it, as if it were protecting itself against intruders or the weather. The two houses were supposed to be the men's house and the women's house, but the sexes were not strictly segregated. Early marriage was encouraged and married couples lived in either house. Dining was communal, and the work was shared by everybody. The smaller houses were for the old and infirm or for newly married couples.

Children lived with their parents, but were very much part of the communal system. Education was minimal and simple. One of the large houses had a meeting hall on the ground floor with rows of simple wooden benches. For a few hours a day, this was the school room, but its main purpose was as a religious meeting hall. The Doukhobors never built churches or even little chapels. The meeting hall was completely bare, with neither candles nor pictures nor flowers to interfere with contemplation and prayer. Half a dozen oil lamps hung from the bare wooden ceiling, and there was neither altar nor pulpit. The men sat on one side and took off their hats. The women sat on the other and covered their heads, Russian style, with scarves.

There were at least a dozen such houses scattered widely up and down the valley, and there were others in neighboring valleys, The pairs of large houses that looked rather like cubes with pointed roofs on them were easy to spot, but sometimes hard to get to. Very often, they were almost abandoned, with just one or two families living in the smaller houses. The original settlers had also built sawmills.

The houses were solidly constructed, each with a small dormer window in the roof for an emergency exit when the snow piled high around the doors and windows. The inside walls were lath and plaster, which was made from local clay mixed with straw, an ancient and practical method, but one that led non-Russians to claim that the Doukhobors plastered their walls with horse manure.

I wandered through quite a few old buildings, but there was usually nothing in the rooms but dust and cobwebs. An old timer often appeared and warned me about rotten floorboards or missing steps on the very steep staircases. One day, one of my students took me up into an attic crammed with old tools and ancient kitchen utensils, where he showed me how to operate a hand-cranked apple peeler, and I showed him how to use the draw knife and the adze. In the corner sat a well-used spinning wheel. It was in excellent condition, and my student said that I could have it if I wanted, but I had no room in my tiny apartment, so we left it there in the corner.

Another day, when another student offered to show me the old flumes, we drove for miles up a rough road into the mountains. We stopped and got out where some old planks of wood lay at the side of the road. One of the first things the pioneer settlers had done was to provide water to irrigate their crops during the long hot summers. For this purpose, my student told me, they had painstakingly built a series of wooden troughs that twisted and turned down from the mountains to their fields and orchards. Hauling the thick planks from their sawmill on the river and anchoring them firmly against the winter storms and the spring floods had obviously been a huge task. The constant maintenance must also have been a major problem, but the flumes had worked well and had lasted for years until the whole communal system began to fall apart.

Some say it was religious differences, with charismatic leaders dividing the community. Others say it was the inevitable pressure of the modern world as English-speaking strangers settled in their valleys. Still others say the Doukhobors were the victims of ruthless land speculators, clever lawyers, and a hostile government. Whatever the reason, more and more Doukhobors left the big houses and took paid jobs or farmed their own little plots. But they still remained members of the Doukhobor sect.

I became quite good at spotting Doukhobor farms and private houses. Because their religion frowned on ostentation and unnecessary frivolity, their houses were usually unpainted and severely functional. They used cars and pickup trucks, but they bought only the basic model without a radio and removed the chrome hubcaps and all the decorative trim. The women wore long, dark skirts and white head scarves, while the men tended to wear black and never wore ties.

Toward the end of the school year, I contacted the *Canadian Geographic Magazine* and suggested an article about the Doukhobor houses. Although they were quite eager to see what I had and wanted to look at my photos, with one thing and another, I never got around to finishing the article and the photos got lost somewhere in the many boxes of photos and slides that I have accumulated over the years.

A little after Easter during my year there, my landlady, a large Doukhobor woman who delighted in bringing me bowls of extraordinarily tasty borscht, suggested that I might like to go to a religious meeting. She knew of my interest, though she was still rather hesitant to speak. "Just go by yourself," she said. "Don't take anybody with you. And please don't talk to anybody about it."

I agreed, and well past sunset one evening, I drove out to one of the few old communal houses that were still occupied. I followed the small crowd from the parking area into the meeting hall, where I found a corner of a bench in the back row of the men's side. There were a few oil lamps burning, but the room was not brightly lit. There was no minister and no apparent service. Nobody crossed themselves, and there was no kneeling or standing, either, just a tightly packed room with rows of people sitting facing a blank wall. Suddenly, a man stood and faced the congregation and began to speak quietly in Russian. Then, after a few minutes he sat down again, and the whole congregation broke into song.

It was obviously a well-loved hymn, and the men's deep voices and the women's higher voices blended easily in the slow, serious,

Russian church music. When the hymn ended, there was a long silence as the echoes died away, then another man rose and spoke for a while. Again the congregation, without any noticeable leadership, sang another hymn, perfectly and precisely. There was no attempt at polyphony, just plain, heartfelt, communal singing of the hymns their grandparents had sung in Russia so many years ago. It was beautiful.

The entire service consisted of individuals speaking in Russian for a short while, following by congregational singing. I didn't understand a word of what was said, but the music was so amazing that I just sat there, soaking it all in. Some of the hymns were quite lively and cheerful, while others were sad and sung slowly, but nobody in the entire congregation needed a book of any kind. The magical night flew by until, at midnight, everybody just stood up and left.

I sat for a while in the corner, trying not to look like an intruder, then made my way out into the cold night with the stars brilliant in the sky. It had been an extraordinary experience, one that I could never forget.

At the end of the school year, almost all the teachers in my school quit. I headed back to Vancouver with a sigh of relief, and I have never been back to that small town in its deep valley. After I was hired by the Vancouver school district, I tried again to settle down. I found a good apartment near the beach, bought some bits of furniture, and looked up all my university friends. Sitting on the beach soon became boring, however, so I explored Vancouver and its suburbs, and then I explored Victoria and Vancouver Island. Next I drove down to Seattle to visit my brother and explore that city. That was the first summer in many years when I didn't have a job that called for hard labor. I could just relax and enjoy myself. It felt strange.

Chapter 30
Teaching Law

In the fall I reported to my new high school (a step up, I thought, from the junior high school of the previous year). It was a large, two-story building in an affluent part of Vancouver, and one of the first things I noticed was that the students' cars were all more expensive than the teachers'. It was a well equipped school with a print shop, a woodworking shop, an electrical shop, and a large automobile shop, where, I found out later, many of the teachers had their cars tuned up.

I reported to the vice principal and was handed my assignment, which, to my horror, included three classes of business law. I had been assured that I would teach some social studies, but mainly English, and when I said, "Law! I don't know anything about law!" the vice principal, a giant of a man, looked down at me and said coldly, "You're a teacher, aren't you?"

The next few days I scurried around to law students I had known at the university and asked a hundred questions and borrowed a ton of books. But, still, I was far from ready when the first day of school dawned.

All my classes were jam-packed. Some of the students even had to perch on the radiators, there were so many of them. As I soon learned, they were all seniors looking for a snap course to finish their schooling. To add to my misery, the textbook was thirty years old and, according to my lawyer friends, completely out of date, so the first few weeks were a nightmare as I fumbled along. Fortunately, the students were well behaved and very patient with me, and I gradually put the text aside and tried to bring the law down to the level of 1960s teenagers. As I relaxed and involved the students more in class discussions, I began to take an interest in the subject.

The students also began to see how the law affected them almost every day. At first, they only wanted to know how to get out of paying a traffic ticket and were a trifle annoyed when I simply said, "Pay the damn thing and drive properly." This led to discussions about the problems involved in buying a car, new or second-hand. They all had cars, and they had all signed, at one time or another, some type of contract. For that reason, we were soon digging quite deeply into the intricacies of contract law. Because many of them were involved in "garage bands" and were writing their own music, we next discussed copyright law. I was not surprised to find that many of them knew more about copyright law than I did. They showed no interest in the Magna Carta or the makeup and duties of the Supreme Court, but they were extremely interested in their liability in case of an accident on the ski run.

One cold winter day I found my classes almost empty. When I asked where everybody was, the students still in the room pointed out of the window at the fresh snow gleaming on the mountains over on the North Shore.

"There they are," they laughed. "On the ski slopes."

Next day, the classes were full again…and many of the students had suspiciously sunburned faces. It was about that time that I was discussing my students in the staff lounge when an older teacher said, "You realize, of course, that a lot of your students have parents who are lawyers?" When I looked surprised, he added, "Yes. Many of those kids are aiming to go to law school as soon as they graduate. I just hope you have your facts right."

For the next few days I worried about just what they had been telling their parents about me. Up to then, there had been no complaints.

The really big complaint came late in the year. I had had the brilliant idea of sending all my students, all 120 of them, down to the law courts to spend a day sitting in both civil and criminal courts and witnessing the process at first hand. I took this step because I had taken a rough survey of my law classes and been astonished to find that almost none of them had ever been in any courtroom, so I had made up a list and divided everybody up, told them where to go, and set a date.

I was feeling quite pleased with myself when, a day before the field trip, the vice principal summoned me to his office. His face was red as he shouted, "How could you? What kind of a silly game are you playing? I'd like to fire you right on the spot!"

For a moment, I just stood there. When I regained my voice, I tried to explain that it was a well-planned field trip that fit right into the curriculum, but he ignored me and continued to shout and threaten me with instant dismissal. I didn't like the man so I stood my ground, and eventually he explained that he had been visited by a very prominent lawyer who was also a very important person in Vancouver. That worthy had marched into the principal's office and demanded that I be fired on the spot. The principal, of course, had passed the buck to the VP. It seems that the "very important citizen" was involved in a messy divorce battle that had been in all the papers during the summer.

The decision was due on the very day that I had chosen for my field trip. Said citizen had insisted that I had done it on purpose and was preparing to pack the divorce court with my students, one of whom just happened to be his daughter.

For the next ten minutes, I tried to explain to the vice principal that I had been down in Seattle with my brother during the summer when the papers had enjoyed themselves with the details of the citizen's divorce. I also told him that I rarely read the local paper and never read about divorce cases, anyway. I knew absolutely nothing, therefore, about the case. I even offered to give him my brother's phone number so he could verify my explanation. It was some time before he grudgingly accepted my story, but when he persisted in ordering me to cancel my field trip, I again put my foot down. It was too late, I said.

"Then it's on your head." he said "If even one student gets into that court room…you're fired!"

As fast as I could, I drove down to the divorce court and found the sergeant-at-arms who handled security. When I explained what had happened, he said, "Don't worry, sir. We don't allow children in, and, anyway, that case is being heard in private. None of your students will get past me."

The field trip went off beautifully. The students all went where I had sent them, and I walked around checking on them and telling them where to go next. My only specific instructions were to pay attention and not talk. The various judges, who were all quite pleased to see the students, invited them to move up to the front seats. Most of them said to the students, "Now, if you have any questions, just ask away. I'll be happy to explain anything you don't understand." In some of the courts, one or two of the lawyers were recent law graduates who knew me and called a cheerful greeting. This raised my standing with the students immensely. I also went over to the divorce court and found a guard standing in front of the door.

One of my lawyer friends had directed me to one particular

court, commenting that it would be "most interesting." I sent a large group of girls there and seated them close to the front. When they came out they were giggling and excited.

"Mr. Fulford," one said, "did you know all those women you seated us next to were prostitutes? Such terrible makeup and really ridiculous outfits!" The students were from affluent and very protected homes and had probably never seen a prostitute before in their lives. I wondered what they would tell their parents when they went home.

I had put a large group of boys in a similar court and stood at the back watching their reactions as the drunk tank was emptied and the prisoners paraded past the judge. It seemed to be a sobering experience for the boys, who said little when they came out except, "The judge seemed to know most of them by name," and "Did you see how he really jumped on the drunk drivers?" Other students found themselves in a jury trial and next day, back in class, had a lot of questions about the court system…some of which I actually knew the answers to.

There was a very quiet student in one of my history classes who smiled very rarely but worked hard. One day another teacher pointed to him and said, "That kid's a Haida Indian from up the coast. A chief's son, I believe. He's in my class, too, and he says he carves argillite stone figures. He says that only a chief's family is allowed to dig the rock and carve it."

I was very interested in learning more, and one day I spoke to the student about it. He was happy to find someone who was genuinely interested. "Only a few people know where the best argillite can be found," he said. He then explained that argillite is a type of slate. "It's a bit soft when we dig it up," he went on, "so we have to work fast before it dries hard."

He smiled shyly, "I guess I'm one of the best carvers, but that means nothing because there's only a few of us left." He shrugged his shoulders. "The other kids aren't interested. They don't want to learn to be carvers."

I thought it was sad that the ancient skill was dying out and I asked him if he would carve something for me.

"Sure," he said. "It takes a bit of time, though." And that was that. Many months later, when I had almost forgotten about it, he appeared one day with a parcel containing a shiny black argillite totem pole about eight inches high. It was beautiful. He had typed out an explanation of the sacred animals, starting with the bear at the base and working up to the raven on the top, and explained how they told one of the ancient legends of the Haida. He had even signed and dated it under the base. When I admired it and congratulated him on such an exquisitely carved masterpiece, he only smiled shyly. I also made out a check that took over a month's salary, but it was worth every penny.

Such a beautiful object could not sit around my apartment where any visitor might knock it over, so I gave it to my brother George as a thank-you present for all the help he had given me during my time as a student. George had a small, but carefully chosen art collection, and he was ecstatic when he saw the argillite totem pole. He canceled all my student loans from him, saying that the piece of art was worth more to him. He hung on to it through many moves, a few hard times, and even a couple of divorces. I learned later that my student had gone to Paris to learn to work in silver and then returned to Canada to recreate the ancient Haida legends in bright silver instead of the gleaming black argillite.

As the school year was coming to an end, I had to make up my mind whether or not I wanted to remain in that high school. Almost all of the other teachers were elderly, so I had made few friends. In addition, the administration was aloof and bureaucratic, and it had already been made clear that I would be teaching business law again next year rather than the English classes I wanted to teach. It was a good school with high standards, but I was not comfortable there. In addition, although I had plenty of friends in the city, I had not put down any roots there and it was ten years since I had left England. So I decided to take a year off and go to Europe to visit my family.

My brother George had moved to California, so I drove down to San Francisco to see him again, then across country to Toronto to visit my brother Paul. I sold my old car for a few dollars to a junk yard and next took the bus to Montreal, where I found a freighter going to England. It was a tiny Swedish vessel with only three passengers, and the crossing was glass smooth all the way to Bristol. Back in England at last, I visited family and old friends. But soon I became restless and headed down to Barcelona in Spain.

Chapter 31
Teaching in Spain

I wasn't quite sure what I intended to do in Spain. Looking back on it as I write this, I suppose I was looking for my roots. I was born in Barcelona of English parents. My father's sister had married a Spaniard and still lived there. My father's mother was Cuban, and both sides of my family had branches in Madrid and the Canary Isles. I had always been fascinated by Spanish and Latin American culture and history and considered myself to be more than a little Spanish.

I had visited Barcelona many years before and remembered it as a quiet, slightly run-down city that had not recuperated from World War II, so when I exited the train now, I was surprised to find a dramatically changed city. Business was booming, the streets were choked with traffic, the pensions were full of tourists, and new buildings were going up everywhere. Catalan flags flew from balconies, and in the Gothic Quarter on Sundays, people danced *sardanas* to traditional music played on traditional instruments and chatted in Catalan. I promptly fell in love with the new Barcelona and began looking for a job there.

My aunt, Luz Maria, had become a grandmother since my last visit and was as charming as ever. She suggested that I teach at the language school in the Ramblas, the major street in Barcelona, where my father had taught many years before. When I inquired, the director, an elderly gentleman, remembered my father and immediately offered me a job. He gave me one full class per day and a number of individual students, who came three times a week. There was also a young Frenchman teaching at the school, and we made arrangements to share a small apartment.

My morning classes consisted of about fifteen men and women of all ages. They were mostly in the hotel and restaurant business. I enjoyed these classes because the students were bright and eager and quite stimulating. Using Spanish only as a last resort, I tried valiantly to speak only in slow and precise English and give them time to work out what I was saying. Then I made them repeat everything in English and corrected their pronunciation. We also read from the textbook.

The individuals I taught were mostly university students who wished to perfect their English. One was a young lady who was learning English, French, and German all at the same time. Another was a young man whose father wanted him to handle the English side of his business. It was fun teaching these students the finer points of English. I soon discovered that some of them had gone to English classes sponsored by the British government and others had gone to classes sponsored by the United States government. The main difference seemed to be contractions. The British schools dissuaded their students from using contractions, whereas the American schools emphasized the use of them.

The real problem for all of my students was writing. They could all read and speak English quite well, but they hated to write in English. It took me a while to find out why. Spanish spelling is reasonably simple, with very few quirks. Most words are spelled the way they sound. But they found English spelling to be a complicated maze with neither rhyme nor reason. "We spend all our time looking up words in the dictionary," they said. I did my best to explain that there is a pattern to English spelling and it has rules, too, but it was an uphill battle.

This problem of explaining English spelling started me thinking, and spelling became an obsession with me. Eventually, after many years of research and study, I wrote a book titled *The Complete Guide to English Spelling Rules*, in which I explained that there are indeed rules that govern English spelling and that, generally speaking, English spelling is quite logical.

My students in Barcelona had to buy the school textbook, which was small and not expensive. But I found it rather old-fashioned. It was, in fact, about thirty years out of date. One day I asked the director about the book and suggested that it needed revising. He laughed out loud and said, "Well, that is probably because your father wrote it!"

I had plenty of spare time that year, so I explored the city and found the apartment house where I was born, which was very close to La Sagrada Familia, the lovely basilica that Antoni Gaudí designed and where I was baptized with the middle name Josemaria. When I visited Park Güell, I found the spots I vaguely remembered from my childhood. I also found the Picasso museum, and now and then took a bus or train to little towns up and down the coast or inland to the monastery at Montserrat. Often I sat in a plaza and studied my Spanish textbook, but my Spanish improved only slightly because my roommate only spoke English with me and I always spoke English with my students. My relatives all spoke Spanish and Catalan, of course, but when I visited them, they invariably switched to English, even the children. Even shopkeepers and businessmen seemed to guess at once that I was an English-speaking visitor to Spain and almost always switched to English. This was nice, but it was no way to learn Spanish.

When winter arrived, I learned an uncomfortable fact. Barcelona can get very cold. Most of the buildings are designed to stay cool in summer. The rooms with their tall windows and marble floors are wonderful in the summer, but in the winter they're impossible to heat, especially as many of the buildings have no central heating. In my classroom, we had an electric heater under the table, but it only kept our knees warm. At home, we had just one two-bar electric heater for the whole apartment. I wore a heavy sweater almost all the time, and in the evenings after school I often went to a cheap cinema just to warm up.

The movies with their dialogue dubbed in Spanish helped me a little in my struggle to learn the language better, but it was always strange to hear Hollywood actors talking in Spanish and with voices that often were quite different from what I knew they sounded like. And they always sang in English with their regular voices. It was most amusing.

At Christmas, I made a short trip back to England for the family festivities, but when I got back to Barcelona I soon realized that I was digging into my meager savings too deeply. My teaching job just did not pay enough to cover my expenses. The director of the school found more students for me, but, as he pointed out, the other teachers relied mainly on private classes. It would take some time and money, he said, to advertise and acquire enough private students to make a decent living. Meanwhile, I was going broke.

For the next few months, therefore, I counted every penny and worked hard at spreading the word that I was available for private classes. But nothing came of it. So one day I took a careful look at myself. Although I had been in Spain for nearly a year, I was not a Spaniard. No matter how hard I tried to fit in, I would always be a foreigner. I loved my birthplace, but I still felt like an outsider. And, I concluded, it was not Vancouver, which was where I really felt at home. Also, I suspected that I would never make enough money to live well in Barcelona.

When I travel abroad, I sometimes have a nightmare about being stuck in a strange place with insufficient money to get home. I have come pretty close to it a few times and it's no fun. So now I checked my finances carefully and made some calculations. I had almost reached the point of no return. Soon I would not have enough to get myself back to Canada. I had to make a decision.

Reluctantly, I gave my notice at the school then took the train to Madrid, where I spent an enjoyable holiday with relatives from my mother's side of the family. I also explored the city and visited Toledo. It was well into the summer when I took the train to Paris and rode across the channel to London, where, after visiting more family and friends, I caught a small Dutch freighter headed back to Canada. Teaching in Spain had been a wonderful experience, and I had enjoyed myself, but I had also discovered that, although I had roots in England and Spain, I was no longer a European. My future lay in North America.

Chapter 32
Winter in Winnipeg

The crossing back to Canada from England on a tiny Dutch freighter with only four passengers was easily the wildest voyage I have ever experienced but I wasn't seasick and rather enjoyed it. When we reached the port of Montreal, the captain presented me with a certificate declaring me the only passenger who had turned up for every meal during the voyage. Considering how good the food was, the mock award was easily won. As soon as I was on land again, I went straight to the railroad station and booked a seat to Vancouver on the transcontinental express, with its glass domes and fancy restaurant car. It was expensive, but cheaper than flying, and certainly faster than hitchhiking across the continent.

As the train made its way through the forests north of Lake Superior, I suddenly realized that I was in deep trouble. I would arrive in Vancouver with just a few dollars in my pocket. I would certainly not have enough to rent an apartment, look for a job, and buy food for a month before my first paycheck. Worse, as it was doubtful that the city school board would take me back because I had taught for only one year and then quit, I would also need a car to visit surrounding school districts and go over to Vancouver Island and Victoria.

I had only one choice. The school year would be starting soon. I had better find a job immediately, no matter where. The next major stop was Winnipeg, so I talked to the conductor and arranged for a stay-over. As soon as we arrived, I made straight for the headquarters of the teachers' union.

"Yes, it's a good district and the pay scale is fine," the secretary told me. "I'm sure there's still a high school opening somewhere. Here, let me phone the school board office and tell them you're coming."

I headed for the school board office, where I was hired immediately and given a school. I now had a job, so, with my contract in my pocket, I dashed back to the railroad station, cashed in the rest of my ticket, bought a newspaper and a small map of the city, and began to look for somewhere to live. To solve the problem of meals, I scanned the *Room and Board* advertisements and marked places close to the school I had been assigned to. The first establishment proved to be just what I wanted, so after a quick trip back to the station to retrieve my luggage, I found myself sitting in a comfortable room with all my problems solved. It had happened so quickly that my head was still spinning, and so it was a while before it dawned on me that I was going to spend a year in the coldest major city in Canada, over a thousand miles from either the Pacific or the Atlantic.

The school, which was a combination junior and senior high, was within walking distance of my new home. It was very big and very modern, with a large indoor swimming pool and all the latest teaching equipment. The staff were young and very friendly, and I felt right at home almost immediately. I was given senior English classes, plus a few history and geography classes, and the first days of school went quite smoothly, My home room, and favorite class, was an interesting bunch of problem students who were mostly on probation or were struggling to make up courses so that they could graduate. At least one of the girls was pregnant, though it did not show. At first, the students were suspicious of their new teacher, and it took me some weeks to gain their confidence. In time, however, we became a team. I like to think that the friendly atmosphere of the class stopped quite a few of my students from dropping out of school. Also, when they heard that I had taught business law in Vancouver, their opinion of me went up ten points. I never had any trouble with them.

During lunch one day a couple of the physical education teachers, big, muscular young men, sat down at my table. "Keeping discipline in your class is your problem," one of them said to me, "but if any student gets physical with you, or with anybody else, just send him down to us. We have ways to persuade obnoxious kids to improve their behavior." I had noticed that about the only behavior problem in that school was smoking in the washrooms.

With a full load of classes and extracurricular activities, the time flew by. When the principal assigned me to be teacher-director of the journalism club, I prepared myself to mentor future writers. But the students had other ideas. The club had an expensive color movie camera, and they wanted to make a documentary movie. I knew nothing about making movies, so I played it safe and let them do what they wanted. For about six weeks, I sat in the back of the class and listened to highly technical discussions and agreed to just about everything they proposed. It worked out quite well. One day they turned the auditorium into a cinema and showed their film. They had simply driven around the city, filming whatever caught their eye, and the result was a unique view of urban life. It could have done with a lot of editing, and the shots were a bit blurry at times, but the end result was bordering on excellent. The principal complimented me on the good job that I had done and all the hard work I must have put into it.

A few days later, the vice principal asked me if I would like to teach night school. There was an opening for an ESL teacher to take two classes, three evenings a week. Since I had no social life, I said, yes, I was interested. I would be teaching basic English to newly arrived immigrants. About a week later, I arrived at the school to find a room crowded with adults, all eager to learn English. But I had absolutely nothing to work with. There was no text or guide of any kind. I was completely on my own.

I had to think quickly. After my experience in the Spanish language in the school in Barcelona, I was ready for almost anything. Most of the first class were Greeks and Portuguese with limited education. They were more interested in conversing in English than reading or writing it, so speaking was what we did. I had no trouble getting them to speak English whenever possible. In fact the problem was to keep the conversation down to reasonable levels and get them to use *correct* English.

The second class was quite different. It was made up of professionals and businessmen who had immigrated from many countries and hoped to continue in their professions as soon as they had mastered English. Many of them, however, lacked even enough English to pass the Canadian driving test, and some of them had not found a decent place to live because they could not read the advertisements in the papers. One middle-aged gentleman, who was a fully trained optometrist, was working in a restaurant for minimum wages. After hearing their stories, I phoned the head of the night schools, and a couple of evenings later I came in to find a stack of newspapers and a big pile of official driving test manuals stacked up on the floor.

Using these donated materials, both of my classes made good

progress. They learned how to read the small ads offering rooms for rent, cars for sale, job openings, used furniture, and similar things…but our attempts to read the comics were a dismal failure. Humor does not often translate well. The driver's manuals were such a roaring success that I had to ask for more, and they proved to be so handy that they actually became the text for the course. Because we concentrated on what the students actually needed in their daily lives, the classes went well and the students turned up regularly, even during the dark and bitter cold of winter.

I was boarding with a Ukrainian family in a lovely older house on a beautiful, tree-lined street. I had a large, comfortable room with excellent heating, and the bathroom was right next door. My basic laundry was done once a week, and each morning and evening, except Sundays, one of the sons brought me a tray with my breakfast or supper. The food, which often included Ukrainian delicacies such as cabbage rolls, was excellent.

Across the hall from me lived a university music student who was also the music critic for a local newspaper. He had gotten the job by simply applying for it, but he was not paid. I envied him because, as a critic, he received a constant flow of brand new recordings that publishers hoped he would review favorably. He was allowed to keep the records in lieu of pay. What he liked, he kept and the stuff he didn't like, he gave to friends. His record collection was immense. Fortunately, he listened to the records with headphones.

The beautiful summer ended abruptly. One morning I stepped outside to find the trees all red and gold, and for a few short days, the avenues were ablaze with color, and the lawns were knee-deep in leaves. But just as suddenly, the street sweeper came by, autumn was over, and the trees stood dark and bare against a graying sky. Daily, the temperature dropped a few more degrees.

Because there is no mountain range between Winnipeg and

the North Pole, any little air movement over the northern tundra picks up speed as it roars hundreds of miles south, crosses Lake Winnipeg, and slams into the city at "The Forks," where the Assiniboine River flows into the Red River. Much to the unhappiness of the prairie farmers, the snowfall was very light that winter, whereas the wind was mean. Winnipeg is Canada's "Windy City," and the light snow was soon blown away, so it was no problem. But the cold wind was another matter. I soon bought a winter coat with a lined hood that was not only warm, but, according to the salesman, also wind-proof. I also bought fur lined gloves and ear muffs.

I had noticed a row of electrical outlets in the parking lot at school. Come winter, I also noticed that many cars parked there appeared to have electrical cords poking out of their front grills. It was not long before I discovered what the cords were for. They were plug-in engine block heaters, and every car in town had one. They kept the engines of the parked cars just above freezing point. The driver merely had to remember to unplug the cord when he drove off and to plug it in again when he arrived. This service was provided by the school board; otherwise, they would have had to provide a covered and heated garage just for the teachers' cars.

Extreme cold does strange things to a car. Not only can the water and other fluids freeze, but the various oils can also become thick and almost useless, so that brakes don't work, the steering stiffens and the engine refuses to turn over. The tires freeze solid, and when the driver finally gets the car started, he has to bump down the road for a block or two until the flat, frozen surfaces round off and the rubber becomes flexible again. Ice forms everywhere, inside the door lock as well as on the windshield, so everybody has a plastic window scraper attached to the sun visor and little bottles of alcohol handy for de-icing. Fortunately, Winnipeg is quite flat, so people seldom need snow chains, although everybody carried them in their trunk, along with the necessary sack of sand. It is not surprising that some people put their cars up on blocks, drain all the liquids, and abandon them in their backyards for the winter and rely on the excellent public transit system.

With the first cold weather, the city erected low, wooden barriers around the baseball diamonds in the parks, and the fire department flooded them to form ice skating rinks. On weekends, the rinks swarmed with children of all ages, even tiny tots, slipping and sliding and showing off their skill. I knew from experience that I was hopeless on skates, so I contented myself with photographing the colorful scene.

And it was indeed colorful. Winter is the time to wear brightly trimmed parkas of every color, to wear brilliantly colored woolen toques with the edges pulled down over the ears. This stocking-like head cover had to have a woolen bobble on the end, and some toques were so long they could be used as scarves or as mouth covers against the lung-searing cold. On a bright, clear winter day the parks and streets were a riot of color.

The river froze over, of course, and a road grader cleared a long, smooth stretch for the serious ice skaters to glide back and forth for hours on end, some of them clearly aiming for the Olympic Games. A few hours' drive west of the city are some low hills that looked like nothing to me. But when the wind had packed enough snow against them, they were fine for skiing and were busy every weekend. Meanwhile, out on the frozen lakes, ice fishermen set up their shacks, and in the forests, snow mobiles roared down forest trails. But none of those winter sports appealed to me except as subjects to photograph and film. One bright day I was busy taking photos when I heard a strange sound. The film in my camera had frozen and snapped and the shutter was frozen open.

At school, the students started building ice sculptures and my homeroom class set out to build a rather ambitious ice castle. For days, they spent their lunch periods hurrying in and out with bottles of colored water, and the structure grew outside my window. It was weirdly colored and not exactly like a castle, but it was big and quite impressive and they were very proud of it. Out on the football field, the school had sled races and, by tradition, the lone passenger on each sled had to be a teacher. As everyone in my class hauled on the ropes, I bounced across the frozen snow, lungs burning in the cold air, hands frozen in my gloves, yelling encouragement to my "huskies." It was a most uncomfortable ride, but we came in second.

Eventually, spring came, and it came in a hurry. One day the trees were bare and dark, and the next day they were shimmering green with tiny leaf buds on every branch. Within a week, all the leaves were out, bulbs were blossoming in the lawns, and there was life in every garden and new life out on the vast prairie.

I flew down to San Francisco to visit my brother for Easter and found him lounging in the sun on his patio in shorts and light shirt. There was a lemon tree just over his head and a glass of something cool in his hand. "So," he drawled, "how are things up in Winnipeg?" He grinned. "Had a nice winter?"

Then and there, I decided that, no matter how much I loved Canada, I loved bright, hot sunshine even more, and as soon as I returned to Winnipeg, I began the long process of applying for legal immigration to the United States.

As the academic year drew to an end, teachers' work loads increased, with tests and reviews and piles of paperwork. All year, I'd had had the usual problem of trying to hold the interest of those students who were only interested in their cars and their evening jobs. Sometimes a student fell asleep in class because he had worked all evening, then gone to a party.

The biggest nuisances were the students going on to college.

They were so worried about their grades that almost every day I heard, "Mr. Fulford, will this be on the test?" What they thought would not be covered, they ignored, and if something did not appear on a test when they had expected it, they became quite angry. Their testiness took quite a bit of pleasure out of teaching. One evening when I was walking home after working late, I saw a light on in an elementary school along the way. I walked in and found a teacher just tidying up his desk. After I introduced myself, I asked, "What's it like, teaching elementary?" He smiled broadly. "Great! I used to teach high school, but I soon switched to elementary. The little ones are so receptive. It's lots of fun and I love it. Maybe you should consider it."

When school ended and I handed in my resignation, the principal sighed. He complimented me on my work in night school and said I had done a good job with my home room students. He had hoped that I would remain in his school. "That's our problem here in Winnipeg," he said "We have an excellent school system and a first class university, so our kids get a fine education. But then they leave." He shook his head. "They're off to Toronto or Vancouver or Chicago, or even Europe. That's the price we pay for being so far from everywhere else." He looked at me and asked, "You're not interested in winter sports, are you?" When I said that I was not, he sighed again and nodded. "That's a pity. Myself, I'd rather spend a day ice fishing than lounging about on some beach." Then he laughed and said, "Well, John, good luck."

Chapter 33
Getting to California

With the help of my landlady's teenage son, I found a cheap but reliable old car and set off for Calgary, where I picked up my mother at the airport. She had flown in from England, and it was her first visit to North America, so I took her to the Calgary Stampede, a cowboy parade and rodeo bigger than any they have in Texas. Then we drove to Banff and over the Rockies through the most scenic parts of British Columbia that I could think of, stopping at nearly every viewpoint. After I showed her Vancouver and Victoria, I put her on the plane for San Francisco, where my brother George was waiting for her. Then I drove down the wild and scenic Pacific Coast Highway from Astoria in Oregon to San Francisco, taking my time and stopping wherever I felt like stopping. I arrived in San Francisco a few days before my mother returned to England. That was the last time I ever saw her.

As I drove, I gave some serious thought to switching to elementary teaching. I soon found that there were plenty of openings in schools in the San Francisco area for a male elementary teacher. But first I had to finish the immigration process.

To try and speed things up, I phoned around and eventually reached an immigration official. The first thing he said was, "You realize that you have to be out of the country before you can enter?" I agreed that that was logical and pointed out that I was staying with my brother in San Francisco at the time. "That's not good enough," he said. "You can't enter if you are already here. You applied in Winnipeg, so that's where you have to enter the United States from."

My heart sank. Despite all my protests, the official was adamant. I would have to retrace my steps back to where I had made the initial application and wait there.

I had my doubts that the old car would survive the long trip back to Winnipeg, so I flew back and found a cheap hotel, where I sat and waited. I suspected that the bureaucrats would take their time, so I signed up as a substitute teacher for summer school and was surprised to find that I was called two or three times a week. The classes were small and the work was quite easy, so the summer passed quickly. In fact, it passed too quickly. When the new school year arrived, I was still in Canada. Eventually, however, all the immigration paperwork was finished. Eager to find a new job and get back to work, I caught the next plane back to San Francisco.

Those few short weeks of delay waiting for my immigration papers had completely changed the picture. Now I found that every school district in the Bay Area that I applied to had all the teachers that they needed. So I set off again to search for teaching jobs. For transport, I found an old Chrysler that looked in reasonable shape, then I mapped out a route down the coast. Day after day, I worked my way south stopping at every school district and sleeping in the cheapest motels that I could find. My route took me through some of the most beautiful countryside in California, and there was many a town I would love to have settled down in, but I heard the same thing everywhere. "Oh, if only you had been here last week!" Or "We have been looking for a male elementary teacher all summer. We found one only a few days ago." Most disappointing was Carmel, one of the loveliest towns on the coast, where the secretary said, "Oh, if only you had been here a few days ago!"

After three weeks of driving south, during which I became an expert on the geography of coastal California, I arrived in Los Angeles and made my way to the home of an old friend. He advised against applying in Los Angeles because it was a huge district, and I would probably be sent to one of the problem schools where no other teacher wanted to work. I applied in the surrounding school districts and struck it lucky.

It was a small district in Orange County with just a few elementary schools. A teacher had suddenly quit because her husband had been transferred by his company, so I was hired immediately, which was lucky because I had barely enough money left to rent an apartment and stock the kitchen.

Chapter 34
The School in Orange County

That school in Orange County, California, was easily the worst school I ever encountered. It was a fairly new elementary school located in a working class neighborhood, and it had six grades and about a dozen teachers. Although it looked quite attractive from the outside, it wasn't long before I realized that the school district was using it as a dumping ground for their deadbeat teachers and staff. About half the teachers were good, hard working people, but they were swimming upstream against a tragically incompetent administration. The other teachers were a useless waste of taxpayers' money.

The principal (rumor had it) only kept his job because he was a personal friend of the superintendent. The man was a nervous wreck, completely unable to make a decision on anything without first conferring with the superintendent and getting his permission. He always tried to keep his hands hidden under his desk or in his pockets because he was constantly scratching and picking at his fingernails, making his cuticles a beautician's nightmare. During the year I was there, he rarely left his office and never visited my classroom.

The school secretary was a skinny, elderly lady who had wrapped a large sheet of brown construction paper around the lower half of her desk because she believed that everybody was staring at her legs. She prevented visitors from seeing the principal, avoided communicating with the teachers, and ate her lunch at her desk. One of the students was called Boy Child because that was what it said on his birth certificate and she had never bothered to learn the child's proper name.

There was only one other male teacher in the school. This was a young man who taught a sixth-grade class and was supposed to be our math expert, although he never offered the rest of us any advice or gave a demonstration lesson. His overwhelming interest was baseball, so he often took his class out onto the school's athletic field to have a game of baseball…no matter what they were supposed to be studying.

Across the hall from me was an overweight female teacher who was counting the days to her retirement. All she required of her students was complete silence and no movement. She had an endless supply of outdated work sheets, but she didn't care whether the students finished them or not, since she never graded—or even looked at—them. The children in her class could read or draw or simply take naps, just as long as they were silent and remained in their seats for the whole class period.

Another teacher dressed in weird outfits and proclaimed herself to be "very artistic." She was also keen on the children "expressing" themselves. Whatever she was supposed to be teaching, she invariably produced colored paper and crayons and scissors and smiled while the children happily spent the period "expressing themselves" but learning nothing. At one time, her class was festooned with so much art work hanging from the ceiling that it looked like a jungle. When the fire department inspector made a surprise visit, he almost exploded.

These deadbeat teachers spent most of their time in the staff room drinking coffee and complaining. It was a poor neighborhood in a rich county, and most of the families who lived there were poor whites from the Southern states. At that time in the 1970s there were very few minority students in the school, which was fortunate because most of the teachers were prejudiced and extremely racist. They blamed the blacks and the Mexicans for everything. Having lived and traveled in Africa and South America, I was horrified at their attitude, but I quickly learned that it was useless to argue with them.

For the one year I was at that school, we never had a planning session or even a staff meeting devoted to curriculum. Actually, there were very few staff meetings at all, as the principal dreaded them. So we all did our own thing, including making up tests and grading the students.

On Friday afternoons, some of the upper-grade teachers herded all their children into the lunchroom to watch old movies, mostly cartoons and ancient "educational" films that they had seen countless times before. One student was put in charge of the projector, and then the teachers left the lunchroom and sat in the staff room drinking coffee, often leaving the children completely unsupervised. This was a regular Friday routine. The principal never said a word.

The district superintendent was one of those administrators who enthusiastically endorse any new idea that comes along, tested or untested. The year before I arrived, he had embraced the "team teaching" fad that was then in vogue and had ordered classroom walls removed in many schools across the district. Since nobody ever told the teachers how to handle the now doubled classes or explained how two teachers working as a "team" with sixty children would do a better job than one teacher working with thirty students, the experiment was an utter failure. It was, in fact, soon abandoned, and the walls that had been knocked down were replaced with moveable canvas walls. They were a nuisance, but better than no walls at all.

Opening the wall did, however, have one great benefit for me. I met Lillian Christensen, my future wife. Hers was the classroom next to mine, but I didn't notice her during the first week of school. She was tall, and a few years younger than me, with long, fair hair and gray-blue eyes. She was a friendly, outgoing person, but she didn't drink coffee and she preferred to read, so she was rarely in the teacher's lounge. It was her love of books, in fact, that first attracted me.

One lunch period, when I opened the sliding wall and introduced myself, I was struck by the dozens of children's books on the shelves by her desk and scattered over the students' tables. I commented on the wide selection.

"Yes," she said. "I majored in children's literature. I like to see them reading. It's so important."

She then offered to stock my classroom shelves with books at the appropriate reading level. We spent the rest of the lunch period discussing books, and I learned that she had bought every single book herself and even let a student take a book home if the student was really interested in it.

Born in Long Beach, Lily had been out of California only twice, when she went to visit the family farm in South Dakota where her father was born. She was fascinated by accounts of my travels and the many jobs I'd had and soon caught the travel bug from me. Our friendship grew, and I was soon invited to meet her parents, who were very welcoming but a trifle wary of a Canadian Catholic who was interested in their only daughter. Her father was a master chef and baker who specialized in elaborate wedding cakes, so there was always something delicious in the refrigerator when I visited.

We decided to get married during the Easter holiday, and everybody suddenly became very busy organizing the wedding. When I approached the priest at the nearest parish church, he was very friendly but pointed out that, as a stranger, I would need to show him a baptismal certificate. I immediately wrote to my parents in England, but they couldn't find it. Next, my father wrote a letter in impeccable Spanish to the bishop of Barcelona, who very quickly sent a copy of my baptism certificate, which said I had been baptized in the crypt of the famous Sagrada Familia Cathedral.

Everything was finally arranged down to the last detail, and hotel reservations had been made for Lily and me in Carmel and for guests in Long Beach…when the principal called me into his office.

"You'll have to postpone your wedding until the summer," he announced. "The superintendent won't allow a married couple to teach in the same school."

I stood there with my mouth open for a half minute, then said, "Why?"

The man plucked at his fingernails. "He says it's not a good idea"

"Then move me to another school."

He shook his head. "The superintendent says that's impossible." And he sat back with a smug look on his face.

I was suddenly very angry at the idea that a petty bureaucrat thought that he could tell me when I could get married, but I controlled myself and leaned across his desk. "You're going to look very silly explaining this on television," I said. His eyes opened wide and he sat up straight. "A couple of phone calls," I continued, "and every newspaper and radio station and television station in Southern California will have a reporter here in five minutes."

Then, feeling quite proud of myself, I walked out of his office

and immediately pushed the incident to the back of my mind. I
tried to forget it, but I suspected that I had made a dangerous ene-
my and that repercussions would soon follow.

The wedding went off perfectly. Lily had told her class that
they would all be welcome, and about twenty parents and students
turned up, all dressed in their best. She was a well loved teacher.
The rest of the school year was trouble-free, and, occasionally, we
would open the dividing doors and take turns teaching our combined classes.

But there was one problem we hadn't foreseen. Rents for even
third-rate apartments in Orange County were astronomical, and
even with our combined salaries, we would have had serious trouble making ends meet, and we could not continue living with Lily's
parents in their little house in Long Beach for much longer. There
was only one way to increase our income and that was to get our
master's degrees as soon as possible. I estimated that getting my
M.A. should not take much longer than a year, so at the end of the
school year, I handed in my notice and Lily remained at the school.
Our agreement was that when I had my degree and a permanent
position, she would work on her master's. It was a simple plan, and
it all went horribly wrong.

Lily was involved in a traffic accident just before our wedding.
She was out of hospital and walking quite well for the wedding,
and the insurance settlement provided enough to pay her medical
bills and buy us a fairly new car. It also added a nice sum to our
combined bank account.

Lily and I had spent a day or two in Tijuana and Ensenada,
Mexico, and we both wanted to see more of Mexico, so despite her
father's deep reservations, we headed off to Mexico City. After seeing all the sights in Mexico City, we took a bus south to Oaxaca, and
from there our trip snowballed into an extraordinary adventure.

When we reached Panama, we still had money and time, so we continued south. Using any available transportation, we traveled through Venezuela, Colombia, Ecuador, Peru, Bolivia, Chile, Argentina, Uruguay, Brazil, and Paraguay. The end of the line was in Asunción, Paraguay, where we ran out of both time and money. We had to use a credit card to fly Lily home.

I remained in Bolivia, where I had an old college friend, and spent the next three or four months traveling around that fascinating country and exploring its every nook and cranny. I was diligently collecting information and literature for my projected master's thesis, but when I returned to the university and discussed the subject with my thesis committee, my proposal was rejected outright. There was nobody on the faculty who knew anything about Bolivia.

But my research was not wasted. I remained deeply interested in Bolivia and eventually wrote a history of that extraordinary, landlocked country. When *To Reach the Sea* was quite well received, I also wrote a book about my travels in Bolivia and titled it *Last Plane to Cochabamba*.

Meanwhile, back at the school, Lily was having a terrible time. The principal, on the orders of the superintendent, began harassing her. They couldn't do anything to me, so they picked on her, and the spineless principal took every opportunity to call her into his office and bully her about trifling little details. He criticized the length of her skirts, so she wore tailored slacks until he banned her from wearing "men's trousers." When this silly rule reached the ears of the other female teachers, they descended on him in a very angry group. He had to change his mind in a hurry. Almost daily, he found something else to complain about, but Lily was an excellent teacher and a sensible person, so she put up with it, knowing that they would never find grounds to fire her.

The superintendent and principal, unsavory pair that they were, realized that Lily had right on her side, so they changed their tactics. One day, she walked into her classroom and found three men sitting in chairs at the back of the room and holding large yellow notepads. They were the superintendent, the principal, and another man who I later learned was the district lawyer and was billing the district by the hour. They did not introduce themselves and said not a word, but sat there scribbling notes and staring intently at Lily as she went about teaching her class. They sat there silently for the whole morning and then returned after lunch. Sitting. Staring. Writing. It was extremely uncomfortable for Lily, but she survived the day and sighed with relief when they left.

They were back the next day. For a week, they sat in the back of Lily's class and glared at her silently through every class period, making notes on everything she did. It was very effective psychological torture, and it worked. By the end of the week, Lily, usually a strong and sensible person, was a wreck. But she could not tell her parents and carefully wrote not a word about her torture to me as I scrambled over mountains and wandered through the jungles of Bolivia.

After that first week, the trio changed their tactics and appeared at random intervals, sometimes in the morning, sometimes in the afternoon. But their behavior was the same every time: they sat and stared. The worst part was that they never said anything, and the principal never called her into the office to comment on what they had observed. It was the silent approach, to which Lily had no defense.

Her reaction was to eat. Lily was living with her parents in Long Beach while I was gone, and the refrigerator always contained cakes, pies, and other delicacies that her father had brought home from his bakery. Those goodies were just too tempting, and she began to put on weight. When I returned to California and she met me at the airport, I hardly recognized her. She saw the look on my face, of course, and as soon as we were alone, she broke into tears and explained everything.

My first reaction was to drive down to the school and confront the principal. But I soon realized that he was merely obeying the superintendent's orders, and, as Lily pointed out, "He will just say that he is observing a teacher. That's part of his job." But it was obvious that this was blatant harassment, so my next step was to contact the teachers' union. When I eventually got through to somebody at the California Teacher's Association office in Orange County, however, nobody was particularly interested. Neither Lily nor I were members, and even though we offered to sign up immediately, we could find nobody who wanted to handle the tricky issue of teacher harassment.

So I decided to confront the superintendent. But first, I tackled the school principal with the question, "What exactly do you want?"

He said, "If Mrs. Fulford hands in her resignation, we will give her a good letter of recommendation. If she does not resign voluntarily, we will continue observing her, then dismiss her and blackball her and make sure that she never gets another teaching position anywhere in California, ever again." And he gave me a smug smile.

I said nothing and drove to the superintendent's office.

"What exactly do you want?" I asked him. His reply was exactly, word for word, what the principal had said.

I held on to my temper. "You're harassing a perfectly good teacher out of her job just to get back at me," I said. He smiled and said nothing. "This is not only harassment," I said, "but it's blackmail and illegal."

He simply shrugged his shoulders and said, "Prove it."

After half an hour of futile argument, I gave up. We finally agreed that Lily would quit at the end of the school year, and the principal would write her a good letter of recommendation. I was very suspicious of the man and asked him to put our agreement on paper, but he shook his head. "I'd rather have nothing in writing," he said.

Lily never received a letter of recommendation, of course, and when she went looking for a teaching position the next year, she bumped into an invisible wall. District after district turned her down with no explanation. Even districts that were pressed for teachers. Years later, I learned that the vindictive pair had blackballed her by simply refusing to give her any recommendation, good or bad, to districts that inquired. It was a clever trick that avoided putting anything down on paper. It also served to arouse suspicion among prospective employers.

For the next year, all Lily could get were substitute jobs, usually only for a day, though occasionally for a week. More than once, we had to ask her father for help as I hurried to finish my graduate studies and get that all-important master's degree.

Chapter 35
Motel Manager

With Lily out of a job, we were in serious trouble, and to add to our problems, I had to take extra education classes to enable me to apply for an elementary teaching credential. These were the usual Child Psychology and Theory of Education nonsense created by academics and delivered by other academics who had obviously never taught in a real elementary school. I had to suffer through them, and they took time.

Our initial plan had failed. We were still living in one room in her parents' small house, and the future looked grim. I needed a real job. One day Lily showed me an advertisement. "It's for a couple to manage a motel," she said, "It's only a small salary, but it includes a free house with utilities."

Since finding somewhere to live was our biggest problem, we drove a few miles up the coast from Long Beach to have a look at the property. The motel was quite old, and the rooms were tiny and very close together, but it was only two blocks from the beach, and the adjoining manager's house was very attractive. So we applied for the job.

What we soon discovered was that two young business men had bought the old motel with the intention of tearing it down and building a tall condominium building on the site. Unfortunately, they had not done their homework. They soon discovered that the city had a ban on any building higher than two stories within a certain distance of the beach. They were stuck with running a motel, something they knew absolutely nothing about. Either they were impressed by our enthusiasm or nobody else applied for the position, because we were hired almost immediately.

The day we took over, one of the owners was waiting to hand over the keys. "Your job is quite simple," he said. "Just handle the money and keep good records."

"But a motel takes a lot of work," I said. "Who handles cleaning the rooms and other stuff?"

He waved a hand vaguely in the direction of the units across the parking lot, "Maria takes care of everything else. Maria Guivera. She gets a rent-free unit for doing the rooms. I gather that she's been here for years." He smiled confidently and added, "No problem. Just leave that part to her." And he handed me the keys and left.

The owner had not taken me on a tour of the motel or spoken a word about the mechanical and electrical equipment, including the washing machines, or the neon sign. I had the clear impression that he knew nothing about them himself.

As I was standing there, clutching the huge ring of keys and wondering what I had gotten Lily and me into, Maria came up and introduced herself. She was a short, round, cheerful, Mexican lady who, fortunately, spoke perfect English. Lily liked her immediately.

"You will have nothing to worry about," she assured us. "I handle everything. This is a pretty quiet place, not much business and never any trouble."

That evening we switched on the No Vacancy sign and went to bed, happy in our good fortune.

Next morning was different. We awoke to find the parking

lot filled with unmarked vans and a police car sitting across the street. There were about a dozen men with short haircuts bustling about and shouting in bad Spanish at a swarm of Mexican men and shoving them into the vans.

I dashed out and asked the first official I came to, "What's going on?"

"Immigration," he yelled, waving his arms. "Get back into the house."

Then Maria appeared, and we went into the house and watched through the window. "It is *la migra*," she said. "The immigration people are taking all the boys. It happens now and then, but don't worry."

I had heard vague stories about illegal immigrants, so I asked here where they would be taken.

"Oh, they usually just take them across the border and drop them off." She laughed and said, "Most of them will be back in a couple of days."

She was right. That very evening, one of the deported men was back. I'm sure he set some kind of record. When I asked him how he did it, he just smiled and shrugged his shoulders.

While we waited for the officials to finish the roundup that morning, Maria told us that the majority of the units were rented out long-term to illegal immigrants from Mexico who worked in the local restaurants and hotels. "There is not one of those fancy places on the beach that could survive a week without wetbacks," she said. "Who would do all the work? No *gringo* would work for those wages."

Then she took me across to the motel to see the units. There were two rows of very small, attached units and some slightly bigger, separate units. "Only rent out the separate units to visitors," she advised. "They're nicer. These others we keep for the boys."

I understood then that "the boys" meant the illegal workers. The units were barely large enough for a Murphy bed that folded up into one wall, plus a large, shabby sofa and a chest of drawers. The bathrooms, with their ancient fixtures, were tiny and cramped, but the hot water was hot and everything seemed to work.

"Well," I finally said, "I suppose two men could live here quite well."

Maria gave me a look and shook her head. "Two? There are nine men living in each of these units!"

I was horrified and looked around the tiny room again. "Nine? But there's no room."

Maria pulled down the Murphy bed and said, "They all work in shifts, so they sleep in shifts, too. Three sleep while three are working and the other three are off somewhere, probably chasing girls. Don't worry. They've worked it all out. And they save a lot of money this way." She smiled. "It's a good system for you because they never have parties in the rooms because there's always somebody sleeping. The *migra* only caught the ones who were sleeping this morning. The others will be back soon."

And this was my introduction to the illegal immigrant problem that I had read about but had never really paid any attention to.

Over the next few months, Lily and I got to know "the boys" quite well. They ranged in age from teenagers to older men and came from every part of Mexico, mostly the poor mountain villages. Some of them were completely illiterate, and their Spanish was a strange mixture of English, Spanish, and words from languages like Nahuatl and Zatopec, but since we all had a smattering of Spanish, we got on quite well. Often, when Maria was not around, one of them would ask Lily or me for advice or ask us to translate some document.

Since they were in the country simply to earn money to send

back to their families, their earnings were of prime importance. I was often horrified at the way their employers cheated them. Some were paid in cash, but many had printed pay stubs. One day I was asked to explain a pay stub from a major restaurant. There was the "gross pay," and below it were listed all the deductions and the "net pay," which was obviously considerably less. Leaning on the hood of a parked car, I went down the list with the man. There was absolutely no mention of overtime pay, yet I knew that they all worked long hours. Union fees were deducted, but the men were not in any union. Pension contributions were deducted, but the men were not in any pension plan. There were deductions for medical, but the men were not covered by any medical plan. And there were a few other items that were quite unexplained. Naturally, there were deductions for state and federal taxes, but these looked excessively high. After I explained all this to the men and they had walked away unhappily, I explained it again to Lily.

"You know what they're doing, don't you?" she said. "None of that money ever goes where they say it's going. Those businesses keep two sets of records, screw the workers, and pocket the difference." When I nodded, she added, "And since the men are here illegally, there's absolutely nothing they can do about it."

Despite the fact that they were being overworked and underpaid, the men were quite philosophical. "We have work and make some money," they said. "Better than back home." And then they added the Spanish equivalent of "half a loaf is better than no loaf."

One day I was clearing out the trunk of my car when one of the Mexicans said, "That's a big trunk. Lots of space. You could get three men in that trunk quite easy."

I laughed and asked, "How much could I make?"

He mentioned a very high figure.

"Well, that's very tempting," I said, "but I don't want to spend ten years in prison for bringing wetbacks across the border."

He shook his head. "No, the *coyotes* bring them across. All you would have to do is bring them up the coast to Los Angeles."

I knew the freeway quite well and said, "But what about the immigration checkpoint twenty miles north of San Diego?"

"Oh, that," he laughed. "You go around it through the mountains. There's a way."

Nevertheless, I declined his generous offer of employment.

There were two permanent residents in addition to Lily and me. The first was a bachelor house painter who worked for the city and was very quiet, the second, a slatternly woman who lived on welfare and was always drunk. I replaced the glass in one of her windows at least three times after she had thrown something through it. Many months after Lily and I had left the motel, we got a subpoena from a law firm. I ignored it, but the letters kept coming, so one day I sat down in a corporate conference room at a large oak table surrounded by serious men in expensive suits. It had transpired that this woman was suing the motel for injuries sustained on the premises. After a great deal of legal formalities, the lead lawyer mentioned the large sum that the woman was claiming.

"Do you know this woman?" he asked.

I nodded and said, "Everybody knows her. She's usually drunk, smashing windows and things like that."

The lawyer glared at me. "That is only your opinion."

I smiled. "Well," I said, "you can ask any of the Mexicans who live there. They call her La Boracha." (Which means female drunkard.) There was a dead silence in the room, then several of the lawyers closed their notebooks, and somebody said that my deposition was no longer needed.

The motel we managed was not very attractive, so we had few

real customers. I always allowed potential guests to see the rooms before I took their money, but quite often they took one look and left. On the weekends, we got plenty of young men who only wanted a place to sleep after a wild day on the beach or in the local bars. If they brought a girl with them after dark, it was no business of mine. Now and then, we had a drunk who just needed a room in which he could get seriously plastered for one night, but once we had a middle-aged man, quite well dressed, who paid for a week and stayed drunk the entire time. Maria had a master key and stopped by to change sheets every day, but he was always flat out and unconscious on his bed. Although we watched carefully, we never saw him go down to the liquor store; we found out later that he had bribed one of the boys to keep him supplied. Eventually, after a week, we could not wake him up, and I called the ambulance. We never did find out what happened to him.

Quite often, a male customer would ask if we rented by the hour, about which Lily usually said, "If we rented rooms by the hour, we could make a fortune." But the owners had expressly forbidden it, not because of any moral standards, but because the city inspector had warned them not to.

Once we had a very well dressed customer, a middle-aged man, who insisted, "Don't tell anyone I'm here. Nobody!" and wrote an obviously false name on the registration card. He had scarcely vanished into his room before a woman drove up and demanded to know if her husband was there. There was quite a scene as I denied that her husband could possibly be in our motel, all the while telling myself that, as I did not know who her husband was, I was technically correct. After she threw a minor tantrum in the parking lot and threatened to call the police, she was still so angry I was sure she would kill the poor man when she caught him. But eventually she drove off, and the man slipped away after it was dark.

About half of our customers were just normal people looking for a cheap place to spend the night, but the other half included some interesting characters, including thieves. Maria took it for granted that things would be stolen, so we had a good supply of ash trays, water glasses, and towels, but one thief really set a record. He was a college student who said, "I just need a room for one night while the paint dries where I live. The smell of wet paint just ruins my sinuses." So I gave him our best room.

Next morning, Maria ran into the lobby. "Gone!" she exclaimed. "Everything is gone!" She took me to the room, where everything was indeed gone. Our student had taken absolutely everything, including the entire bed and mattress, the chest of drawers and the dresser, all three chairs and a small table, even the mirror off the wall. He had also taken all the linens and towels and even the toilet paper, the shower curtain, and the light bulbs. The only thing he had not taken was the Gideon Bible. Maria picked it up and said, "Bah! What else can you expect from an atheist?"

I spent the rest of the day asking the neighbors if they had heard anything during the night, but nobody had heard a sound. We had to guess that he had friends who'd parked a pickup down the back alley and helped him. It was so smoothly done that I had to admire him, but the policeman who took the report did not share my feelings, and neither did the motel's owners.

Customers were not the only thieves. The owners had contracted with a local laundry to do the linens, and one day Maria said, "You know, I don't think these are our sheets." She held up a particularly worn sheet and looked more closely at it. "No," she said again, "this is not one of ours."

So I phoned the laundry, but they insisted that there was no mistake. We had a stack of brand new sheets in the storeroom, so Maria replaced all the worn sheets and we forgot about the incident. And the next week, we discovered that all our new sheets had been replaced with old, worn out sheets, some of which were even torn. Again I phoned the laundry, and again they denied it. When I phoned the owners and explained the problem, they were not interested enough to do anything, so we simply replaced the sheets. For the next few weeks, the laundry systematically stole every new sheet and substituted old, tattered, and torn sheets, many of them with the names of other hotels and hospitals clearly printed on them.

The matter came to a head one morning when Maria showed me a sheet with a name printed clearly right across the top. "Madre de Dios!" she said as she crossed herself. "Just look at that." It was the name of a local mortuary.

I phoned one of the owners and demanded that he come and look.

"Good God!" he said when he saw it. "Imagine waking up and seeing that! It could give you a heart attack. We could be sued for half a million." We soon had a new laundry.

The most interesting character, and the sleaziest, to arrive at the motel was a bum with three small children. He turned up on our street one day and began begging on the street, conveniently close to the local newspaper offices. The editor sent out a young female reporter, who wrote a beautiful sob-story, complete with photos of the children. The editor printed it without bothering to check anything. The public reacted immediately and donated used clothing, food, and even sent money. The paper set up a fund and did follow up stories. Next, a city agency found the money to house them at our motel. They moved in to our largest unit.

But I was suspicious from the first time I met the bum…er, father. His story about losing his wife and his car breaking down and having a job waiting for him slipped off his tongue too easily, and he was vague about places and times. The two little girls spoke not a word, and I suspected that they were not even his children. His son, an overweight boy about nine or ten, was rude and insolent, but he also had a big mouth and eventually gave the game away. He boasted that they had traveled all over the southwest states living off the charity of gullible citizens. Their method was to find a town that had a local newspaper or a radio station so they'd get plenty of publicity with their well rehearsed sob-story. Then the offerings would pour in and they'd live well for a month or longer. Often there would also be cash gifts, and a number of times they had been given a secondhand car, which they sold as soon as they arrived at the next likely town.

The boxes of donated food and clothing poured in to the motel, but the "poor, hungry and thinly dressed little family" merely picked out one or two items that caught their eye and threw the rest into the back alley. It was a neighbor who finally advised me of the pile of rotting food and ruined clothing that was almost blocking the alley. While I was moving it all into the big dumpsters, I caught the boy urinating in our parking lot, just feet away from the bathroom in his unit. When I yelled at him, his language was so foul that I phoned the city agency and told them to get the bums out of my motel. It was while I was arguing with a bureaucrat that I learned that some kind soul had donated a secondhand station wagon to the fund that had been created for the "poor little family." Two days later, the father smiled for the photographers as he received a nice check. Then they all drove away in the donated car.

To try and make the place look a bit more attractive, Lily planted all kinds of flowers in the sadly neglected garden out front. They were an astonishing success. During much of the summer, a narrow band of early morning fog would sit over the two or three blocks closest to the ocean. It would be gone by noon, but in the furnace heat of a Southern California summer, this fog produced just the right mini-climate for her garden. When she had crammed flowers into every available square inch, it was quite a sight and people often stopped to admire it. Unfortunately, it made the rest of the motel look even shabbier.

Far from being the easy job that the owners had promised, keeping the motel running proved to be a lot of work. The very first week, one of the hot water heaters stopped working, so I phoned the owners and asked if I should call the plumber or would one of them fix it? "No need to call a plumber," I was told, "I'm sure it's something you can fix." And this became the answer I always got when anything broke down. The owners did not want to spend a penny on plumbers or electricians, and they did not want to fix it themselves, either, so, since I was the manager, I could fix it. We were being paid only a tiny stipend, and we had been assured that we would only handle the office, but I hadn't finished my thesis yet, and we needed the job. So I did all the maintenance.

The water heater that broke down was in a cockroach and spider-infested hole under the floor of one of the units. I had not the faintest idea what to look for as I wriggled down into the cramped space and started tinkering. Naturally, I soon had an audience of Mexicans, all eager to offer advice. One of them proved to have some experience in plumbing. After a trip to the store for a part, we had the water heater put back together and working. In the weeks that followed, I rebuilt all the water heaters. I felt quite proud of myself.

The next thing to break down was the clothes dryer, which was heavily used by the Mexicans. I didn't know how it worked, but I was curious, so I took it apart and found that it was a simple machine. I also found a sock jammed into the pump, and the drive belt had worn down so much it was useless. But the dryer ran fine when

I put it back together. I kept the receipts for everything I bought and took the cash from the motel receipts. I didn't charge for labor, however, because I knew the owners would never pay me and also because I got personal pleasure in fixing things.

The only thing at the motel that I never touched was the pay phone near the office. Few of the illegal immigrants ever wrote letters; they preferred to phone home, and often the machine would be so stuffed with money it would not accept another coin. I frequently had to phone for the phone company man to come and empty it. Despite the fact that this happened so often, the phone was never vandalized. That link with home was just too precious to damage.

Some of our regular customers seemed to like breaking the light switches and shorting things out, and I became quite good at fixing electrical appliances. Tracing the old wiring and finding the correct fuse in the ancient fuse boxes was always a problem, however, and after a few rather nerve-wracking mistakes, I learned to be very cautious with electricity. Fixing sticky doors, changing locks, replacing broken window panes, and nailing down loose floor boards and steps became routine jobs.

But plumbing was another matter. There is a great deal of plumbing in any motel, and it gets blocked up frequently. Fixing a leaking shower head was simple compared to removing a blockage in a pipe, and I soon got sick and tired of doing that. But it had to be done, sometimes late at night. The ancient, cast-iron pipes should have been replaced decades ago, and I often had to resort to extreme methods to get the water moving again. One gadget a plumber sold me was rather like a small bomb. It was squeezed into the drain and covered with a heavy cap, then detonated. The explosion usually did the job.

A major problem I had to deal with involved two of the units with back-to-back bathrooms. I thought their drainage pipes would be separate. I was wrong, and I found that out the hard way. When I thought the customers had left both the units, I slipped a bomb into the blocked shower drain, set it off, and watched as the water flowed quickly away. Happy that the drain was clear, I started to tidy up when I heard a yell of anger from the adjoining unit. Within minutes, the customer, a man dressed only in a towel, opened the door and began swearing violently and very loudly. I guessed immediately what had happened, but I was not prepared for the mess I saw when he eventually stopped swearing enough to let me into his unit. The light plastic shower curtain was black and strangely heavy, and then I pushed it aside to find a completely black shower stall instead of gleaming white tiles. The bomb had blown off the chrome drain cover and had blasted an astonishingly large amount of foul waste all over the shower stall. Even the ceiling was splattered. It was hard to believe that so much filth could come from just two showers. It was running down the walls and dripped from the faucet handles and shower head. As we stood there staring, the stink began to rise.

"I heard the bang just as I was getting ready to take a shower," the man said, marginally calmer now that he had my attention. "If I had opened the shower curtain a few seconds earlier, I'd be covered in that shit! What the hell happened?"

My first thoughts were of liability and lawyers and law courts. My heart sank. "I'll take a look," I said to him, "but first you have to get dressed. Use the shower next door." I propelled him into the adjoining unit and followed with an armful of his clothes and shoes.

While he was taking a very hurried shower and dressing, I considered the situation, and when he came back for his wrist watch, I was ready with an explanation.

"Gas," I said. "Methane gas. It builds up in the sewers and it stinks. There must have been a bubble of it and it burst through." I watched his face and hoped he had not paid much attention in his high-school chemistry class. "I'll talk to the city engineer and they'll fix it," I added, hoping that mentioning the city would somehow reduce the matter of liability.

He seemed satisfied with my explanation and even laughed a little. "Hell, just think," he said. "One minute earlier and I would have been covered in stinking shit."

I sighed with relief as I escorted him to his car, then I went back into the house and sat down to write faster on my thesis.

Chapter 36
Bilingual Teacher

When my thesis was finally accepted and I had my M.A, I went job hunting again and found a school district that needed a Spanish-speaking teacher in a hurry. It was a medium-size district with a good reputation, and the principal of the elementary school that needed a teacher saw me at once.

"Damn idiots say I have to have a bilingual teacher," he said in an angry voice. "New regulations. We are not in compliance. We have to have a Spanish-speaking teacher." He ignored my application, which was lying on the desk in front of him, and glared up at me. "You speak Spanish?"

My Spanish was quite basic, and I could hardly call myself bilingual, so I said, "I was born in Spain," and held my breath.

"Start on Monday," he said.

And I was hired.

As soon as we could, Lily and I gave notice to the motel owners and moved as far away from the motel as we could. It had been an interesting experience and we had both learned a lot, but we would never run a motel again. Many years later, we drove past the site, expecting that our motel had been long ago torn down, but it was still there. Somebody had fixed it up and turned it into an expensive little "boutique" motel with wrought-iron railings, shade trees, hanging lamps, and flowers everywhere. In contrast to what it had looked like in our day, it was quite beautiful.

Epilog

That job at the motel was the last nonacademic job I ever had, and it always surprises me when I think back to that sudden change in my life. For nearly thirty years I had wandered from job to job and from place to place, constantly looking for the greener grass on the other side of the hill. Then, suddenly, I knew that I had found what I was looking for. I was a teacher.

In a few days Lily and I had rented a house within walking distance of the school and were busy scouring second-hand stores for furniture. I soon moved to a nearby school in the same district where the students were almost all Spanish speaking and began training for my ESL (English as a Second Language) credential. The teachers at that school were friendly and cheerful, and the students were bright and eager. It was a pleasure to teach there.

Eventually we scraped together enough money to buy a "fixer-upper" house in Long Beach and, with the experience I had gained over the years, we fixed it up ourselves. We even added a master bedroom with separate bathroom, a laundry room, and a large family room with a fireplace and a skylight. Between us, we did everything from wiring and plumbing to installing hardwood floors, and the city building inspector never found anything to complain about. We never moved from that house.

I became involved in the teachers union and was twice elected local president. It was an interesting post and gave me a great deal of insight into how school boards work (or don't work) as well as union politics. Almost every summer, Lily and I managed to travel somewhere in our old Rambler, and in time we managed to visit every place of interest in the U.S. and Canada west of Chicago. We became quite expert at tracking down the cheapest motels and finding interesting off-the-beaten-track places to go.

I taught in the same school for thirty years until, inevitably, it came time to retire. But Lily's diabetes grew worse, and we only had a couple of years to enjoy my retirement and do some traveling. When she died, I was shattered. She had been my stabilizer, my anchor, for thirty-six years, and I didn't know what to do with myself. My reaction was to travel. To get far away from our house with all its memories.

I backpacked in Australia and wandered around New Zealand. I sailed in a four-master to Tahiti and the Polynesian Islands. I took a round-the-world cruise and a round-South-America cruise. I sailed through both the Suez and the Panama canals. I visited friends and relatives in England and in Canada and drove hundreds of miles. But without Lily beside me, it was not as much fun as it once had been.

Eventually I settled down to write. Lily had always encouraged me to write, so at first I wrote just for the fun of it. My pension and our savings were enough for one man to live on, so I didn't try too hard to find an agent and didn't send anything to any publisher. Instead, I paid a few dollars to register as a publisher and created my own Astoria Press.

But since I knew absolutely nothing about publishing, it was, to put it mildly, a very interesting learning situation. But I learned. My first book was an embarrassment and never sold enough copies to cover costs. So I joined the California Writers Club and with lots of friendly advice, I turned out an African travel book. *Hitchhiking to Serendip*, a south American travel book. *Last Plane to Cochabamba*, and a history of Bolivia. *To Reach the Sea.*

Throughout my teaching career, I had been fascinated by English spelling and had been researching the subject for more than twenty years. I eventually worked out the many rules that seem to govern the way English words are spelled. I put them together in a book and published it and found that those who read it were very enthusiastic. The travel and history books sell very slowly but sales of *The Complete Guide to English Spelling Rules* have been increasing steadily. So now I am a published author and I can take time off to travel to exotic places whenever I please.

I suppose I could call writing another job, but it's not work. I consider it to be a pleasure and a labor of love.

Not quite The End.

Made in the USA
Monee, IL
07 July 2026